THE SOVIET UNION THROUGH FRENCH EYES, 1945–85

The Soviet Union through French Eyes, 1945–85

Robert Desjardins

Foreword by Archie Brown

St. Martin's Press   New York

First published in the United States of America in 1988

Printed in Hong Kong

ISBN 0–312–02068–6

Library of Congress Cataloging-in-Publication Data
Desjardins, Robert.
The Soviet Union through French eyes, 1945–85.
Bibliography: p.
Includes index.
1. Soviet Union—Politics and government—
1945— . 2. Soviet Union—Study and teaching
(Higher)—France. I. Title.
DK267.D369   1988   947.084′072044   88–4544
ISBN 0–312–02068–6

To my dear parents,
Bernard Desjardins and
Réjane Taillefer

Contents

Foreword

Though the work of a select few French scholars on the Soviet Union is known wherever Russian studies are conducted, citations of French Sovietology are surprisingly sparse in the vast English-language literature on the USSR. Robert Desjardins has therefore performed an immense service by writing a guide to French published work on the Soviet Union (1945–85) in all its diversity and by placing it in its historical and ideological context.

It is a service to the non-French scholar who can draw upon Desjardins's several years of painstaking research and discover by leafing through these pages which parts of the French body of writing on Soviet affairs correspond either to his or her interests or appear to break new ground. It may be a boon also to French readers with a particular interest in the Soviet Union, for nothing like so full or so well-informed an overview of Soviet studies in France exists in the French language.

There are several reasons why this should be so, among them the fact that Soviet studies there have been quite widely scattered and lacking in specialist interdisciplinary institutes. Of equal importance has been the high degree of partisanship and politicisation characteristic of French writing on the Soviet Union which has made it hard to achieve as much scholarly cooperation on a national scale as exists, for example, in the United States, Britain or West Germany. While it is difficult for *anyone* to write an account of French Soviet studies acceptable to all of the contending schools of thought discussed in Desjardins's work, it would be well nigh impossible for an actual participant in the French debates to do so.

The author of this book has the advantage of being an outsider – and at the same time one who shares several of the attributes of an insider. On the one hand, Robert Desjardins provides ample evidence to support the view that the spectator sees more of the game. On the other, as a French Canadian, he has roots in French culture and an easy entrée into French intellectual life. His background at once distances him from the heated controversies he analyses and yet provides him with ready access to the special knowledge of the insider to complement the detachment of the outsider. He has made good use of his conversations and interviews in France as well as of his voluminous reading.

After studying law at the University of Montreal, the Free University of Brussels and the University of Ottawa, Robert Desjardins turned his attention to politics as a graduate student at Oxford University. Having acquired, *inter alia*, a thorough knowledge of the British and North American literature on the Soviet Union, he is in a good position to relate French Sovietology to that body of work without being tempted, as a native English speaker might be, to regard the French writing as no more than an odd deviation from the Anglo-American norm.

That temptation could be a real one. From a British perspective it seems as if at a time when the Soviet system was at its harshest and when the totalitarian paradigm was the dominant one in English-language Sovietology, a surprisingly large proportion of French writers on the Soviet Union saw that country as embodying the very principles of socialist democracy. Then, as late as the 1970s, long after the main features of the Stalin oppression had been assimilated into the Anglo-American consciousness and Sovietological writing, and a majority of British and North American specialists had begun to take note of the developing diversity within the Soviet Union which lay behind a monolithic façade, and were debating what kind of authoritarian (as distinct from totalitarian) state the USSR had become, totalitarian interpretations of the Soviet system gained a new lease of life and many adherents in France.

Robert Desjardins helps to explain how this development came about and at the same time shows convincingly that there is much more to French Soviet studies than such an oversimplifying summary can begin to convey. It is one of his reasonable contentions that even those writings which may strike the English-speaking reader as one-sided and extreme often contain insights which it would be unwise for other Western readers to ignore. Desjardins documents also the remarkable variety of theoretical standpoints to be found in French writing on the Soviet Union, while pointing to shortcomings as well as some achievements in detailed empirical research.

He does not restrict himself only to 'Sovietology' in a narrow sense, but takes account of the whole range of serious writing on the Soviet Union in post-war France with its diversity of political and academic standpoints. As a result, this book can be viewed as a case-study in recent French intellectual history as well as a work of importance for those whose particular interest is in the USSR. Even readers who do not find themselves in agreement with all of Desjardins's own judgements on Soviet developments and prospects and on the literature he discusses (and I would myself differ from some of them) can hardly fail to find his account illuminating. And after laying down this most comprehensive survey and interpretation of French perspectives on the Soviet Union, we shall have no excuse for not paying due regard to past and future French work in the Soviet field.

St Antony's College   ARCHIE BROWN
Oxford

Preface

The purpose of this book is to survey and interpret a relatively wide body of specialised French literature which has been devoted to the understanding of the Soviet Union. In reviewing this hitherto relatively neglected body of work, I concentrate on the most interesting and influential analyses and interpretations of French Sovietology. The book, need I say, does not claim to exhaust the entire subject. It is a contribution to that category of writing which has expounded the various approaches and 'conceptual lenses'[1] which have been utilised in Western (mainly Anglo-American) studies of Soviet politics. I have in mind, for instance, the concise but comprehensive appraisal of this scientific and scholarly literature carried out over a decade ago by Archie Brown, in his book *Soviet Politics and Political Science*.[2]

Anglo-American specialists (to the best of my knowledge) have been generally neglectful of French Sovietological literature. It may well be argued that such unfortunate neglect has deprived them of a wealth of interesting ideas about the Soviet system and of a set of theoretical positions which, however debatable they may be at times, are undoubtedly intellectually stimulating. It is my hope that this book will, perhaps, contribute to an increased awareness of French efforts. I trust it will serve both as a guide to French Sovietology for those whose lack of French prevents them from exploring it for themselves, and as an introduction to that literature for those who possess the language but have not hitherto had the time or motivation to find their bearings in the work of French specialists.

For the purposes of this book, I adopt a broad definition of Sovietology which will include not only the work of Soviet specialists but also the major writings of some French historians, economists, sociologists and political scientists who, although unfamiliar with the Russian language, can be regarded as having made a significant contribution to the understanding of the Soviet Union. I exclude from the scope of the book the study of the Soviet Union's foreign policy and international relations *per se*. None the less, I shall occasionally mention the factors which are perceived as lying behind that country's conduct in the international arena.

The period I cover runs from the mid-1940s until 1985. The choice of 1945 as the starting point of my survey fits in with the rise of the

Soviet Union to international stature, and with the strong need then felt in numerous Western circles for a thorough investigation of the inner workings of the Soviet socio-economic and political structures. As Hélène Carrère d'Encausse, one of the most prominent French specialists, remarked:

> at the end of the war, the U.S.S.R. is, in the eyes of world political leaders and international public opinion, no longer a transient state of an indeterminate nature but a permanent and stable reality . . . The acknowledged stabilisation of the Soviet regime made its study urgent; [the regime's] expansion into Eastern Europe and the budding cold war turned such urgency into an affair of state.[3]

My introductory chapter aims at shedding light on some elements pertaining to the social, cultural and academic spheres which have, at one time or another, directly influenced the development and orientation of French Sovietology. This field of study has periodically been viewed by specialists as being in a relative state of under-development. The first step of my research consists of taking a look at this question of under-development. In this respect, a brief depiction of the French effort prior to 1945 is offered, in order to provide the necessary historical perspective. The first chapter also attempts to locate French Sovietology within the larger framework of French political science.

Following this general introductory survey I proceed to examine selected interpretations of the Soviet Union. These discussions constitute the major part of the book. Thus, the second chapter considers a number of interpretations which belong to the Marxist tradition. Attention is paid, in particular, to the writings of C. Castoriadis, P. Naville and C. Bettelheim. The following chapter, concerned with totalitarianism and ideology, lays particular stress on the ideas developed by R. Aron, J. Monnerot, C. Lefort and A. Besançon. The fourth chapter, in addition to a consideration of the work of Carrère d'Encausse, seeks to provide a description of French theorising about some specific institutional questions such as the role and influence of the army in the Soviet Union. In the brief concluding chapter I devote some attention to the failure to establish in France an important centre for interdisciplinary research on the Soviet Union.

This book draws essentially on research conducted at Oxford University for a postgraduate dissertation. Needless to say, I feel greatly indebted to my former thesis supervisor Archie Brown, of St Antony's College, without whom this book would never have been possible. His advice and most perceptive comments on the whole manuscript have been of prime importance. I also want to thank Alex Pravda of the Royal Institute of International Affairs, Chatham House, who made a number of constructive suggestions at an earlier stage of the project. I wish to extend my gratitude to a number of French academics and researchers who gave up their valuable time to be interviewed: Jean Bonamour, Hélène Carrère d'Encausse, Francis Cohen, Jean-Guy Collignon, Marc Ferro, Michel Heller, Basile Kerblay, Georges Lavau, Lilly Marcou, Marie Mendras, Zdenek Strmiska, Michel Tatu and, lastly, the late Raymond Aron, who was particularly forthcoming and whose modesty made a great impression on me. Finally, the help received from various friends has been much appreciated. Errors and misjudgements are, of course, my own responsibility.

ROBERT DESJARDINS

1 The Development and Orientation of French Sovietology

The question of the development, or rather the under-development, of French Sovietology will constitute the fulcrum upon which a good part of this first chapter will turn. Soviet studies in France have often been considered by French scholars themselves to be relatively under-developed and backward. Thus, even though this book is essentially concerned with post-World War Two studies, it is appropriate to pay some attention to French work in this field prior to 1945. The weight of the past, with its traditions and specific features, cannot be overlooked. This kind of 'genealogical' scrutiny provides a necessary perspective within which to view French Sovietology in the immediate post-war decade. Even a brief scrutiny of this earlier period reveals that the field of Soviet studies had, in comparative terms, not been endowed with substantial scholarly or material resources.

THE FRENCH EFFORT PRIOR TO 1945

It was normal practice, during the period 1900–45, to speak and write of Slavonic studies and rarely of Russian or Soviet studies. Even if this may appear to be merely a matter of form, it is of some consequence that after 1917, despite the new and multi-faceted phenomenon created by the Russian Revolution, no case was presented for singling this country out as a distinctive subject of specialisation.

The central concerns of developing Russian studies were essentially grammatical and philological. Taking an overview of the years preceding 1914, one cannot avoid the conclusion that 'Slavic studies could still be perceived as a province of the empire of erudition, the fief of linguists, grammarians, philologists, archaeologists and palaeographers'.[1] These Slavonic studies were carried out by people largely unfamiliar with and uninterested in economics, sociology and politics. Moreover, such studies were undertaken by a few isolated scholars, 'hardly more than could be counted on the fingers'[2] and

1

they had a marginal status within the French university system. As Jean Bonamour, former director of the Institut d'études slaves located in Paris recently put it:

> For a long time, studies on the countries of Eastern Europe were of only marginal significance in French university life. Until the First World War – and to a large extent even up to 1945 – they remained the work of isolated scholars . . . After the First World War . . . Slavic studies remained of only marginal importance, especially since cultural relations with the USSR proved difficult to develop.[3]

At the end of World War One Paris was considered by some as a possible international centre for Russian studies, partly because of the conspicuous presence of numerous Russian *émigrés*. This expectation was disappointed. On the other hand, the war illuminated the need for a change in the global approach to Slavonic studies. A new door had to be opened.

In July 1917 Ernest Denis succeeded in publishing the first issue of a periodical called *Le Monde slave*. This scholar's intentions included the idea that the publication should diffuse and popularise intellectual currents and literary writings and, more surprisingly, show some interest in the political institutions of the Slavic peoples. The door had been opened. Sadly, this first attempt was to perish only months later with the signing of the Brest–Litovsk Treaty.[4]

Determined to go ahead regardless, Denis's biggest concern was the absence of any focal point for French Slavists. The idea of setting up a permanent institution was germinating, and in 1919 the Institut d'études slaves was founded in Paris. Among its various objectives was the sense that this newly created institute had 'to strive to follow and make available to an educated public the political, economic, intellectual and moral evolution of Eastern Europe's peoples'.[5] The door remained ajar. In 1921, the year which saw the death of Denis, a periodical purporting to be the official organ of the institute, the *Revue des études slaves*, was launched. One would have expected this publication to fulfil, at least partially, the above-mentioned aim. Such expectations were dashed however, since, according to the Foreword of the very first issue, the real business of the journal was to report on, and to echo, the latest developments taking place in the realm of linguistics and philology. The original intention of the Institut d'études slaves, to shed some light on the economic and political condition of the Slavonic peoples of Eastern Europe, remained unfulfilled. The consolidation of the Soviet regime did not change anything: the literary and philological orientations were scrupulously adhered to, and what could have been a new opportunity in Slavonic and Soviet studies had been missed. Nevertheless, some resolute minds decided that the time was ripe for changing the dominant direction of Slavonic studies. Louis Eisenmann, a professor at the University of Paris, played a notable role in bringing about this development.

It is interesting to note the quiet envy expressed by Eisenmann with regard to the 'nation-study' already well established in Britain, especially at the London School of Slavonic Studies. In an article published in 1922, he pointed out that the very structure of the French higher education system made it more difficult 'to find room for studies which have practical ends in view'.[6] In 1924 he combined his efforts with those of Auguste Gauvain of the Académie des Sciences morales et politiques, Henri Moysset of the Ecole de guerre navale and of Jules Legras of the University of Dijon, in order to resurrect the periodical of *Le Monde slave*. In a way, the affiliation of these men indicated that a new course of action was being proposed:

the Western world can no longer leave the study of the Slavic world, as if it were a mere curiosity, to a few scholars who would cultivate this field the way others cultivate the field of ancient India, primitive Greek civilisation or pre-columbian America.[7]

It must be stressed that these men had agreed that *Le Monde slave* would specifically devote more space to Russia, a country viewed as 'the great unknown of the problems of tomorrow'.[8] They expressed a sincere intention to study with objectivity and impartiality the new Russia, this political phenomenon which, as they speculated, 'will, perhaps more than any other phenomenon since the end of the Middle Ages, have changed the shape of Europe and . . . exerted the strongest influence on the destiny of our old continent and of the world'.[9]

For the first time in the history of French Sovietology such questions as the national or the Jewish problem were to receive attention. The programme of the periodical speaks for itself:

In the realm of politics: boundaries, constitutions, administrative systems, forms of government, life of political parties . . . military organisation and psychology of the military. In the realm of socio-economy: social structures, agrarian questions, labour legislation . . . financial and banking organisation.[10]

This ambitious programme may be seen as the beginning of modern French approaches to the study of the Soviet Union. A thorough examination of the contents of *Le Monde slave* over its fourteen years of existence reveals a number of topics which illustrate this breakthrough. Following the call by Marcel Mauss for a sociological study of Bolshevism,[11] one encounters titles explicitly referring to matters which still come within the compass of modern Sovietology, such as 'The XIVth Congress of the Russian Communist Party',[12] 'The Soviet government's nationalities policy in the Ukraine',[13] 'Women in Soviet Russia' (a study assessing on the basis of official figures the role and influence of women in the various soviets, the Communist party and trade unions),[14] 'Political, economic and intellectual life in the USSR' (a long chronicle of the events occurring in the Soviet Union),[15] 'The Komsomol',[16] 'Stalin's politics',[17] 'The second Russian agrarian revolution',[18] 'The Soviet press in 1932',[19] 'The Soviet Academy of Sciences',[20] 'The 1933 harvest in the USSR'.[21] As can be seen, there were constant efforts to assert the Soviet Union's uniqueness and examine some of its new and prominent features.

Nevertheless, one must not exaggerate the scope and repercussions of this noble effort. Thus, in the opinion of some sociologists, the attention given, in the pre-World War Two period, to the Slavonic reality had been virtually non-existent.[22] But much more crucial was the simple fact that the progress referred to did not, at any time, spark off a similar effort within the French higher education network, which remained impervious to the advances which had been achieved. For example, until 1939, no specialised courses on the Soviet Union were offered in French universities.[23] However, it is certainly pertinent that this academic 'darkness' also affected many other areas and countries and that the Soviet Union was by no means a singular or isolated case. Africa, for instance, where France had numerous interests as a colonial power, had been greatly neglected during the same period. Indeed, it seems quite remarkable that the colonial connections between France and Africa did not actually serve to stimulate French university study in the area.[24] Of course, the general pattern of intellectual indifference to 'area studies' must be taken into consideration.

Also illustrative of such important blind-spots is the case of the famous Ecole libre des Sciences politiques in Paris (ancestor of the Institut d'études politiques), which was not, as recalled by R. Szawloski and H. Terlecka

> prepared to devote a complete 'area-studies' course to Russia, although the presence of Leroy-Beaulieu on its staff for thirty years offered a unique opportunity to do so.[25] . . . the School offered, from time to time, apart from the 'Russian subchapters' in a few courses, individual lectures on topical aspects of Russia such as 'The Russian Parliament' or 'Socialism and the workers and agrarian movements in Russia'.[26]

With regard to the university system, one may note that the teaching and curricula have generally been characterised, even until recently, as continually trailing behind the various new currents of research taking place outside the university.[27] Furthermore, the university tradition of predominantly individual work has always been an obstacle to the launching of research in new fields.[28] The domain of Russian or Soviet studies, therefore, has suffered, and is still suffering, from those ingrained patterns within the university system, namely the disregard for area studies, lack of interest in the study of foreign countries, and a tradition of scholarly individualism rather than of cooperative effort.

All in all, it can be safely said that the endeavours which, prior to 1945, aimed at depicting existing Soviet realities and at propounding a serious analysis of some of the features, objectives and policies of the Soviet Union, were essentially carried out outside the aegis of the French university system by a relatively small group of dedicated observers and enquirers. Thanks to such men as B. Souvarine,[29] whose book *Staline – Aperçu historique du bolchevisme* is a classic,[30] topics of the kind which needed to be pursued if there were to be any further advance had begun to be investigated with a degree (albeit uneven) of insight. It remains to be seen whether the end of World War Two led French Sovietology to embark on a less precarious and more dynamic course.

THE POST-WAR PERIOD

On the face of it, the immediate post-war years presented an opportunity for systematic and sustained study of the Soviet Union.

A fresh chance to dig more deeply into that new world power had arisen and was apparently just waiting to be put into the concrete form of scholarly analysis. According to Y. Delahaye, France had more than one reason to undertake thorough study of the Soviet Union. Such a need was justified, for instance, by the alliance which had united France and the Soviet Union against the Nazis, and by the somewhat similar nature of many of the problems, economic as well as social, confronting both countries at that specific period.[31] Such study, therefore, was seen as being 'of obvious significance in the service of the state'.[32] For others, the 'new man' in the Soviet Union (and in Eastern Europe) could not be passed over in silence by French sociological research.[33] Thus, much was working in favour of an upsurge in Soviet studies. The sociologist E. Sicard, writing in 1946, stated that it was unacceptable 'that . . . such a vast area of research as the Soviet Union and the Slavic Republics of Central and Eastern Europe be abandoned by French science'.[34]

However, a growing disappointment with regard to the effective realisation of such necessary research did not take very long to be voiced:

There is no other country where [Soviet] studies have been more neglected. In France, there is no research or documentation centre especially devoted to the Soviet Union. Nothing, or virtually nothing, has been done in universities. It therefore comes as no surprise that the French contribution to the body of knowledge about the U.S.S.R. is insignificant when compared with that of Anglo-Saxon countries where important resources and sound working methods have benefited this discipline, which one could call 'Sovietology'.[35]

This critical judgement was delivered in 1956, which makes some of its points, such as the absence of research centres, obsolete. One is forced, however, to take note of the degree of the poverty this statement underscores, as well as the weakness of the French contribution to the knowledge of the Soviet Union in contrast to the situation in other countries. Of course, this judgement should not be misunderstood as meaning that nothing had been achieved in Soviet studies. Indeed, there is no doubt that in France a relative increase of interest in the Soviet Union was displayed after World War Two. For example, as was correctly pointed out by one of the leading French Sovietologists, Basile Kerblay, several groups, whose goal was the augmenting of knowledge of the Soviet Union, emerged in the decade subsequent to 1945, only to expire a few years later. Their demise was not undeserved in view of their biased publications of a generally mediocre standard.[36]

The truth is that the expected rapid growth of real scholarly work failed to materialise, even though the relevant conditions seemed to exist. In this context, the importance of continuity must be raised. Some hitherto essential features of French Slavonic studies, such as the inert attitude of the French universities, were bound to have a direct impact. Given that historical weight an overnight change was highly unlikely, however desirable it might have been. So, Delahaye might have been well advised to cast a glance over his shoulder to assess what exactly the whole period prior to 1945 had been like. This would have perhaps lessened his high expectations and perhaps softened his tone.

The general ideas conveyed by his account were, however, to be corroborated over the following years by many other people. In fact, the landscape of French Soviet studies is dotted with a spate of testimonies expressing concern about the unsatisfactory level attained. In 1969 R. Szawloski wrote of the gap existing in the field of Sovietology between France and other western countries, notably West Germany (a more reasonable partner in a comparison than the United States, when one considers the resources involved). Speaking of the urgent need for the French to catch up, he observed:

> If considerably more efforts, and human and financial resources, are used, this could perhaps, be achieved in one generation. If not, the situation around 2000 will not differ very much from the present one. The latter, on the threshold of the seventies, does not, in turn, differ very much from that existing in the twenties. This is not encouraging.[37]

Interestingly enough, Szawloski, on the point regarding generational delay, was quoted with approval by the jurist Michel Lesage in his most important book,[38] and also accepted by another French specialist, Georges Mond.[39] In 1971 the most prominent of contemporary French specialists on the Soviet Union, Hélène Carrère d'Encausse, recognised that France lagged considerably behind in the field of Soviet studies.[40] Finally, in 1979, G. Wild, in his review of the latter's book, *L'empire éclaté – la révolte des nations en U.R.S.S.*, notes 'the ignorance of Soviet realities that exists in France. One of the merits of Hélène Carrère d'Encausse is precisely to point out the necessity of more research and reflection on the USSR.'[41]

It has generally been understood by specialists that the development of Soviet studies in France has been impaired historically by the influence of two factors of a contrasting nature, the one structural and the other ideological. There is little doubt that these factors have combined to adversely affect the growth of French Sovietology.

Structural obstacles

Structural obstacles, as was suggested briefly in the first part of this chapter, lie in the French university and research systems. As far as the university structure is concerned, there has simply been no place in it for the production of specialists on the Soviet Union. The system has been concerned with the education of students for whom the Russian language constitutes an end in itself, and not a necessary adjunct to a grounding in the social sciences.

It has been generally acknowledged that the source of this failing has been the rigid division separating the disciplines (recognition that this is a problem is by no means a new phenomenon).[42] The persistent difficulty has consisted in the line drawn by the system between the teaching of the Russian language and the teaching of law, politics, and sociology.[43] This deep-seated feature, involving a basic rejection of any idea of integration, has produced results which have robbed French Sovietology of a potential pool of well-trained researchers. According to Michel Lesage:

> Under these circumstances, it was very difficult to train experts on Eastern Europe in the various social sciences. The system could only lead to the training of specialists of language and literature who were not introduced to the other problems of East European societies. It also generated economists and jurists who, with certain exceptions, had a poor knowledge of the specific problems of such societies. The few existing specialists were often self-taught, their approach being more or less artisanal.[44]

The organisation of teaching has inhibited the kind of interdisciplinary studies required in order to lay the foundations of a sustained growth in Sovietology. Even today, the prospects for securing a degree of integration within the university sector appear to be somewhat remote. This is particularly so if one takes into account the perennial university emphasis on the study of Russian language and literature, together with the fact that the social sciences have generally found a more receptive home in diverse research centres and institutes.[45] As noted by Lesage, the French effort in Soviet studies has for a long period relied upon and revolved around self-taught specialists. To rely on such a 'do-it-yourself' policy has proved insufficient and the numerous accusations of under-development in this field of study drive home the point that a price has been paid for this policy.

Attention must also be drawn to the fragmentation of the research effort as a whole – that is, including research conducted outside the universities. The specialists of the 1950s and 1960s ended up labouring in, as it were, a closed circuit. Those years were ones of great isolation for the researchers, and the 'individual, piecemeal research' has been condemned by one leading French specialist as an anachronism.[46] A few years earlier, another writer tried to convey a sense of urgency; Jean Train went so far as to link that isolation with the critical backwardness of the general French Sovietological endeavour.[47] Train's plea was for the harnessing of the dispersed efforts of researchers without which French Sovietology would carry on dabbling. The underlying idea was to instigate better 'organised research',[48] the need for which was highly apparent.

The place to locate the planning of this organisation would, at first sight, appear to be the Centre National de la Recherche Scientifique (CNRS), which constitutes the official body in charge of promoting, coordinating and orientating scholarly research in France. The reality is that the CNRS has never initiated any kind of plan or had any research strategy with regard to Eastern Europe and the Soviet Union.[49]

Part of the problem is also the multiplication of small research units, attached or unattached to the universities. Indeed, this undoubtedly represents a far cry from the situation which prevailed in the 1950s. This particular phenomenon, it is worth noting, must be seen in the more general context of the French social science policy in which there is a tendency to conceive of progress in research as arising from merely an increase in the number of teams and institutes. At first sight, it might seem that a proliferation of research should signify a new vitality affecting the French Sovietological endeavour.

There is, no doubt, a grain of truth in this, though it should not go without qualification. Indeed, it must be stressed that interest shown in the Soviet Union and the institutional energy expended on furthering its comprehension vary enormously, with the demand for specialists fluctuating from one institution to another. In some cases, the image conveyed is one of a token Sovietologist. Thus, not only are the researchers widely scattered, but they find themselves working in institutions whose work is orientated only incidentally towards the Soviet Union. Jean Bonamour has ably captured this feature when he writes of 'the extreme scattering of researchers in Soviet and East European affairs' who 'often belong to institutions that are by no means specializing in Soviet . . . research but are concerned in general terms with world history, the legal sciences, comparative economic science'.[50]

It is dubious, to say the least, whether such an increase in the number of institutes should be associated with a better-organised research effort. One may argue that if the latter is to be achieved, attempts to remedy the rather weak intercommunication existing between these institutions have to be made. In this respect, the effort undertaken by the CNRS has amounted to virtually nothing. However, one may point to the agreement signed in 1975 by seventeen French universities, the Ecole des Hautes Etudes en Sciences sociales and the Institut d'études politiques in Paris. That convention created a new body, the Institut National d'études slaves (INES), placed under the authority of the Ministry for the Universities.

According to the first clause of the agreement, the signatories agreed to coordinate their actions through the INES in order to ensure the development of scientific research in the field of Russian and Soviet studies. However, a quick survey reveals that no progress in terms of coordination has been achieved. Moreover, the INES no longer exists.[51] A new entity, the Institut du Monde Soviétique et de l'Europe Centrale et Orientale (IMSECO) was created in March 1986 and superceded the INES.[52] Among the various objectives underlying this recent creation was the need to have in France a centre for research on the Soviet Union and Eastern Europe that will seek, yet again, to coordinate the works emanating from various French academic and research institutions. Time will tell whether such coordination will materialise.

As far as the question of collaboration among scholars is concerned, one is forced to conclude that very little headway has been made. Leading specialists readily acknowledge this fact.[53] Of course, the picture is not entirely bleak, since there have been a number of common efforts in some areas. A problem, however, in so far as collaboration is concerned, lies squarely in the nature of the subject of study itself. Given the ideological baggage which study of the Soviet Union has long carried, Sovietology has been somewhat partitioned into what may be called 'ideologico-methodological coteries'[54] which have made up the rather loose research infrastructure. The nature of these cleavages has curtailed the possibilities of collaboration.

Leaving that aspect aside, one must also observe another significant trait of the social sciences in France – that is, the well-known relationship between mandarin-patron and research worker. Even though this feature is not completely applicable to the field of Sovietology because of the lack of team work, the foreign observer generally notices a glaring contrast between a small group of 'big names' much sought after in France and on the international scholarly circuit, enjoying all the rewards associated with that fame, and the rest of the researchers working in relative obscurity. Indeed, there is a danger that these 'big names' may be somewhat distracted by their own success, since these specialists have to face a great many demands. This risk of 'over-exposure' may cause the quality of their work and research to suffer.[55] Because it has been left to a sort of spontaneous growth for so long, and because its infrastructure has suffered from fragmentation and dispersion, French Sovietology could not avoid being fertile ground for the emergence of several leaders presiding over limited fiefdoms.[56]

On the whole, our brief examination has demonstrated that the French scene is still plagued by organisational problems. Among other things, the French university system has remained a disappointing educational and research instrument as far as the Soviet Union is concerned – at any rate, in disciplines other than language and literature. According to the well-informed scholars Jean Bonamour and Jean-Guy Collignon, what was said by Michel Lesage in 1969 still fundamentally holds good.[57] The important catching-up effort facing French Sovietology in the 1960s required, to some extent, a concentration of human and financial resources. As has been pointed out, nothing of the sort took place. The harnessing of the research appears to have been insufficient. Collective, interdisciplinary work has been rare, and it may well be argued that the flourishing individualism has also been yielding inadequate results.

Passions and taboo

It is necessary to examine how seriously ideological considerations have at times dramatically impeded the progress and growth of

French studies devoted to the Soviet Union. This was most notably apparent between 1945 and 1956, when there was a near paralysis of such studies in France. In this period the Soviet Union could hardly be subjected to scholarly investigation without arousing all sorts of polemical storms. It constituted an exceptionally sensitive and controversial subject matter. 'For years', recalled Pierre Sorlin, 'it was almost impossible to broach the subject without unleashing passions'.[58] It is fair to mention here that passion had not been absent before World War Two. To be sure, the Soviet Union, as far back as the 1920s, was often looked at, as remarked by *Le Monde slave*'s Conseil de Direction, with 'the eyes of an inquisitor or exorcist'.[59] In the Introduction to his book *La Russie Soviétique* (1927), Jacques Lyon confirmed this fact and underlined the necessity for students of the Soviet Union to assert their primary concern with scientific objectivity.[60] In 1947 the sociologist E. Sicard touched on this problem by referring to 'the difficulties and passions of a political nature that have always accompanied the discussion of Russian research topics'.[61] This being said, one has to bear in mind that, as far as passions are concerned, the decade 1945–56 represented an unrivalled peak.

In order to understand this period, we should briefly evoke the intellectual climate of those years. In post-war France, as pointed out by the sociologist François Bourricaud, 'Marxism and the Communist Party become obligatory reference points for all those pretending to belong to the Left'.[62] In the general context of the ideological disqualification of the Right, the Left intelligentsia became, in the words of Jean-Marie Domenach, 'the dominant intelligentsia'.[63] This intelligentsia dreamt of a revolution which, as it well knew, could not possibly take place in France. Thus, as Gilles Martinet once observed:

> The Left intelligentsia dreams of a revolution that cannot occur in France. Therefore, it projects this dream elsewhere and wants to discover in a far away land . . . that [which] does not exist in France. Such political exotism causes it to lend its own aspirations and phantasms to societies which are in fact extraordinarily remote from this imagery . . . The Soviet intervention in Hungary deals a decisive blow to these illusions . . . The USSR can no longer be the object of such projections.[64]

The Soviet Union, 'wearing the halo of glory earned at Stalingrad',[65] constituted the homeland of socialism in the minds of a great many French intellectuals who 'invested in it all the dreams of an emancipated humanity'.[66] For them, though with varying degrees of enthusiasm, the Soviet Union had gained the title of 'most ideologically privileged nation'.[67] Any person daring to level a criticism against the Soviet Union was automatically accused of playing into the hands of the class enemy and labelled as a member of the imperialist and fascist camp. Naturally, few people were ready to run such a risk. In a 1948 issue of *Les Temps modernes*, Claude Lefort, writing about Victor Kravchenko's book *I Chose Freedom*, made this particular point very clear:

> There is a fundamental ambiguity in the subject of the U.S.S.R.: any criticism of the U.S.S.R. necessarily implies a defense of the interests of world capitalism. Such reasoning obviously goes very far. Indeed, all those who get caught in this trap are obliged – regardless of their moral scruples and mental reservations – to follow the sinuous path of Stalinism and to justify its politics either with fallacious arguments or silent complicity.[68]

Obviously, under such conditions, the Soviet Union could not be subjected to serious, reflective scrutiny.

It is evident that the role played by the French Communist Party (PCF) was of the utmost importance. The PCF had made it an absolute priority to defend the Soviet Union, by any means and whenever requested.[69] Intellectuals not belonging to the Party frequently found themselves, as mentioned by Lefort, in a position where they had to align themselves, tacitly or not, to the party line. Equally, the ideological ascendancy of the PCF in the social sciences has to be reckoned with. The sociologist Alain Touraine, in his memoirs, recollects that state of affairs:

> Today, one can hardly appreciate the extent of the Communist domination . . . Those who were not Communists, as was frequently the case in social sciences, were manifestly considered to be on the fringe. There are very few social scientists whose life has not been dominated by their relationship with the Communist Party.[70]

By enunciating a number of dogmas and by its hostility to the social sciences, seen as the product of American imperialism,[71] the PCF was able to exert considerable leverage as far as the methods and concepts applicable to the Soviet Union were concerned. For instance, the concept of totalitarianism was discarded without appeal because it was judged reactionary, and simply a ploy diverting minds from the real enemy, that is, the capitalist system.[72]

The PCF sought to be the only 'authoritative' source able to speak about the Soviet Union. It managed to do so, being successful in what was seen as its function 'in authenticating truth' (*rôle de pôle d'authentification de la vérité*) about this revolutionary country.[73] In this connection, the theoretical approach and terminology developed by the sociologist Pierre Bourdieu may prove useful.[74] One would constantly find the PCF, an actor engaged in the 'political field' as a producer of proposals and programmes and as a seeker of a share of political power, articulating a set of 'authorised' images of the Soviet Union. The PCF, in its own interests, infiltrated the 'scientific field' attached to the study of the Soviet Union and short-circuited its possible or normal functioning. The PCF's success did, for some time, have serious consequences for the advent of a sustained French Sovietology. Raymond Aron once deplored that regrettable distortion and went so far as to link the strong development of British Sovietology with the numerical and political insignificance of the British Communist Party.[75]

In short, the most unfortunate effect induced by the intellectual environment prevalent in the post-war decade was the unwillingness or reluctance of interested people to initiate research into the Soviet Union.[76] This was accompanied by the general attitude prevailing in the university community, which has been called 'academism' by the historian Alain Besançon. This term refers to the great degree of timidity caused by important social considerations which have impeded 'the search and expression of the truth'.[77] Although few university professors were members of the PCF, it seems that they had cautiously taken notice of the *Zeitgeist* and were behaving accordingly. At that time, the Presses Universitaires de France could be accused by some observers of being complacent towards the Communists and suspicious of everything that could offend them.[78] A secondary effect was, as pointed out by B. Kerblay, that the work done on the Soviet Union had to be gauged only by 'external criteria', that is, to be qualitatively 'assessed by their formal guarantees' such as familiarity with certain techniques and the adequacy of the bibliographic references.[79]

1956, largely because of the Hungarian Revolution, constituted an important turning point in so far as those historical events broke forever the sacred image of the Soviet Union: 'The intervention of

Soviet tanks desecrated the motherland of socialism and, indeed, "relativized" Communism.'[80] Budapest significantly reduced the appeal of Communism for a great many French intellectuals. The environment conditioning the near paralysis of Soviet studies started to change and, importantly, it became, as emphasised by F. Bourricaud, 'possible to talk about the Soviet Union in almost the same manner as any other country'.[81]

That essential qualitative modification carried the potential of an advance from the hitherto dormant state of Soviet studies and research. However, it must be noted that the years following 1956 saw the French intelligentsia more interested in condemning 'Soviet imperialism' than in studying thoroughly Soviet politics and society.[82] Interestingly enough, the same general attitude may be said to apply to a large extent to the intellectuals whose final 'reconversion' took place either with Prague in 1968 or in the 1970s with the 'revelations' of Solzhenitsyn.[83] There is no other country in which this famous dissident made a bigger impact.[84] What had been known and regularly denounced in France since the 1920s, that is, 'institutionalised' police arbitrariness as well as the existence of the prison-camps, suddenly entered the public consciousness.[85] It has been acknowledged that ideological residues deriving from a Leftist experience had barred many intellectuals from an earlier discovery of the highly oppressive nature of the Soviet regime. (Mention ought to be made that this general line of explanation has been questioned by a number of writers who have been more inclined to underline the more basic idea of self-imposed intellectual blindness.)[86] In any case, it is well beyond dispute that Solzhenitsyn induced a very profound change in French intellectual circles. Some of its members even felt compelled to commit to print their revised thoughts on Marxism and the 'real' Soviet Union. However, they did so in a fashion which was generally anything but scientific.[87]

That having been said, it is worth reiterating that 1956 marked the end of the great ideological freeze which had been so adversely affecting the growth of French Sovietology for more than a decade. It is also worth pointing out that the background of the 1950s has produced interesting long-term effects. This is particularly so in the case of former Communists or supporters of the Soviet Union who became Sovietologists at a later date, who have swung to the other extreme on the ideological spectrum. These people represent the 'right-wing' tendency in modern French Sovietology. For them, the Soviet Union constitutes a phenomenon unique in human history.

They tend to guard themselves against the use of conceptual tools developed within contemporary political science which, they believe, cannot properly advance the understanding of this unique Soviet phenomenon. In this respect, a somewhat extreme viewpoint was expressed a few years ago by Michel Heller, a Russian *émigré* who arrived in France in 1969 and who is currently *maître-assistant* at the Sorbonne. Closely associated with this tendency, he once made clear that, in his opinion, Jerry Hough, one of the most prominent American specialists, 'delves very deeply where there is nothing to find. It is an abstract analysis that serves no purpose.'[88] The interpretation of Alain Besançon, who is also representative of this tendency, will be examined at a later stage.

So, in the aftermath of Budapest, 'all can be said'.[89] However, such possibilities were to be conditioned in some respects by the very development of French political science.

Soviet studies in French political science

Among the questions to be examined in this final section is the one encapsulated in a comment by Roger Kanet, an American political scientist and observer of French Sovietological work. He has pointed out that most of the French writing on Soviet politics 'fits into the category of institutional–legal studies'. He amplifies:

> Detailed discussions of the organizational structure of the state and party apparatus, careful dissection of the intricacies of the Soviet constitutions, and surveys of the highlights of the historical development of the Soviet Union dominate most French studies.[90]

Kanet's opinion must be taken for what it is – an undoubtedly useful generalisation, but one which involves some element of simplification. There are other categories, outcomes of long-standing and evolving interest which, though at times less voluminous, could lay claim to having established the reputation of French Sovietology. Nevertheless, it would be pointless to deny that institutional–legal studies have been much to the fore over the last 25 years. They constitute a major facet of French Sovietology.

Any sensible treatment of this question can hardly be separated, as we have indicated, from the larger frame of reference represented by political science itself. Rudolf L. Tökés once observed that most American area specialists involved in studying Communist politics were also 'practicing *political scientists*' and that, as such, they were bound to be aware of and influenced by the intellectual and methodological dilemmas of their discipline.[91] Although the word 'dilemmas' may be quite inappropriate in the French context, the rest of the proposition may still hold true. It may show how Sovietology in France exhibits some of the basic features of French political science. French Sovietology, a few cases notwithstanding (analysis of bureaucracy, for example) has rarely been innovative for French political science as a whole. Rather the reverse, in that it appears to have clung on to the themes and approaches already provided by that political science. French Sovietology has generally not ventured into areas left uncharted by mainstream French political science. This cautious attitude, it may be argued, has coloured its own sense of direction, since it has meant overlooking areas of scientific interest such as policy analysis.[92] In this respect, Sovietology has been negatively cross-fertilised, as it were, by French political science.

As far as institutional–legal studies are concerned, the reasons for their prominence do not present the observer with a problem. Simply, French Sovietology has reflected and, one may argue, outlived the main approach which dominated French political science until the early 1960s, that is, 'the history and the "formal–legal" analysis of the state with a strong emphasis laid on the institutions examined from the viewpoint of public law'.[93]

The years after World War Two witnessed, despite the strong influence of Marxist dogmatists, a significant boom in the social sciences which had some effect on political science. This growing interest was channelled into the creation of the Fondation Nationale des Sciences Politiques, entrusted with the task of ensuring the progress and diffusion of political science as well as of the social sciences more generally. The creation of a number of Instituts d'études politiques followed.

Finally, from the mid-1950s, political science became a minor but systematic appendage to the official programmes of the Facultés de droit. A major problem arose here. Prior to this educational innovation there had been no specialised 'training' connected to this 'fashionable science'.[94] The new teaching cadres had to be found, but who had the competence? What took place has been explained by Professor Georges Burdeau: 'As there was no autonomous teaching of political science, until recently, one came to it from other domains. Political science did not train its own researchers but, instead, borrowed them from other sciences.'[95] Thus, and this is important to remember, historians, experts in literature, philosophers, professors of public law and others who were not political scientists by educational background, were incorporated into this enterprise.

For the historians, this involvement was by no means a step in the dark. Historians – especially, perhaps, diplomatic historians – had been flirting with political science in the Facultés des Lettres throughout the first half of the century. This close relationship may be illustrated by the nomination of the eminent historian Pierre Renouvin as the second President of the Fondation Nationale des Sciences Politiques. As for professors of constitutional law, the foundations for a serious penetration of political science by them had, as was pointed out by political scientist Jean Leca, been laid down at the turn of the nineteenth century by famous jurists (Léon Duguit, for example).[96] For the jurists, the question of the state clearly constituted public law's essential object of reflection and study. Their writings dealt with constitutional developments within the various political regimes and described their respective political institutions. Indeed, post-World War Two jurists began by pursuing and insisting upon that classic orientation.[97]

All these academics were confronted with the uneasy task of improvising as political scientists, and they were naturally inclined to resort to the general methods and approaches with which they were most familiar.[98] There is little doubt that the original disciplines of these men and women had a profound effect on the initial orientation taken by French political science (and, as a result, the one taken by Sovietology). Thus, the original background of many political scientists, together with the French intellectual tradition, kept them away from large domains of investigation eagerly explored by their American colleagues and, for some time, instigated mistrust towards American methods. On this particular question, an observation made by political scientist Alfred Grosser in 1960 is very relevant:

> Almost none of the French political scientists, the majority of whom are well *experienced in the methods of literary or juridical analysis*, has penetrated the domains in which the American 'political scientist' has been evolving since the early years of his academic training. The French political scientist can and must develop an interest in psychology, sociology and . . . statistics; in general, however, he will not master them.[99]

While French Sovietology was beating the drum of institutional–legal studies, its American counterpart was involved in a scholarly process characterised by an important qualitative change, shifting 'from isolationism to comparativism' (to use the words of J.-G. Collignon).[100] There is no need to linger over this phenomenon here, since it has been well described and documented. It is worth noting, however, that the American awareness of the isolation associated with the area studies orientation came hand-in-hand with the general expansion in comparative research. As pointed out by Daniel Tarschys, there was an increasing interest during the 1960s in integrating research on Soviet government with comparative political studies. This provided Sovietologists with new instruments and fresh theoretical frameworks.[101]

This evolution attracted some French attention. Basile Kerblay, for one, considered that the study of the Soviet Union could only be 'fructified by advances in the social sciences'.[102] Some years later, Hélène Carrère d'Encausse emphatically welcomed the newly opening horizons in Soviet studies.[103] Of course, for some, especially those in Marxist circles, the picture was not at all that promising. The jurist Robert Charvin, for example, considered the Anglo-Saxon quantitative methods as a clearly useless tool when applied to the task of understanding the political reality of the Socialist states, and condemned the artificiality of transferring to those states instruments and themes developed within the womb of Western (particularly American) political sociology.[104]

This particular Marxist response may be regarded as an over-reaction. Firstly, at the time Charvin vented his concern, numerous 'American intellectual fashions' were already on the decline and had never, in any case, been (even at the height of their influence) in a position to produce any real impact on French Sovietology. Secondly, the present situation demonstrates only too well that what has emerged from years of sometimes heated academic debate remains of marginal significance in France. Hélène Carrère d'Encausse is unreserved on this specific point: 'the influence on French Sovietology of the American research on the Soviet Union has been weak, if not non-existent'.[105] (Interestingly, as Kanet has remarked, the latest writings of Carrère d'Encausse show a clear influence of American scholarship in her approach to the study of Soviet politics.)[106] Indeed, the 'insularity' of French Sovietology may be said to be anchored in French political science, which has itself been relatively autarkic. Thus, Pierre Favre has recently underlined the undeniable reality of the 'very weak penetration [in France] of foreign political science, most notably that of the Anglo-Saxon countries'.[107]

2 Analyses in the Marxist Tradition

INTRODUCTION

This chapter examines certain general analyses of the Soviet Union which belong, broadly speaking, to the Marxist tradition, as well as some of the specific issues raised by *hommes de gauche*. It also looks briefly at the work of the economist Marie Lavigne. It seems entirely fitting to conclude this chapter with a discussion of Lavigne, since she has generally found fault with the basic line pursued by various Marxist economists in search of a conceptualisation revealing the 'true' nature of the Soviet system.

One introductory remark is in order. The critique of the Soviet system made by Leon Trotsky has been a source of inspiration and the starting point for some of the writers considered in the present chapter. We should not be surprised to find, therefore, an emphasis on the USSR as a bureaucratic phenomenon holding considerable sway within French Marxist circles. The precise nature of class relationships within Soviet society and the problem of relating a characterisation of the power of the bureaucracy to class analysis have been questions of central importance in Marxist accounts of the Soviet Union.[1]

In France the group 'Socialisme ou Barbarie', led by Cornelius Castoriadis, forcefully equated, in the 1940s and 1950s, the bureaucracy with a new dominant class. However, the group was following in the footsteps of others such as the economist Lucien Laurat who, in the 1930s, had already produced a similar characterisation of the Soviet bureaucracy. Laurat was of Austrian extraction, his real name being Otto Maschl. After spending three years in Moscow in the mid-1920s, he finally settled in France. During his lifetime Laurat was very often associated in his work with Boris Souvarine.[2] Then a member of the Parti socialiste français (SFIO), Laurat edited *Le Combat Marxiste* between October 1933 and April 1936. This periodical offered Laurat the opportunity to criticise Trotsky's analysis as well as to further explore the nature of the Soviet Union. In a book published in 1931, Laurat, borrowing an idea expressed some years earlier by Souvarine,[3] took the view that the Russian bureaucratic oligarchy, though not owning any means of production, constituted a new exploiting class: 'What characterises a class . . . is its function in the whole economic process as well as the source of its income. A study of this question reveals that the Soviet bureaucratic oligarchy is indeed a class deriving its income from the exploitation of the population.'[4]

These early assertions did not influence Pierre Frank, who was Trotsky's secretary in 1932 and 1933 and a well-known figure in the Fourth International.[5] In fact, Frank derided comrade Castoriadis, as he then was, when the latter started laying the groundwork of *'Socialisme ou Barbarie'*.[6] Frank's viewpoint remained relatively constant, and he rejected the assimilation of the Soviet bureaucracy to a new class, still viewing it as a 'parasitical element in the new mode of production'.[7] Frank has generally remained faithful to the teachings of Trotsky. In an essay written almost 30 years after the polemic with Castoriadis, Frank asserts:

> the main theses developed by Trotsky on the nature of the Soviet society and on the role of the bureaucracy in this society still constitute, in our view, the framework from which it is possible to understand the evolution as well as the contradictions of the Soviet Union.[8]

In Frank's opinion, there is little doubt that the bureaucracy has, for some time, been in a period of decline. A political revolution, far from being an unlikely possibility, appears to be a genuine one. Such a revolution should aim at destroying bureaucratic privileges, keeping the socialist base and 'restoring' full socialist democracy.[9] One cannot but be amazed by Frank's bold affirmation that 'there is no doubt that the greatest future in the Soviet Union is promised to Trotskyism'.[10]

For some time such theories of the bureaucracy as a new ruling class left Jean Elleinstein unimpressed. Appointed historian of the PCF, a position he held for a number of years, he published two books in 1975, the fourth volume of his *Histoire de l'U.R.S.S.* and his *Histoire du phénomène stalinien.*[11] According to the French political scientist Georges Lavau, Elleinstein, at this particular period, 'can be regarded as an unofficial spokesman and advance guard for the party'.[12]

The picture of the Soviet Union which can be drawn from these books can be briefly summarised. For Elleinstein, the Soviet Union, despite numerous difficulties, represented the 'Land of Socialism'. The relative superiority of the socialist system over the capitalist one would prove to be absolute in a few decades. Indeed, he saw in the Soviet Union a more rational economic organisation than in the West. Though admitting the existence of social classes, he constantly refused to view the bureaucracy as a new exploiting class:

> The phenomenon of bureaucracy must not be mixed up with the existence of a bureaucratic class – management posts were neither hereditary nor were they held for life. One does not find a group of people who occupy the same position in the process of production and the circulation of capital and there is no social reproduction of groups of leaders.[13]

Elleinstein left the PCF in 1980. In that same year he wrote the Foreword of the French edition of Michael Voslensky's book *La Nomenklatura – Les privilégiés en URSS*. In these few pages one finds a radical reappraisal which only serves to stun the reader. On Elleinstein's own admission, Voslensky's book caused him to adopt a completely new interpretation of the Soviet Union:

> The reading of Voslensky's book has finally convinced me of the existence of a genuine dominant class in the Soviet Union.[14] . . . a class – the Nomenklatura – . . . exploits and dominates the majority of the population through a totalitarian State.[15]

Elleinstein goes on to affirm that this class wields an unprecedented power, reigning in a system which boasts methods of government unique in the whole of human history. The assimilation of the Soviet Union to a variant of 'Asiatic despotism' is rebutted by Elleinstein, who claims that such an explanation totally omits the originality and modernity of the system.

Elleinstein is an interesting case for us, in that he has painfully broken away from what he calls 'a now ancient tradition and a sufficiently sophisticated mythology'.[16] This idea of mythology vindicates, if much vindication were needed, the large majority of French specialists who have for decades turned a blind eye to, or retained a healthy scepticism for, the various works on the Soviet Union published under the auspices, or with the 'holy' benediction, of the PCF. Such scepticism was brought about by the profound scientific poverty of these works.

When it became impossible to be content with strictly adhering to and repeating the best passages of the Stalinist catechism, the typical and devout Communist writer launched into an interpretation of the Soviet Union which essentially, and for a long period of time, confined itself to an apologetic idealisation and sanctimonious admiration of the system. However, in the 1970s, under circumstances marked by the Eurocommunist wave and by what has been dubbed 'the Gulag effect', this uncritical theoretical position ebbed. In some Communist quarters there was a sense of the need to develop a more credible global picture of the Soviet Union. A book published in 1978, *L'URSS et Nous*, embodied the thoughts of five intellectuals trying to achieve this objective of 'modernisation'. Francis Cohen, who wrote the Introduction, spelled out the new state of mind:

> For a long time, we have persisted in considering the negative aspects of the Soviet Union merely as diseases that attacked the system but which did not originate from it.
>
> Nowadays, we want to examine the system as it is and as it functions . . . We want to recognise its contradictions since only they will enable us to understand the contrasts as well as the possibilities for progress.[17]

In spite of all its caution, 'prudish' tone and silences which skipped over various important issues, the work constituted, in a sense, a qualitative leap forward. It allowed the attentive reader, as observed by Lavau, the opportunity 'to form a half-positive and half-negative judgement on the Soviet regime'.[18]

It is worth taking note that the book did not go unnoticed in interested Muscovite circles, where unpleasant surprise was provoked by such a daring novelty which had received warm support from the PCF's leadership.[19] Four Soviet commentators contributing to *Kommunist*, the theoretical organ of the CPSU's Central Committee, condemned the book. The condemnation was also reprinted in its entirety in the Soviet periodical *New Times*. Their message was put across in a clear fashion: 'the book is not objective and is in many respects untruthful'.[20] They were also severe in their comment that 'the book leaves one with the depressing impression that the authors wittingly or unwittingly have viewed Soviet reality not with their own eyes but through the coloured spectacles of anything but friends of socialism'.[21] One finds the four Soviet authors trying to understand, to plumb the depths of what they saw as a 'radical turn in the thinking of Francis Cohen and his co-authors'.[22] It was as if they felt the necessity to undermine the credibility of Francis Cohen and ironically remind him of his previously large contribution to an 'objective' description of their country. Indeed, here they had a point.

As a Communist intellectual, Cohen may be regarded as one of the main figures of French 'Communist Sovietology'.[23] Cohen is at present one of the directors of the Institut de Recherches Marxistes (the IRM was founded by the PCF in 1979), where he heads the 'socialism' section in charge of research projects on the Soviet Union and other socialist countries. Between 1946 and 1949 Cohen was correspondent of the PCF's newspaper *L'Humanité* in Moscow, and, between 1966 and 1980, he was editor of the periodical *La Nouvelle Critique*.

When one examines Cohen's 'objective and sound' writings, which were but pleasant memories for his Soviet critics, it is difficult to resist the temptation to recall some propositions which undeniably bordered on absurdity. In fact, there is a surfeit of choice. As a dedicated Stalinist,[24] Cohen was once proud to celebrate the glowing superiority of the socialist civilisation over the decadent capitalist one, and to write of a 'superior sort of man, who progresses steadily on the road to Communism'.[25] Fourteen years later, in a book which came out in 1963, he confidently advanced that 'in the pursuit of science and technology . . . the Soviet Union has gained an insurmountable lead'[26] and that 'the ongoing economic and social transformations are leading to an apparently limitless development of the human being'.[27] Cohen was also dauntless enough to state that 'there is not a single major problem of our times to which the Soviet Union does not propose a solution through its example or suggestions'.[28] Furthermore, in line with this last quotation, one comes across Cohen in 1965 arguing that, apart from being a source of anti-Soviet propaganda, the American Institutes studying Soviet affairs were also attempting 'to find, in socialism, methods that . . . would help capitalism to prolong its survival'.[29]

The contemporary Cohen has certainly distanced himself from this type of discourse and, as it were, acknowledged his sins. His more recent writings, indeed, bring to light some points of interest. The first concerns his attitude to the idea of a new ruling class. In a book published in 1974, he was forthright about this idea of a new class, denying it any scientific value: 'No Soviet citizen enjoys the slightest possibility of investing in means of production . . . The notion of a "new class" is entirely disconnected from the means and relations of production, and has no scientific value whatsoever'.[30] In 1981, Cohen seemed to have made a move in favour of a more scientific approach to this issue, at the expense of his orthodoxy. In the face of what he considers to be a social group enjoying important managerial power, he wishes to see a comprehensive study concentrating on important social aspects of the question, such as the formation, mobility and reproduction of the leading bureaucratic layers.[31] Despite this concession, Cohen remains committed to his rejection of the idea that the Soviet bureaucracy does, or could, form a ruling class. Finally, in a Summer 1983 issue of *Recherches internationales*, an IRM publication, Cohen dismisses, albeit while avoiding any categorical judgement, the suggestion made by some that the Soviet intelligentsia now constitutes a new ruling class. In the same article Cohen reckons that, in the context of the whole discussion bearing on this class, the Nomenklatura represents an avenue worth exploring.[32] However, Cohen is then quick to eschew any pronouncement on this particular social category on the grounds of lack of information and data.

This aspect of Cohen's reflection brings in its train the fundamental question of who holds power in the Soviet Union. In 1977 Cohen had little hesitation in affirming that 'for the first time in History, there exists a regime in which the labouring masses hold the power'.[33] In *L'URSS et Nous*, one can read a more moderate Cohen, then writing of a 'power oriented towards the working class and partially by it'.[34] Five years later, in a 1983 issue of *Cahiers du Communisme*, the theoretical organ of the PCF's Central Committee, Cohen comments that there is no simple answer to this question, but goes on to assert that 'serious studies reveal the hegemony of the working class, through its organisations and social weight'.[35] On the other hand, Cohen has long recognised that, at all levels and in all spheres, the party leads and decides. To reconcile this reality with the preceding theoretical point, Cohen likes to resort to the social structure of the CPSU. Particularly significant, in his eyes, is the priority given to the working class in the recruitment of new members. As he confesses, 'it may perhaps not be sufficient, but it is a very important political act that affirms the role of the working class. This act has considerable consequences.'[36] One regrets that Cohen does not explain the real extent and nature of these consequences.

An interesting recent emphasis made by Cohen is on the concept of social pluralism. Essentially, this conjures up the question of the social complexity of the Soviet Union. In this regard, Cohen underlines the numerous and important social differentiations which have emerged concurrently with the *rapprochement* of the social classes and their serious effects:

> Our attention is drawn to a new social differentiation that is becoming more important as class differences tend to disappear with the systematic structural evolution of socialist countries . . . The categories and social groups based on qualification, professional activities, . . . sex, nationality . . . education, etc., have different interests. These interests may not coincide, and may even come into conflict.[37]

The above-mentioned conflicting situations constitute, in Cohen's analysis, a key phenomenon in the contemporary Soviet Union. At times, Cohen squarely speaks of struggles taking place between various social groups or categories.[38] To be sure, he underlines the fact that it falls to the party to conciliate the interests and iron out the divergences. However, in an interrogative fashion, this Communist observer then raises important questions as to whether the party can properly assume the totality of such a role and achieve a satisfactory degree of soundness in the innumerable decisions it has to make. At this juncture, the question of political pluralism is broached by Cohen. In his mind, political pluralism in the Soviet Union would be unlikely to produce features which have become common in the Western democracies, but would mean rather a diversification of the organisational forms, coupled with a real development of the latter's specific powers. As Cohen asks:

> should forms be found to enable trade unions and other organisations . . . and the representative organs to rest upon this social pluralism in order to allow each segment to take part in the decision-making process and, therefore, participate in the broadening of socialist democracy that is officially pursued in socialist states?[39]

It remains to be seen whether Cohen will pursue his reflections on the question of political pluralism in the Soviet Union. However, one would support the view that any further development along this line will almost inevitably share in the major shortcomings which generally afflict Cohen's analytical efforts. One would particularly point to

Cohen's hesitations and lack of depth, as well as his propensity to skirt issues which for a Communist are complicated and sensitive. Alternatively, could Cohen imitate Elleinstein? This is highly unlikely. Myths die hard; indeed some myths appear to be too well entrenched in Cohen's mind. Also, fully admitting that Soviet socialism has grown alongside a substantial and undesirable degree of rigidity, Cohen insists on the fact that it entered into an era of reforms more than a decade ago. He could hardly be more explicit about this state of affairs: 'Everywhere critique, experiment'.[40] In short, as he puts it, Soviet socialism has entered a period of 'self-examination'.[41] The recent arrival of Gorbachev on the Soviet political scene has most certainly strengthened Cohen's conviction. So long as Cohen remains sincerely convinced of the existence of such a powerful and promising trend, it is difficult to imagine how he could suddenly adopt the same kind of radical step once taken by his former comrade Elleinstein.

FROM A TROTSKYIST LINE TO 'TOTAL BUREAUCRATIC CAPITALISM'

Socialisme ou Barbarie

In the late 1940s a number of young Trotskyists left the ranks of the International Communist Party (PCI), to found an independent political group, Socialisme ou Barbarie, and to begin publication of a journal of the same name, the first issue of which appeared in March 1949. Among the 'rebels' were Cornelius Castoriadis and Claude Lefort, who had met in August 1946. The most important figure and the real driving force behind the whole existence of the group (which came to an end in the Spring of 1966) was Castoriadis. Accordingly, the following pages will concentrate mostly on his reflections.

Born in 1922, Castoriadis is of Greek extraction. During World War Two Castoriadis, then a member of the Greek Communist Party, took part in the resistance movement. He came to realise, during the occupation, the true nature of Stalinist politics. He thus broke with the Stalinists and joined the Fourth International. As D. Howard put it, such a move meant avoiding 'not only the Nazis but Stalin's thugs as well'.[42] At the end of 1945 Castoriadis moved to Paris, where he remained involved in revolutionary politics. He gradually found himself opposed to the main tendency of the Fourth International 'not simply on conjunctural questions but on such major issues as the nature of the Russian regime, the structure of capitalism . . . and the role and function of the Party'.[43] After more than two years of discussion within the PCI, Castoriadis and others, including Lefort, 'came to understand Trotskyism as fundamentally incapable of perceiving the nature of bureaucracy'[44] and decided, in the Summer of 1948, to form an independent group.

Castoriadis's importance in the group is unequivocal, for he provided Socialisme ou Barbarie with the initial theoretical foundations on which it was to flourish. Lefort who, incidentally, left Socialisme ou Barbarie in 1958 over a serious disagreement concerning the nature of the organisation, has recently restated this fact: 'At the time, Castoriadis was formulating an analysis of the relations of production in the Soviet Union that provided Socialisme ou Barbarie with an essential theoretical foundation'.[45] Some years ago, in the same vein, Lefort recalled his first impression of Castoriadis, when he heard him lecture the PCI on the Soviet Union: 'His analysis overwhelmed me. I was convinced by him before he even reached his conclusion. I would have never been able to articulate the economic foundation that he provided for his conclusion. Castoriadis' arguments seemed to me worthy of the best Marx.'[46] Castoriadis's ideas had been aired in an embryonic form in issues of the *Bulletin intérieur du PCI* between 1946–7, before he developed them in their mature form in *Socialisme ou Barbarie*.[47] Owing mainly to his status as an alien in France and to his position as an international civil servant, Castoriadis wrote his contributions to *Socialisme ou Barbarie* under pseudonyms such as Pierre Chaulieu and Paul Cardan.

The critique of the Soviet regime initiated in the post-war period can be regarded as the first leg of a fruitful intellectual trajectory, which has since seen Castoriadis make deep inroads into more abstract sociological and philosophical thought. These, however, will not concern us here. It is accepted that his thinking is marked by 'a certain dynamic quality that constantly pushes analysis forward, beyond the complacent assertion of what it already knows as given by the categorical structure of the moment'.[48] A good example of this quality concerns Castoriadis's clean break with Marxism. Indeed, Castoriadis's thought evolved from a full and proclaimed acceptance of Marxism in the first issue of *Socialisme ou Barbarie* to a rejection of the doctrine a decade later. Curiously, Castoriadis's understanding of the Soviet Union remained a stable one for more than 30 years.

Of course, this stability did not by any means shelter it from critical reassessment. Indeed, Castoriadis, on the occasion of the republication of his *Socialisme ou Barbarie* writings in the 1970s, made plain that aspects of his thought had proved ill-conceived or had been made irrelevant by events. That said, one may come across, in a 1978 issue of *Esprit*, a report presented at the *Biennale consacrée à la Dissidence dans les pays de l'Est*.[49] Here Castoriadis openly tapped the ideas elaborated many years earlier in the journal *Socialisme ou Barbarie*.

However, as the significant Soviet military build-up developed in the 1970s and as the Soviet Union's increasing use of its might on the international scene came to attract much concerned attention, Castoriadis felt that a fresher conceptualisation of the Soviet Union had become a necessity. The result has been the publication in 1981 of *Devant le guerre – Les réalités*, in which Castoriadis puts forward the concept of 'stratocracy'.[50] This development will be examined later in the chapter concerned with institutional questions. This new concept, as its creator affirms, must not be taken to entail a repudiation of his previous characterisation of the Soviet Union.

In the 1970s, the republication of Castoriadis's writings led one intellectual to wish 'that justice be done to a theory that, despite its profound originality and crucial importance, has remained, up to the present, widely and scandalously unrecognised'.[51] This wish has since been fulfilled. Castoriadis has found a niche for himself in the French intellectual establishment where he joined, in a sense, his former colleague Lefort, now hailed as a leading thinker on totalitarianism. Lefort had indeed paid very early attention to that political phenomenon in *Socialisme ou Barbarie* and elsewhere, and demonstrated his interest in the question of bureaucracy. (Lefort's first serious attempt to grapple with the phenomenon of bureaucracy under 'socialism' may be traced back to an article published in 1948 in *Les Temps Modernes*.)

The late discovery of Castoriadis clearly indicates that the entire analytical corpus developed by Socialisme ou Barbarie (which, it must be stressed, comprehends much more than a critique of the Soviet regime) remained generally unknown.[52] Part of the blame may be attributed to the sectarianism and smallness of the group. Lefort once noted that 'the circle was narrow. Beyond its borders, our respective works were ignored or deliberately passed over in silence.'[53] Socialisme ou Barbarie was portrayed by René Lourau, a French sociologist, as a 'very small group which confined the organisation to intermittent gatherings . . . in the back-room of a café, to a small number of public meetings and to the publication of the journal'.[54] At best the journal sold 1 000 copies.

One of the most important merits of the group was that, as pointed out by M. Poster, *'Socialisme ou Barbarie* was the first French group effectively to criticize Stalin's Russia'.[55] Bearing in mind the quasi-paralysis affecting the French intelligentsia on this question, a point underlined in the first chapter, one has to realise the boldness of Castoriadis's journal. In ridiculing as it did the 'Land of Socialism', Socialisme ou Barbarie went against the grain, paying in the process the price of being often deliberately overlooked.

Soviet bureaucracy: A dominant class in a system of exploitation

Castoriadis's point of departure was a questioning of the principal tenets of Trotsky's analysis. In Castoriadis's view the insistence that the Soviet Union constituted a 'degenerate workers' state' arising from isolation and backwardness, together with the assessment that this regime was merely transitional, were theoretically indefensible.[56] What he has called 'the sociological and historical *exceptionalisme* of Trotsky's conception' had to be refuted.[57]

In short, according to Castoriadis, the outcome of World War Two and its aftermath took the ground from under the Trotskyist position. There could be no doubt whatsoever about the stability of the Soviet Union, whose industrial power was second only to that of the United States. Moreover, the crude imposition of 'revolutions' in Eastern Europe (which were anything but proletarian) precluded any idea of a 'degenerative' process. As he put it:

> Russian bureaucracy emerged from the ordeal of war greatly strengthened; if its regime, like any other class regime, contained contradictions, it had nothing in common with the house of cards depicted by Trotsky. The 'isolation' was eliminated by the bureaucracy that extended its power over half of Europe and over China and installed in all these countries regimes that were on all points identical with the Russian regime which, as became evident, it was ridiculous to describe as a 'degenerate workers' state'. The idea that nationalisation and planned economy can result only from a proletarian revolution and thus furnished a demarcation line between a capitalist regime and a 'workers' state' was thus reduced to naught.[58]

The two fundamental assumptions in the Trotskyist line of reasoning – the Soviet regime has a socialist base characterised by the abolition of private property, linked to a deviant superstructure defined in terms of 'bureaucratic deformation' – were subjected to merciless criticism.[59] For Castoriadis, the only sensible way to ascertain the nature of the regime was to go beyond juridical forms and concentrate on the economic foundations *and* their social implications. As he pointed out, 'Trotsky's error lay in confounding the *juridical forms of ownership* with the *effective social and economic content of production relations*'.[60] Castoriadis could hardly refrain from finding the Trotskyist analysis grossly superficial, of even transgressing an important tenet of Marxist teaching – namely, the necessity to track down all mystifications, regardless of their form.

Denying any kind of socialist significance to nationalisation and central economic planning *per se*, he went on to argue that 'it is the structure of the *relations of production* that determines whether or not "nationalised" property has a socialist character'.[61] In May 1949 an article entitled 'Les rapports de production en Russie' appeared in *Socialisme ou Barbarie*. In it Castoriadis lampooned Trotsky's attribution of a 'bourgeois' character to the distribution of the surplus and, at the same time, a real 'socialist' character to the relations of production.[62] He then set out his definition of the relations of production:

> The relations of production, in general, are defined: a) by the mode of *administration* of production (organisation and co-operation of material and personal conditions of production, definition of both the objectives and methods of production); b) the mode of *distribution* of the social product . . .[63]

The basic relation of production between the workers and the state, as expressed by the law, is an abstract one, which is best approached in terms of a relation between the workers and a very ramified structure, namely the bureaucracy. Castoriadis argues that an examination of the Russian reality reveals that the bureaucracy wields overall managerial power, exercising total authority over the means of production as well as over the distribution of the surplus. With regard to the means of production, continues Castoriadis, the Soviet bureaucracy possesses the *jus fruendi, utendi et abutendi* (the right to enjoy, use and abuse), and this is sufficient reason to ascribe a class character to the relations of production.

From the proletariat's viewpoint,[64] the class character emerges vividly from total subservience to a 'production process that completely escapes their control',[65] as well as in the subordination to the needs of the bureaucracy and in the loss of the surplus. In a word, exploitation. Claude Lefort once summarised the thoughts of Socialisme ou Barbarie on the bureaucracy as an exploitative class:

> Undoubtedly, there is a ruling class in the USSR . . . What determines the proletariat as an exploited class is its exclusion from the administration of production and its reduction to merely mechanical functions. What determines the position of a ruling class facing the proletariat is the fact that all decisions concerning economic life (i.e., concerning the volume and distribution of investments, wages, intensity and duration of labour, etc.), are made by a particular social stratum.[66]

Socialisme ou Barbarie's originality lies in a further step taken by its analysis. The analysis considers the deep division between 'rulers' and 'executants' (*dirigeants/exécutants*), forcefully described in the case of the productive/economic process as having been extended to encompass Soviet society in its entirety.[67] Thus, we arrive at the idea of a Soviet bureaucratic society which subtlely supersedes, as it were, the idea of a bureaucracy within the Soviet society. Lefort explained this in the following manner:

> *Socialisme ou Barbarie* . . . substituted the idea of a *bureaucratic society* for that of a *bureaucracy in society*, i.e., a society which produced and reproduced itself by separating the producing masses from a social stratum which collectively expropriated surplus value. Such a *bureaucratic society* was made possible by the rigorous integration of all bureaucratic strata by the state apparatus.[68]

In this bureaucratic society the action of the bureaucracy, whose active nucleus is the apparatus of the CPSU, is being constantly guided by its own interests to the detriment of the 'general interest of the economy'. Castoriadis admits the difficulty in defining this notion, but translated into reality, this pursuit means heavy industry, armament production and 'especially the production of machines designed to reproduce the same type of production and the same relations of production'.[69] Buttressed by a totalitarian state, the

Soviet bureaucracy seems more firmly established than the classic bourgeoisie. It enjoys a greater liberty as to the ways it can dispose of its capital which 'is "essentially" the surplus accumulated from the exploitation of the Russian people over the last sixty years. In its physical form, it is the sedimented result of the bureaucracy's decisions and of the functioning of its system during that time.'[70]

The use of the word capital must be correctly understood, for it does not indicate that the Soviet Union is a regime of 'state capitalism'. Castoriadis's opposition to this characterisation has never slackened, and goes back as far as 1946. He considers it to be devoid of any meaning, claiming that it has spread confusion 'as it implies that the economic laws of capitalism continue to remain in effect after the disappearance of private ownership, of the market and of competition, which is absurd'.[71] On the other hand, we know already that it is his view that the Soviet Union will not be remembered as the 'Land of Socialism', no matter how the concept of socialism itself has been qualified.[72] So, how *can* one define the Soviet Union? According to Castoriadis, the mode of production, though important, clearly cannot lead to an overall characterisation. As he has recently explained, 'the notion of "mode of production" is meaningful if it is used to characterize production as such, not a society or a group of societies'.[73] Hence, in his opinion, the need to resort to the notion of 'social regime', which in the case of the Soviet Union is one of 'total bureaucratic capitalism'.[74]

The Soviet Union's 'social regime'

The logical process which led Castoriadis to such a characterisation of the Soviet Union's 'social regime' has been summarised by B. Singer:

> The analysis had shown that in terms of the productive relations, the Eastern regimes appeared similar to those in the West, and this similarity would become increasingly evident as the Eastern regimes liberalized and the Western regimes grew more and more bureaucratic. Certainly there were differences, but in large part they only served to confirm the underlying identity; for, at bottom, the Eastern regimes had merely taken that formal 'rationality' embedded in the individual capitalist enterprise and applied it to the total organization of the economy and society.[75]

In short, Castoriadis's formulation essentially means that the Soviet regime is the 'concentrated' or highest form of capitalism. It reveals the 'essence of capitalism':

> We may say that it represents the last stage of the capitalist mode of production, in the sense that the concentration of capital . . . has attained its ultimate limit since all the means of production are at the disposal, and under the administration of a central power . . . It also represents the ultimate stage of the capitalist mode of production in that it achieves the deepest exploitation of the proletariat.[76]

The question of the role of the Communist Party cannot be avoided, as the part it played in the historical advent and development of the Soviet 'social regime' is unequivocal. For Castoriadis, Bolshevism did symbolise the most extreme outcome of a particular conception of revolution – that is, a revolution resting upon essential features such as the equation of the revolutionary theory with a science known by few 'professional specialists', a rigid organisation subject to strict control from above and so on. For Castoriadis, such a conception of revolution was very profoundly penetrated by capitalist ideas, one of which was the capitalist feature par excellence, namely the basic and crucial division *'dirigeants/exécutants'*.[77] 'The party', wrote B. Singer, 'had proved to be the privileged point for the importation of a bureaucratic "rationality" into the workers' movement and its revolution'.[78] According to Castoriadis, 'rationality', a key notion expressing the spirit of capitalism (around which gravitate secondary notions germane to capitalist culture such as technical progress, the expansion of productive forces, the detailed division of labour and quantitative analysis), had found a perfect vehicle in the party. The October Revolution, rupturing the Russian political evolution, installed a new dominant power which necessarily aimed at creating relations of production and the corresponding material infrastructure, thereby stimulating the decisive phase of the 'rational' and bureaucratic transformation of Russia.

The constitutive features of the Soviet 'social regime' are threefold – universal extension of the bureaucratic-hierarchic apparatus, central planning as a mechanism of integration, and effacement of the formal line between the state and the civil society (Castoriadis discards any 'absorption' of the civil society by the Soviet state).

From this deep division running throughout the Soviet bureaucratic society, Castoriadis moves on to uncover what amounts to the fourth feature of this 'social regime', which is its fundamental contradiction. He explains:

> In production, as in all areas of social life, the regime seeks to prevent individuals and groups from controlling their activities and to assign this function to a bureaucratic apparatus. To the extent that it is external to these activities and it runs into the opposition of the people involved, this apparatus is usually unable to direct or control them – or even to know what is going on. Thus, it is constantly obliged to call for the participation of these same people it wanted to exclude and transform into robots.[79]

Thus, the Soviet bureaucracy lives with a permanent paradox, which in turn leads it to an interminable critique of its guiding principles and methods. In short, it is destined to be engaged in a kind of circular and fruitless self-criticism.

As already discussed, a significant problem facing the bureaucratic apparatus lies in a persistent and major weakness which adversely affects the information flow so vital for global central planning. Reacting to their exploitation 'the masses of workers', writes Castoriadis, 'hide the truth from the apparatus'.[80] Thus, the externality of the apparatus, as distinct from the social reality over which it is supposed to preside, is compounded. In a system lacking 'rational' modes of nomination and promotion, this information failure is aggravated by the bureaucrats themselves, as they generally sense a necessity to provide the higher circles with 'embellished' information. Pervading the entire hierarchy, this anomaly is now virtually institutionalised.

The bureaucratic apparatus suffers from another vice. An essential social feature of the system – namely the permanent struggle among cliques and clans – dominates the apparatus and inhibits its functioning. As a result, options which could be regarded as objective become subjected to diverging forces and suffer serious distortions. One could argue that this social feature is not peculiar to the Soviet Union; rather it seems to be a feature of all modern bureaucracies. Castoriadis and Lefort reply to this by pointing out that the Soviet Union is unique because it depends for its coherence on an essentially unifying political element. In the view of Lefort, 'the rivalry of bureaucratic apparatuses reinforced by the struggle of interbureaucratic cliques is only managed by the intervention of a political principle at all the levels of social life'.[81] This shows the particular and crucial importance of the Communist Party, portrayed by Castoriadis as the 'supreme unifying body'.[82] However, the simple fact that the CPSU itself is the epitome of bureaucracy, and subject to the same division, fragmentation and inertia which prevail in the whole system must certainly not be overlooked. Indeed, in the last analysis, Castoriadis sees this unifying factor as synonymous with a small Politburo which must 'each time, *in extremis*, slice arbitrarily through problems that can no longer be put off'.[83]

Such a characterisation of the Soviet Union raises a final question: what holds this bureaucratic society together? According to Castoriadis 'the only cement of bureaucratic society is cynicism. Russian society is the first cynical society in history.'[84] It is cynical, says Castoriadis, because the ideology is extinct and because disillusionment is widespread (acutely affecting Soviet youth). Soviet society, for the first time in history, appears unable to offer and inculcate, except for the grand old values of Russian chauvinism and ultra-nationalism, these 'motivations adéquates' so essential to the reproduction of any society.[85] Consequently, maintains Castoriadis, the Soviet Union has been witnessing the birth of a new, cynical man.

None the less, problems (industrial, agricultural, national) are severe and seem to bite deeper and deeper. With much irony, Castoriadis points out that

> This 'socialist' regime has not yet been able to solve the problems already solved in Neolithic times: how to assure continuity between one crop and the next; nor others, solved at least as far back as the Phoenicians: how to provide commodities to those who are willing to pay the price.[86]

In the face of the blatant insufficiencies and absurdities of the system which cause the Soviet population to be burdened with many deprivations, the inert bureaucracy can do no more than engage in merely tinkering with the system. As any sensible economic reform would, among other things, entail curbing its own discretionary powers, the bureaucracy cannot contemplate inflicting upon itself what Castoriadis calls 'a self-mutilation'.[87] For him, the idea of bureaucratic reform within the Soviet context is virtually self-contradictory. Furthermore, writes Castoriadis, any attempt to put the party's role and power into question 'would be suicide for the bureaucracy, and any Party "democratization", no matter how limited, would be suicide for the authority that embodies, personifies and exercises power, i.e., the Summit of the Apparatus'.[88] Admitting the bureaucratic suppression of the numerous problems and taking into account the negative influence of the new cynical man on the prospects for evolution, Castoriadis none the less maintains that sooner or later some kind of conflict is bound to detonate the explosive Soviet Union: 'Among industrial countries, Russia is the prime candidate for a social revolution.'[89]

In view of the analysis developed by Castoriadis, a number of objections may be raised. One is whether the Soviet system can be reducible to an antagonism pervading the entire society. There seems little to be said for any argument which does not pay attention to the division existing between the decision-making bureaucratic apparatus and the rest of society. As Z. Strmiska, a Czech sociologist now living in Paris and Director of the CNRS's Centre d'Ethnologie sociale et de psychologie, once put it, 'the line between the officials, the political elite or the "bureaucracy" (terminological questions are not decisive here) and the quasi-totality of society expresses . . . the deepest division that exists in the whole society'.[90]

On the other hand, it is also clear that one ought to go beyond such a theoretical posture to embrace comprehensively, on a sociological plane, a differentiated and complex reality. To a certain degree Castoriadis falls within the scope of a criticism made some years ago by A. Brown, who not only considered the idea of 'the bureaucracy' as either a ruling or new class to be over-simplified, but also called for an analytical breakdown of these bureaucratic and class abstractions into more precise power relationships.[91] A further point relates to Castoriadis's assertion that the party is the epitome of bureaucracy. It has been cogently argued by various writers that the party is a reality which does not fit well within the classical concept of bureaucracy as developed by M. Weber. That point, phrased in a more simple fashion, is that the party *apparatchik* is clearly no traditional bureaucrat. Differences between the *apparatchik* and the bureaucrat are too well known to the student of Soviet politics to merit repetition here. It is sufficient here to underline that the party official, unlike the bureaucrat in the classical sense, is essentially committed to ideologically defined goals and that his task is a far cry indeed from the implementation of rationally established legal rules and regulations. As recently observed by Strmiska:

the apparatchik differs from the bureaucrat because he is the central figure in the direct regulation of the relations of power and because he exercises power in a specific fashion. His task, unlike the traditional bureaucrat, is not to assist the power by providing specialised services in such or such domain of social life, but to manipulate the relations of power at every nodal point . . . of the social organisation in order to ensure the preservation as well as strengthening of the existing power.[92]

Castoriadis (and Socialisme ou Barbarie) has, in fact, generally avoided probing deeply into the intricacies of the functioning of the Soviet system. Indeed, this has had unfortunate consequences. The analysis has, more often than not, been confined to repeated generalities. Some of the ideas advanced promise or suggest a more perceptive view of the Soviet system, yet they have by and large remained merely superb intuitions. An interesting example is Castoriadis's destruction of the myth of Soviet 'rational planning'. There ought to be no doubt, especially after the erudite work of the economist Eugène Zaleski, that central economic planning was entirely mythical during Stalin's day (and, dare we add, until the present time). In his book *La planification stalinienne – croissance et fluctuations économiques en U.R.S.S. 1933–1952*,[93] Zaleski convincingly demonstrates that central planning was *never* an instrument for coherent and pervasive coordination of the Soviet economy, if only because of the impossibility of collecting sufficient information. For Castoriadis, central planning is an essentially chaotic operation leading to an astounding degree of waste.[94] In this respect, to use his more philosophical phrase, the modern Soviet society 'seeks only "rationality" but produces only "irrationality" from the viewpoint of this very rationality'.[95] This comment evokes a complex issue which brings a few delicate questions in its train. For instance, can the endemic waste which has long been observed in the Soviet Union be explained without any reference to the notion of "irrationality"? Pierre de Fouquet, a French theorist, suggested this reasoning a few years ago by drawing on the old anthropological principle that a loss may be interpreted as a sign of power. As he tentatively explains:

If, therefore, one understands centralised planning as the instrument of the reproduction of the power of the State within the social formation, one must then acknowledge that the ultimate destination of the product itself is of only secondary importance. As long as production fulfils the following conditions – to reproduce the national economy's labour forces, to reproduce the material capacities of production and to feed the needs of the State *qua* foreign power – the essential thing is being attained: in the centrally planned production process the State controls the entirety of the social organisation which assigns to each individual his place and his function. Through centralised planning of production, the State makes the whole 'social machine' work. Therefore, from such a viewpoint, the waste of a given quantity of the social product may be looked upon not as a weakness of the system but more as the sign of power, as the evidence of the internal power of the State.[96]

De Fouquet's proposition deserves some attention since it translates on a theoretical plane a basic feature of Soviet economic history – that is, the fact that essential economic decisions have always been made under the paramount political considerations 'of power, security and prestige, in relation to which economic profitability . . . seems secondary'.[97] His proposition may also lead one, perhaps not unreasonably, to consider that the *raison d'être* of the centralised economic system has been and still is to feed the power of the state and, ultimately, the power of the party. In such a case, one would have to renounce the widely-held view that the Soviet Union is in the throes of a multi-faceted and deep economic crisis since the faults generally cited in support of such a view – the weakness of Soviet agriculture, the poor standard of living and so on – would clearly not have to be regarded as examples of the failed objectives of the Soviet system. As the economist G. Duchêne recently asked, 'is it not, first and foremost, the strengthening of its power . . . that guides the U.S.S.R.? If this were the case, the socialist world should certainly not be considered to be currently in a state of crisis.'[98]

Finally, before progressing on to Pierre Naville and his 'State socialism', it is worth noting that Castoriadis's new characterisation – that the Soviet Union is a 'stratocracy' – has meant that some important facets of his earlier contribution to the study of the Soviet Union, briefly presented in the last few pages, have been affected. His latest ideas will be examined in due course.

'STATE SOCIALISM'

We move on to the analysis of the Soviet Union advanced by Pierre Naville, Directeur honoraire de Recherche at the CNRS, and at present a member of the Editorial board of the excellent *Revue d'études comparatives Est–Ouest*. Before doing so, it is well worth devoting some space to Naville himself. His path has crossed some of the more striking movements of the century, and in this respect Naville's life appears to have been quite extraordinary.

As a young man Naville became involved in the Surrealist group, being associated with figures such as André Breton, Paul Eluard, and Louis Aragon. For some time he edited, with Benjamin Péret, *La Révolution surréaliste*. In the annals of Surrealism Naville is remembered as the one who sparked off, in the mid-1920s, a crisis which stirred heated arguments and rocked the whole group.[99] The crisis arose on the publication of a pamphlet in which he advocated that Surrealism become more political and adopt the Marxist revolutionary path. Looking back on this episode, Naville writes of his 'efforts to link the surrealist breakthrough to the Communist upsurge'.[100] On another level, Naville became one of the first and most ardent French supporters of Leon Trotsky, siding as early as Spring 1927 with the Russian Left Opposition. His first encounter with the revolutionary took place in Moscow in November 1927. Following a visit to Trotsky in Turkey in 1929, Naville, who had by then severed his links with Breton and the Surrealists, united with others to found *La Vérité*, which between 1929 and 1936 was the newspaper of the French Trotskyists. It would appear that Trotsky valued Naville's literary gifts and propagandist talents.[101] In 1929 Naville sat with Souvarine and others on the Executive Commission of the Cercle Communiste Marx et Lénine, founded in February 1926. Throughout most of the 1930s Naville served on the International Secretariat, which was the administrative leadership of the Trotskyist movement. He left the Trotskyist organisation at the very beginning of World War Two.

Naville, as pointed out by M. Poster, remained an important Marxist theorist. In the 1950s he was one of many who openly polemicised with Jean-Paul Sartre.[102] Naville was also involved in the periodical *La Revue Internationale*, which he recently depicted as one of the instruments he used in his search for new ways to rebuild a socialist organisation in the Marxist tradition outside the PCF and SFIO.[103] Finally, one notes that in 1960 Naville took an active part in the foundation of the Unified Socialist Party (PSU).

Undoubtedly a 'brilliant intellectual', to use the words of the historian P. Broué,[104] Naville's writings testify to a great eclecticism. His published works have embraced various disciplines, such as psychology, philosophy and sociology. As far as his analysis of the Soviet Union is concerned, it is essentially found in the volumes of his enormous work entitled *Le Nouveau Léviathan*.[105] Particular attention will be paid here to the fifth volume, *La bureaucratie et la révolution*, in which Naville, by his own account, reflects upon the connections between the socio-economic structure of the Soviet regime and the institutions preserving its stability while simultaneously furthering its development and crises.

In order to approach Naville's characterisation of the Soviet Union, one has to turn to the key notion on which it rests, namely what he calls the 'socialist system of mutual exploitation' (SSME). The basis of such a system lies in the generalised or universal 'wage-earning relation' (*salariat*) prevailing in the Soviet Union. We find, with some surprise, an early trace of Naville's theoretical preoccupation with the notion of *salariat* in the text of winter 1925–6, which, as we know, provoked a crisis within the Surrealist group.[106] By generalised *salariat* Naville means that everybody in the Soviet Union, from top to bottom, is a wage-earner: 'Cadres and masses, *superiors and subordinates, rulers and ruled, all belong to the new heterogeneous universe of wage-earners . . .*'.[107] Following the disappearance of the capitalist bourgeoisie and landowners, the *salariés d'Etat* form the only productive class in the Soviet Union. However, within it exist various strata, sub-classes and categories (for Naville their precise name does not really matter) whose revenues, rights and prerogatives are visibly differentiated. The question of disparity leads us to underline the basic elements which make up Naville's 'theory of mutual exploitation':

1) the exchange of *goods*, (including exchanges between State-run enterprises) . . . is the fundamental relationship of the system; 2) money and prices determine and regulate the value of these exchanges; 3) these exchanges are unequal, notably those between categories of wage-earners. As there is no longer a ruling capitalist bourgeoisie to dominate this system of exchanges . . . it is the bureaucracy which arbitrates conflicts of interest as well as taking out its own share. Once again, this is the theory of mutual exploitation.[108]

The SSME has been depicted in simple terms by Naville as being a system of direct exchanges unequal in terms of quantity and quality of work.[109] The presence of two conditions inevitably generates this system: that is, firstly, the persistence of essential capitalist features and, secondly, complete state ownership of the means of production. Striking roots in the Soviet Union, this system necessarily entailed the growth of a powerful bureaucracy. Naville has in mind a metamorphosis of the bureaucracy, since, as he reckons, the latter was not created *ex nihilo* from October 1917. Thus, the SSME represents the foundation of the Soviet bureaucracy:

> The bureaucracy benefits from the labour of the society to the extent that it also belongs to it as a salaried, though dominant, stratum. It exists, with all the power it holds, *only because the system of mutual exploitation makes it necessary*.[110]

The necessity of bureaucracy arises from the need to fulfil two functions. In the first place, as pointed out, it has to regulate at the source inequalities, both in distribution and particularly in production. Secondly, it keeps the system which provides it with substantial benefits in 'good working order'.

Naville does not dwell on the point as to whether the Soviet bureaucracy is a 'new ruling class', considering it to be a rather secondary question. Marked by his Trotskyist filiation, he rejects such a theoretical posture, despite making some affirmations which at times smack of uncertainty. Naville takes the position that this bureaucracy is not merely a reflection or expression of the economic relationship taking place within the system. In this regard, he dismisses as rather vague the idea of 'the superstructure'. Instead, the Soviet bureaucracy enjoys, not least through central planning, a full and direct authority over the institution and maintenance of these relationships. In the light of such a development, the bureaucracy would then appear to have displayed its real nature in the Soviet Union: 'it is hierarchical organisation applied to everything, the real framework of social and private life, the authority on everything'.[111] Hence the naming of 'New Leviathan' by Naville to the Soviet bureaucracy.

This has to be seen, indeed, against the sociologist's conception of power, which follows a Weberian line. In our era, writes Naville, the state is, as the repository of power, subjected to a gradual process by which it increasingly develops into a vertical structure of command (on the model of an army). In the last analysis, Naville believes, the bureaucracy wields power since it constitutes the fundamental form of the modern state. Thus, as he puts it, 'the State is the system of power. More and more, the State's name is bureaucracy'[112] and 'the bureaucracy, intangible in the text of the Constitution . . . but real in the functioning of the State, is the power'.[113] Pulling this thread further, Naville is led to locate the focal point of power within the Soviet bureaucracy: the Communist Party, which is the bureaucracy's 'political armature'.

Despite a certain degree of confusion arising from Naville's tendency to express the same point diversely, it emerges that the CPSU is the possessor of the Soviet state. The party 'possesses the State and identifies itself with it'.[114] At one point Naville speaks of the party and 'its' state. Therefore, the party's grip on the country bears absolutely no resemblance whatsoever to the political forms hitherto experienced in history, in the sense that the state and all social organisations are found to be in a situation of total dependence. Naville's only reservation in this respect concerns the army, whose industrial complex and requirements imply the existence of a substantial power. In his opinion, the military entity may at times appear to stand as an autonomous rival to the party.

There is a price to pay for such political hegemony, achieved through an omnipresent state. The reverse side of the coin is obvious. The Soviet economy, owing to an ultra-centralised type of irresponsible management, suffers from an intense lack of productivity. However, as Naville is quick to point out, such a negative consequence is systematically transformed into some kind of permanent motive for political action. Thus, the consequence feeds, as it were, the political element of the Soviet system. This is made clear by Naville when he writes that the 'economic unproductiveness of the bureaucracy has become the condition of its political productivity'.[115] None the less, the Soviet economy is part of the world economy. As a result it is exposed to its fluctuations and, in addition, finds itself competing with the capitalist system as a whole. Its lack of productivity may be perceived in a different manner in Soviet specialists' circles. Indeed, this leads us to the familiar antithesis of the 'progressive' and 'aware' technocrats, and the arch-conservative *apparatchiki*. Surfacing in Naville's work is the question of their conflicting relationship, which he expresses in the form of a question: 'Competition *within* or *for* power?' (concurrence *dans* le pouvoir, ou *pour* le pouvoir?').[116]

To begin with, it is clear that the voices of industrial managers, engineers and economists concerned with improving the running of the economy are listened to in the higher circles of the party. As a matter of fact, the party specifically seeks such professional advice. This said, Naville argues that not only does the framework in which the technocrats operate appear to be far too narrow and over-regulated to leave them with the space in which to aspire to substitute their own rule for that of the *apparatchiki*, but it would also be mistaken to ascribe to them a significant degree of political awareness. In a judgement passed on the whole intelligentsia which is clearly applicable to its technocratic segment, Naville underlines the idea of political inertia: 'It is the first to worry about the bureaucratic domination, but is also the last to draw political conclusions from it'.[117] In any case, the technocrats know only too well on whom their further advancement depends. In this regard, one cannot ignore the process of co-optation which is such an important asset to the party. Playing constantly on technocrats' permanent aspirations to join the inner sanctum of power, the CPSU can assure itself with a kind of self-restraint on the part of those technocrats concerned with keeping as clean a record as possible. In the last analysis, as Naville points out, the higher layers of the technical intelligentsia may be regarded as a 'class of *will* rather than *power*' ('classe de *vouloir* plutôt que de *pouvoir*').[118]

On a more elevated level, Naville turns his attention to the much vaunted legend of a regime without internal antagonisms, only to condemn it as entirely idyllic and foreign to the reality. The Soviet bureaucracy, he writes, lives 'in the imaginary world of harmonious power'.[119] Contradictions of all kinds abound in the Soviet Union. Indeed, owing to the existence of the SSME, there comes to the fore what Naville views as the incompatibility between the way in which surplus-value is formed and the way it is used and distributed. Every social category, each of which is interested at different points in time in these processes, tries to defend its position against each of the others and against the bureaucracy which dominates the system as a whole.[120]

Keeping in mind the point that the fundamental contradiction of 'state socialism' boils down to the dual process connected to the formation and distribution of the 'social product', one may then understand why the criticism which is most ferociously suppressed by the bureaucracy is the one which relates to the organisation of labour.[121] Regulating the inequalities, the dominant bureaucracy is confronted with a steady, general reaction from the wage-earners who, in spite of their own internal opposition, are in search of an extension of their rights, as well as of the respect of proclaimed principles. This sheds light on the peculiar fact that the sophisticated bureaucratic ascendancy over Soviet society does not simply and purely derive from the bureaucracy's own nature. It also constitutes a global response to a fluid situation in which innumerable obstacles are placed in its path. From this viewpoint, then, the bureaucratic omnipotence can also be regarded as paralleling the growing resistance of the Soviet population. Within the context of the fundamental contradiction, Naville later takes the view that 'the conflict has an economic root that immediately turns into political opposition'.[122]

Political opposition represents an issue which is an important part of Naville's intellectual preoccupations, as illustrated by the second element of his book's title – namely, revolution. However, before approaching this radical solution, Naville addresses himself to the question of bureaucratic 'reformism'. Admitting that it is not a theoretical impossibility, he is also quick to stress that it would be a rather special brand of 'reformism' since it would have to be entirely devised and implemented by a Communist Party pledged to preserve the principles on which rest its very existence and domination. Indeed, Naville airs serious reservations about the correctness of the use of the word 'reformism' in the Soviet context. He does not rule out a bolder hypothesis, that of an opportune crisis which could trigger off a 'political revolution' at the very top and would give the key impetus to a general, systemic shake-up. However, such a scenario is, in his view, very unlikely.

In reality, Naville insists, the only sensible avenue of significant change is a revolution coming from below, which would aim at abolishing the *salariat* and the market altogether. Such a revolution depends, according to him, on a kind of collective psychological development which marks the Soviet 'new working class' and against which the bureaucracy remains rather impotent – namely an 'increased awareness of the "irreformability" of the system without a "radical" revolution'.[123] Pushing forward in a more categorical form an idea already sketched in an article published in a 1956 issue of *La Nef*, Naville has recently expressed his belief that the very future of the Soviet Union turns on the behaviour adopted by the 'new working class'.[124] Of course, such a revolution is a formidable task facing enormous difficulties: the elusive nature of the pervasive bureaucracy, this 'hundred-headed hydra',[125] the deliberate pitting of categories of wage-earners against one another, fragmentation of oppositional forces, and a severe repression aiming at eradicating deviant attitudes. With respect to the last difficulty, Naville writes about the reality prevailing in the Soviet Union, where 'there is always a *correct* opinion . . . the bureaucracy deploys all its strength in repressing *incorrect* attitudes'.[126]

However, despite all these problems, Naville seems convinced that some indications of a new Russian revolution are already observable, citing a number of reported and unreported strikes, as well as the creation in 1978 of the Free Interprofessional Association of Workers (SMOT). It seems appropriate to observe that Naville's view of the workers' growing consciousness relating to the revolutionary process is rather simplistic. Indeed, the feature to which he draws attention ought to be weighed against a far more complicated legacy, the one depicted by various works concerned with Soviet political culture. Disillusionment and cynicism are hardly deniable but, as S. White has observed, these negative elements may combine with a genuine commitment to the Soviet system and with feelings of pride in its achievements.[127] Moreover, Naville's opinion is not based on substantial empirical evidence and appears to contain a significant element of wishful thinking.

Naville's work has been hailed by Z. Strmiska as being one of the most elaborate analyses of the development and current state of the Soviet society.[128] There is no doubt that Naville's analysis makes many good and perceptive points about the Soviet regime – his treatment of the question of the relationship between the political apparatus and the technocracy is a good example. None the less, Strmiska's opinion seems to be exaggerated. One would endorse the view that Naville, throughout *Le Nouveau Léviathan*, displays a vast and often critical knowledge of numerous Marxist writings which have sought to cast light on the nature of the Soviet Union. In fact, Naville may be regarded as *the* French authority on such writings. To dwell on such questions as the nature of surplus-value, the regulation of the inequalities and the fetishism of labour is undoubtedly a worthwhile exercise as far as the Soviet Union is concerned and should not be overlooked. This said, one may well consider that such a development bears the stamp of an excessively strong intellectualism. Indeed, an important part of Naville's work remains at an analytical level which begs for a complementary empirical examination of the issues. Aware of this necessity, Naville sets out to deal with some important institutional matters, but does so in a way which is not quite satisfactory. He touches upon many points without actually investigating them in a thorough manner. Although his analysis covers a lot of ground and draws on several sources of information, it remains, for all that, somewhat impressionistic.

It is also clear that basic elements of Naville's analysis may be subjected to some questioning. For example, the notion of *salariat* (a cornerstone of Naville's analysis), as developed in the Marxist doctrine, is not devoid of ambiguity when used in the specific context of the contemporary Soviet-type system. This relates to the constitutional obligation to work, to the essentially administrative or 'statist' ways to determine each worker's wages and, also, to the obligation of the state to absorb all man-power supply. The notion of *salariat* presupposes that labour power comes into play as a commodity whose value is determined by the social costs necessary for its production and reproduction, and implies that the owner who wants to sell his commodity must seek to realise it on a labour market. Thus, the existence of a *salariat* implies, in particular, a market relationship. But, of course, this element is not applicable in the Soviet Union without essential reservations or limitations.[129]

Finally, it is difficult to disagree with Z. Strmiska, who judges as pleonastic the characterisation 'state socialism', since under modern conditions of state interventionism any socialism would be in one way or another a brand of 'state socialism'. Despite isolated praise heaped on Naville's work, it has to be conceded that very little attention has been paid to it in French Sovietological circles. As a matter of fact, in the course of our research, we have come across only a handful of experts or observers who have more or less furtively referred to his voluminous and eclectic writings.[130]

'PARTY CAPITALISM'

In this section we concentrate on Charles Bettelheim's characterisation of the Soviet Union. Directeur d'études at the Ecole des Hautes Etudes en Sciences sociales, Bettelheim is a well-known Marxist economist. Although his writings have embraced a variety of research interests, it would be fair to say that the Soviet Union has occupied a prominent place in his theoretical concerns.

Bettelheim's first lengthy contact with the Soviet Union was in 1936, a year of intense political turmoil. At that time he lived in

Moscow and was engaged in a number of diverse activities, such as journalism and film dubbing. In a fairly recent interview he has recalled his main impressions at this particular period:

> What struck me then was the inequality of the standards of living . . . indeed, I knew that Stalin had started the fight against 'egalitarianism' . . . but I had difficulty accepting the inequalities I perceived. Owing to my membership in the Association of revolutionary writers and artists, I could frequently visit the House of writers; this was . . . a kind of English Club. But, next to this ostentation, I saw the navvies . . . live in barracks . . . I tried to justify such social differences by pretending that they were temporary. None the less, I was struck by the arrogance of the members of the 'nomenklatura', similar to that of the *nouveaux-riches*.[131]

Back in France, he dedicated himself to the writing of his thesis, *La planification soviétique*, presented and published in 1939.[132] With regard to the 'imperfections' and 'dysfunctionings' of the Soviet planning system discussed in this early piece of work, Bettelheim has recently recollected the ideological perspective in which they were seen:

> I do not see in them the perpetuation and development of capitalist relations of production. I think that they are surviving traces of a mode of production swept away by the revolution. For me, the U.S.S.R. was a new society under construction.[133]

In Bettelheim's opinion, the post-World War Two period tended to confirm the steady progress made by the Soviet Union on the road to socialism and communism. The important XXth Congress seemed to indicate the capacity of the party to recognise past mistakes and to adopt a new and rectified course based on greater socialist democracy. For Bettelheim, Khrushchev's denunciation of the camps and the repression, together with the freeing of a considerable number of those who had been deported during Stalin's reign, appeared as elements of a possible democratisation of Soviet society.[134] However, years later, he reached the view that the post-Stalin Soviet Union had failed to live up to these expectations of renewal. It became no longer possible for him to tolerate a series of disturbing realities. Of these realities, Bettelheim picks out the entrenchment of class relationships, the continued concentration of power in the hands of a small minority and an obviously imperialistic foreign policy.

More generally, some tendencies of the post-Stalin Soviet Union induced many intellectuals to 'demobilise' – that is, to abandon the socialist motherland for the still fresh and exciting Chinese cause. High hopes were then pinned on the Chinese socialist experiment. As pointed out by the sociologist Edgar Morin, 'the post-Stalinist crisis in the U.S.S.R. has caused some devotees to find their heaven (*l'ailleurs*) in China, and, afterwards, in the revolutions happening in the Third World'.[135] Morin's remark exactly captures a segment of Bettelheim's intellectual development. At the beginning of the 1960s he had a practical involvement in the Cuban system of central planning and, at the same time, began studying Chinese socialism. In the course of his reflections upon the latter, he became an ardent supporter of Mao's Cultural Revolution, of which he wrote in 1973: 'There is no precedent for such an attempt to transform social relations. It constitutes a decisive and permanent achievement, as decisive and permanent as any scientific or social experiment which discovers new processes or new objective laws.'[136] Bettelheim once held the presidency of the Franco-Chinese Friendship Association, from which he resigned in May 1977. He gave as his reason his profound disagreement with the majority line of the Association, which supported what he considered to be the revisionist position of Mao's successors. Bettelheim's shift in allegiance from the Soviet Union to China gave rise to criticism in some intellectual quarters. Cornelius Castoriadis, for instance, once sarcastically commented on this shift in the following terms: 'he has changed employers: he now pleads in favour of the Chinese bureaucracy'.[137] Bettelheim also fell under a more general condemnation in the same vein, in which Castoriadis castigated all those who 'continue a formidable task of mystification, turning Maoist totalitarianism into the last hope of humanity'.[138]

In the wake of the invasion of Czechoslovakia Bettelheim began an analysis of the workings of Soviet society within a Maoist framework, grounded in the idea of the restoration of capitalism in the Soviet Union. On completion of this study, Bettelheim sensed that it was totally lacking in historical perspective and felt the need to explain how the dominant relations and practices in the Soviet society came about. The result of Bettelheim's historically oriented endeavours is his prodigious and lengthy analysis (more than 1600 pages) *Les Luttes de classes en URSS*, the four volumes of which were published in 1974, 1977, 1982 and 1983 respectively.[139] This work, which covers a period stretching from the October Revolution to 1941, constitutes the principal focus of the following discussion.

In the first two volumes of *Les Luttes de classes en URSS* Bettelheim strives to unravel the complex and progressive process through which a proletarian regime turned into a system of state capitalism in a comparatively short space of time.[140] He set out to identify what he now calls 'a series of "movements" and "ruptures"',[141] trying to correlate them with the evolving state of the class struggle in the Soviet Union. The sociologist Z. Strmiska has effectively summarised Bettelheim's early analysis in relation to two salient issues: firstly, the distortions affecting the Soviet leadership and, secondly, the persistence/resurgence of capitalist relationships within the economic and political spheres of the young Soviet society:

> To summarise this analysis, we could say that the causes of these phenomena are revealed in three spheres: (a) in the survival of bourgeois management practices; (b) in the process of 'autonomization' of political apparatuses, an 'autonomization' which, on the one hand, affects the relationship between the State apparatus and the popular masses, and, on the other hand, the relationship between the Party and its administrative components; (c) in the weakness of the Party's ideological influence in general and particularly in the countryside . . .[142]

On the specific issue of the nature of the 'social relations', Bettelheim unequivocally denies that they have any socialist character. In his view the dominant public ownership of the means of production has left completely unchanged the basic relations of production.[143] The persistence of these capitalist relations undoubtedly determined the installation of a Soviet 'state bourgeoisie':

> As long as capitalist elements persist in the production relations, there also persists the possibility of *capitalist functions*, and the bourgeoisie can continue to exist in a modified form through the state apparatus and assume the form of a *state bourgeoisie*.[144]

At this point, we should remember that Bettelheim's analysis in the first two volumes stems from an interpretation of the October Revolution seen as the first revolution of a proletariat whose power and organisation into a dominant class 'was wielded through the

Bolshevik Party'.[145] However, it must be noted that Bettelheim has now completely rejected this initial interpretation of the revolutionary process. In his 1982 volume Bettelheim acknowledges that international events, academic discussions and further reading have led him to seriously question some of the basic propositions advanced in his first volumes.[146] More particularly, he now regards the Revolution as having been a simple dictatorship by the party imposed on the working class in the name of the proletariat. Bettelheim now takes the view that, following this coup d'Etat,[147] the party's leaders systematically set out to reinforce their authority in the face of the different social forces, those forces corresponding to what he now identifies as the 'multiple revolutionary processes' ('processus révolutionnaire pluriel') initiated in February 1917.[148] Hence, one must note, the eradication of all other political discourses.[149] Central to Bettelheim's recent reflections has been the re-evaluation of the part played by some of the key Bolshevik conceptions:

> Today, I think . . . it is necessary to give a decisive historical role to certain Bolshevik conceptions: the "historical mission of the proletariat" and of its party; a party functioning as the imaginary fount of the production of political and theoretical truth; a socialism that is nothing more – according to Lenin – than "the State capitalist monopoly in the service of the whole people".[150]

According to latest Bettelheim thought, the October Revolution was essentially a capitalist revolution with social upheavals causing a fast expansion of the capitalist relations of production, in particular the wage-earning relation, and leading to an expansion of the capitalist productive forces.[151] In Bettelheim's opinion the Stalinist revolution initiated in 1928 merely constituted the second step of this capitalist revolution or, as he puts it, 'the final crowning of the process inaugurated in October 1917'.[152]

Equally, the reader of the latest Bettelheim thought may be surprised to find out that the historical analysis, as has already been stated, does not go substantially beyond 1941. If that is the case, this is because Bettelheim considers that 'at this time, everything is in place. The U.S.S.R. . . . . reproduces itself according to this matrix'.[153] Indeed, such an affirmation must not be interpreted as meaning that Bettelheim ignores some of the changes which have marked the decades following Stalin's death, such as the decline of State terror, reduced ideological rigidity, as well as the emergence of a collective leadership. For Bettelheim, these changes have not had the effect of instigating new socio-economic as well as political structures. Rather, the foundations of the system established on the occasion of the extreme Stalinist revolution are still essentially underpinning the contemporary Soviet Union.

To characterise the Soviet system, Bettelheim now utilises the notion of 'party capitalism' which, as he writes, is advanced 'de façon problématique'.[154] Bettelheim believes that this new notion relates to the specific conditions which have marked the emergence of the Soviet capitalism. This 'party capitalism' is forcefully equated with a system of exploitation:

> the ruling cadres of the party and their satellites make up the collective capitalist (the *Gesamtkapitalist*), to use Marx's expression who collectively exploits the workers, collectively appropriates the surplus and makes decisions as to its use.[155]

Moreover, adds Bettelheim, this is exacerbated exploitation in the sense that both the Soviet proletariat and peasantry are deprived of the kind of organisational means required in the context of the Soviet class struggle. The exploiting class in such a system is denominated by Bettelheim as a 'party bourgeoisie'. It is evident that he has discarded the notion of 'state bourgeoisie' which was used in his first volumes. Indeed, such a change in terminology is not merely a superficial change of style. On the contrary, the new notion casts a decisive light on what was and still is the immensely important part played by the party in the specific type of capitalism which, in Bettelheim's view, prevails in the Soviet Union.[156] In his opinion, the party's total monopoly of the access to what he calls the functions of the direction of the production and the reproduction of capital[157] is ample reason for forging the new idea of 'party bourgeoisie'. It is essential to keep in mind that this concept bears witness to the fact that the party is, as Bettelheim puts it, 'the political, structural form of the Soviet bourgeoisie's development and of the regulation of its contradictions'.[158]

Postulating that an exploiting class may be divided into 'classes' or 'strata', Bettelheim argues that there exist in the Soviet Union a ruling class and a dominant class. The former, headed by the leaders at the 'summit', is made up of what he calls the representatives of capital as owners ('représentants du capital comme propriété').[159] This class has a monopoly over political decisions and the formulation of official ideology. The latter – the dominant class – is entirely 'bureaucratised' and made up of what Bettelheim calls the representatives of capital as functionaries ('représentants du capital en fonction'),[160] and include those in charge of the production process. It follows from Bettelheim's analysis that the notion of 'party bourgeoisie' excludes any idea of a mechanical identification of this new bourgeoisie and the party. In fact, as Bettelheim notes, a very substantial majority of the CPSU's membership simply do not and never will belong to it. According to Bettelheim, the dominant class finds itself totally subordinated to the ruling class or, more specifically, to a political oligarchy. This oligarchy's crucial 'summit' is comprised of the few men holding concurrent membership of the CPSU's Politburo and Secretariat.

This oligarchy's 'summit' fulfils two essential functions. Firstly, it functions in the role of a collective administrator of the 'party bourgeoisie'.[161] As Bettelheim argues, the Nomenklatura is the institutional means through which this function is essentially exercised. On the other hand, reference has just been made to the contradictions which affect the 'party bourgeoisie'. These significantly point to the serious lack of homogeneity which is intrinsic to the new bourgeoisie. It would be difficult to overemphasise the importance of this question to the central preoccupations of Bettelheim's analysis, for it brings to light a second and decisive function. This second function relates to the divisions existing among the individual fragments of Soviet social capital. Baldly stated, this question concerns the way in which what Bettelheim calls 'the unity of capital' can be achieved in a Soviet form of capitalism. In a system of private capitalism, the economic phenomenon of 'the unity of capital' is basically realised through both the market and competition. This stated, Bettelheim then moves on to discuss an important aspect of his theory of Soviet political economy: in the Soviet Union, 'the laws of capitalism do not operate in the same way; competition exists in other forms. Thus, here we see a transformation of the way in which the unity of capital is attained.'[162] In his opinion, the central planning system seeks to regulate the specific competition among the different fragments of social capital and their administrators. All are striving for a larger share of the available capital, as well as for a greater slice of that part of the global output which can be controlled, and not just seeking the consolidation of their own existing interests. None the less, Bettelheim has no hesitation in concluding that the plan has proved unable to impose 'the unity of capital' in the Soviet Union:

the constraints of a centrally planned system do not take the same form as those imposed by the market where constraints are perceived by economic actors as being objective and inevitable. In contrast, in a centrally planned system, constraints are perceived as externally determined and arbitrarily imposed elements. This causes Soviet agents of capital to avoid the requirements imposed by the plan which are the most difficult to achieve.[163]

Therefore, the failure of the plan essentially means that the ultimate responsibility for bringing cohesion and unification on a permanent basis to the 'party bourgeoisie' lies wholly within the CPSU's leadership.

It must be stressed here that this crucial regulating function, as Bettelheim conceives it, is not restricted to the kind of economic contradiction we have just briefly examined. The regulating function encompasses other instances, such as the conflicts which may run on national or ethnic lines.

If at one time the regulation essentially turned upon the widespread and prolonged use of violence, this is no longer the case. In Bettelheim's opinion the consolidation of the dominant class after Stalin's death, and the accompanying evolution which has fostered a gradual institutionalisation of the major Soviet systemic forces within the party's leadership, have brought about a situation in which continuous bargaining is *the* essential means by which contradictions are smoothed over. Bettelheim, following many other specialists, is quick to remark that a serious degree of 'immobility' pervades the entire political system as a result of this evolution.

Also worthy of note is Bettelheim's macro-perception of the relationship between the party and the Soviet state. On this particular point he rejects an interpretation which suggests the disappearance of the state. Bettelheim disagrees with those who assert, however tentatively, that the state and party have amalgamated in the Soviet Union. In short, he flatly opposes the idea of a 'Party-State' ('Parti-Etat'): 'the interactions between Party and State do not lead to a fusion between the two; in serious crises, the Party and State apparatuses can come apart and even oppose each other'.[164] Rather, Bettelheim develops the idea of the CPSU as a 'Party *of* the State' ('Parti d'Etat'), which he regards as a party separate from the state yet having an especially close rapport – indeed interpenetration – with it.[165] As he explains, the idea of 'Party *of* the State' brings to the fore two essential aspects of the Soviet system, namely the distinction existing between the party and the major apparatuses (administrative, ideological, etc.), as well as the party's permanent need to use these apparatuses to rule over the Soviet population and, indeed, enjoy an exceptional potential to repress.

Another question worth turning to concerns the nature of the ideological relationship between, on the one hand, the party and the state and, on the other, the Soviet population as a whole. The portrayal of such relationships by Bettelheim rightly excludes any given or rigid assumption. In fact he is well aware that these relationships are somewhat fluid, as can be sufficiently demonstrated by Soviet history. Bearing this in mind, Bettelheim emphasises the lack of trust which characterises the contemporary relationships. He calls such relationships, a 'rapport of subjugation',[166] essentially resting upon the image rooted in the population's collective mind of an omnipresent and unavoidable Soviet power. In Bettelheim's analysis that 'image' is compounded by a long-standing absence of any serious elaboration of a *different* type of society. This is principally due to the ideological monopoly which precludes any such attempt. Within the Soviet context, then, it would appear that the notion of 'subjugation' needs some degree of qualification. As Bettelheim points out, it seems that

the idea of rejection of what exists can only lead to a 'vacuum'. The fear of this 'vacuum' is amplified by the effects brought about by decades of lack of any freedom, so much so that the very idea of an overthrow or significant weakening of the power and of its imposed norms generates within large segments of the population a true feeling of panic . . . Thus, the *constraint* is sensed as *safety*.[167]

Leaving aside this 'psychological' aspect of Bettelheim's analysis, there is a more perceptible characteristic in what he sees as the Soviet type of capitalism, namely that which he calls 'absolute overproduction of capital'. Briefly, this phenomenon relates to the economic reality by which investments tend to exceed what is achievable from the existing forces of production.[168] This characteristic of the Soviet economy has, in the last analysis, a direct impact on the life of the Soviet masses, and is at the root of the specific forms taken by the crises of capital accumulation in the Soviet Union. These crises have as their distinguishing feature the fact that instead of generating a surplus production of goods, they cause an overall shortage. Thus, argues Bettelheim, the crises of capital accumulation in the Soviet Union appear in a form opposite to the one occurring in 'classical' capitalist countries.[169]

According to Bettelheim, the Soviet economy is going through a profound structural economic crisis, whose origin lies in the incapacity of the system to move to an intensive type of economic development. Indeed, the structural crisis finds its reflection in the steady decline of Soviet growth rates. Bettelheim explains this decline by pointing to the obstacles to enterprise performance and innovation erected by the centralised economic planning, to the exhaustion of rural and female labour-power reserves and, finally, to the decreasing percentage of the population annually joining the Soviet workforce.[170]

In the framework of Bettelheim's analysis, the economic crisis plaguing the Soviet Union is but one facet of what he describes as a general crisis of the system. Bettelheim sees in this an ideological crisis which must not be underestimated. This crisis is revealed through growing demands and challenges, such as in national claims or in the attempts, however limited, of some elements of the working class to create independent organisations which protect their interests. Bettelheim also stresses what he sees as a political crisis, one of whose principal features he holds to be the paralysis affecting a Communist Party which is unable to instigate the necessary reforms. In passing, one must observe that Bettelheim adheres to the line of reasoning which sees an expansionist foreign policy by the Soviet Union as being, in the context of complex internal difficulties and ills, an escape from reality ('fuite en avant').[171] None the less, he also believes that the ideological tenet of the 'historical mission' of the Soviet Union in the world has long prodded the leadership into the pursuit of this kind of foreign policy. As he pointed out recently, this 'historical mission' may 'generate little popular enthusiasm but . . . it forms an integral part of official ideology (and is enshrined in the constitution). These ideological motifs go to the heart of Russian expansionism.'[172]

Concerning the possible outcome of the Soviet systemic crisis, Bettelheim declines to make any specific forecast. However, he clearly underlines that such a crisis necessitates a number of 'radical mutations'. As he recently observed, 'only radical economic and political reforms can save' the system in the Soviet Union and in Eastern Europe.[173] Bettelheim's view is that the party is too 'sclerotic, too divorced from reality, and too intent on preserving its privileges to undertake the needed reforms'.[174]

It is widely acknowledged that Charles Bettelheim's analysis of the nature of the Soviet Union constitutes an important contribution to French Sovietological studies. However, this recognition has not entailed general approbation of the analysis. Some basic criticism has been directed at the line of reasoning adopted and pursued by Bettelheim, and it is appropriate to conclude this section by paying attention to it.

The crucial issue can be isolated in a comment made by the economist Marie Lavigne: 'To argue that Eastern bloc countries are not socialist, but State capitalist . . . presupposes an *a priori* reference to a socialism which is not to be found anywhere'.[175] The same point has also been made by Wladimir Andreff who, in a lengthy paper appearing in a book edited by M. Lavigne under the auspices of the Centre d'économie internationale des pays socialistes, points out that 'to show that a society is not socialist, one must possess a standard of reference, namely a conception of what socialism is'.[176] Thus, he rejects the comparison of Soviet reality with an imaginary socialist project. Similarly, Strmiska once considered the various theories pivoting on state capitalism as betraying a conservative reflex, and deplored the mechanical aspect of the transfer of Marxist concepts in relation to new empirical realities. While Strmiska points out that Bettelheim and other writers have an illusory image of socialism, he forthrightly exposes what he considers to be a serious methodological flaw in such theories:

> if one proposes to explain ill-known existing societies by imaginary future societies, one then runs the risk of reversing the methodological approach and of explaining *ignotum per ignotum*, *i.e.* more precisely of explaining the unknown by what is more unknown.[177]

Such a reference to an ideal-type of socialism has been linked by Andreff to an implicit methodological bias, which he calls the positivist logic which excludes a third alternative ('la logique positiviste du tiers exclu').[178] As explained by Andreff:

> According to this logic, a society can *a priori* only be capitalist or socialist. This premise prevents one from raising the question of a possible complex interplay between capitalist and socialist elements within one and same society, and *a fortiori*, of envisaging that the latter may be *other* than capitalist *or* socialist.[179]

Indeed, in the light of the postulated ideal type of socialism (a society without, for instance, exploitation, division of labour, a state), one is led to the conclusion, untenable according to Alec Nove,[180] that any future society will necessarily be capitalist as divergences from the ideal type are bound to arise. So, the analysis developed by Charles Bettelheim has been met with legitimate objections, themselves following from the belief, as Strmiska makes plain, that some elements of socialism have been achieved in the Soviet Union.[181]

The arguments we have described about the nature of the Soviet political and economic system should be seen in the context of a long-standing debate. The main themes of this debate, as recently remarked by Nove, quoting Anton Ciliga, were already expressed as long ago as the late 1920s.[182] As J.-J. Marie has put it: 'The nature of the U.S.S.R. The possible or likely evolution. These are questions almost as old as the U.S.S.R. itself.'[183] The evidence of this chapter bears out the perennial character of the search for the elusive nature of the Soviet Union, which has especially agitated Marxist circles.

Ultimately, the question has arisen whether Marxism may be able to yield a coherent and critical understanding of the Soviet Union. Andreff, for one, believes that Marxism, on the whole, has been unable to produce such an understanding. As he once put it, 'Marxism . . . is incapable of rendering an account of the development of the socialist economies . . . The traditional Marxist categories are inapplicable to the reality that arose in the name of Marxism and do not allow one, if kept without modifications, to apprehend how the Soviet-type systems reproduce themselves'.[184]

Though not rejecting Marxism, Andreff has generally been quick to criticise what he regards as the dogmatism of the analyses developed by Naville and Bettelheim among others. In his view, such analyses have too often found refuge in abstraction, thus failing to further a better understanding of the real functioning of the Soviet-type economy.[185] Andreff's basic criticism is fully shared by Marie Lavigne. As we mentioned earlier, Lavigne has generally criticised the conceptualisations which try to assess the nature of the Soviet Union to the detriment, so she thinks, of a detailed analysis of the workings of the Soviet economy. A brief examination of Lavigne's writings accordingly brings this chapter to a close.

'REALLY EXISTING SOCIALISM'

Marie Lavigne heads the Centre d'économie internationale des pays socialistes (University of Paris/Sorbonne). Her reputation, however, extends far beyond French boundaries. Lavigne admits to a methodological *parti-pris* in favour of the use of Soviet economic literature and statistics as a valuable working instrument. She generally emphasises that her most essential concern is to study the economic sphere of the Soviet Union and Eastern European countries with the eyes of the economist, 'equipped with his or her tool-box and having recourse to direct observation'.[186] As she makes clear in her major book *Les économies socialistes soviétique et européennes*, 'the "economism" of our presentation is evident. We will stick to it without examining questions such as the interplay of the various powers (party, State, social organisations) or the "class nature" of these societies.'[187] None the less, one may remark that, despite such proclaimed ambitions, Lavigne is not entirely successful in confining her analysis to the purely economic domain.

Lavigne defines the Soviet economy as being a socialist economy. Such a definition rests upon one criterion, that is, the socialist or collective ownership of the means of production. She has quite recently characterised such ownership as 'an essential attribute of socialism'.[188] It is important to note that Lavigne relates this specific criterion to the historical criterion of revolution. This is why, in her opinion, nationalisations, if not accompanied by profound reforms of the state and society's structures as generally brought about by a revolution, do not suffice *per se* to qualify a regime as 'socialist'.

Interestingly, the classical categories of money and wage-earning relation are regarded by Lavigne as having lost their capitalist content, mainly because of the public ownership of the means of production and central economic planning. In effect, Lavigne considers that these well-known categories have become mere instruments of planning, management and control of the Soviet economic activity. As she points out, 'the utilization of the "monetary categories" completes the central planning to which it is subordinate. These categories result from the economic plan, and not from the spontaneous action of economic agents.'[189] With respect to the specific question of the wage-earning relation, Lavigne first asserts that there exists in the Soviet Union no labour market in the capitalist sense since the Soviet state is *the* collective employer *obliged* to absorb the totality of man-power supply. Bearing this in mind, she thus depicts the 'wages' earned by any working Soviet citizen as a 'right to a certain basket of goods' or as a 'generalised ration card'.[190]

According to Lavigne, the socialist Soviet economy has witnessed the disappearance of 'social classes', defined in the traditional acceptance of 'antagonistic groups opposed through their relationship with the means of production'.[191] Thus, in Lavigne's opinion, classes in their traditional form no longer exist. It is somewhat unfortunate that she does not develop her views on this issue in a more thorough fashion. 'The discourse of the economist stops here', she writes, adding that it comes within the professional province of jurists, historians and philosophers to address such an issue.[192] This is a typical illustration of the 'economism' favoured by Lavigne.

Her postulation that there is no Soviet bourgeoisie, be it a state or party bourgeoisie, demands a quick examination of Lavigne's treatment of the party's role in the economic sphere of the Soviet Union. The party, especially the top leadership, is said by Lavigne to define the fundamental elements of the Soviet Union's economic policy. Thus, the party chooses and imposes the major economic orientations of the regime, takes the decisions concerning any economic reform, closely monitors specific economic sectors (such as agriculture) and is deeply involved in the process of designating functionaries to important economic posts.

Having said that, Lavigne hastens to stress that the party, none the less, does not exercise direct control over Soviet economic activities. The direction of the operations of production belongs to an economic administration. Lavigne insists that one must dispel the widely-held idea concerning the economies in Communist states that 'the party rules everything'.[193] For Lavigne, 'the party is the leading force . . . but its apparatus does not substitute itself in any way to that of the specialised economic administration'.[194] Lavigne considers this bureaucratic administration to be governed by the political principles of democratic centralism and 'esprit de parti'.[195] The first principle is said to ensure that such administration never becomes 'an autonomous body defining its own finalities'.[196] The second principle, in Lavigne's opinion, does not mean the subordination of this economic administration to the party, but rather evokes the necessity for it to conform to the economic orientation defined by the party leadership. Finally, the party also serves as the supreme arbiter in the case of conflict within the economic administration. Such conflicts are frequent between Soviet ministries in competition for greater volumes of various industrial inputs.

Lavigne, like many other economists, believes that the mechanisms of central planning and management in the Soviet economy do not function properly. Adopting Zaleski's theoretical position, she takes the view that Soviet central planning, owing to the greater complexity of the Soviet economy, is 'more mythical today' than it was in Stalin's day.[197] While acknowledging Soviet declining growth rates and what she calls the 'worsening of the qualitative dysfunctionings' – paralysis of economic reforms, inefficiency of labour, absenteeism, growing black market, corruption – Lavigne, unlike many French Sovietologists, refuses to use the word crisis to characterise the current state of the Soviet economy.[198] She accepts that she may be at odds with numerous economists when she argues that 'the USSR is not an economy in crisis'.[199] She makes no apologies for this and justifies such 'heretic' views by pointing to the absence of any significant rupture in the economic development of the Soviet Union and of other Eastern European countries. In her eyes, the key problem for the socialist countries is to prod their economies into a shift from extensive to intensive economic growth. The basic question is therefore to find the appropriate means to substantially increase the productivity of all the factors contributing to industrial production (an overhaul of the central planning system or stress on the market mechanism?).[200] Lavigne believes that the necessary adjustments or changes, be they conjunctural, structural or institutional, may be brought about within the parameters of the existing Soviet system. In this respect, Lavigne would probably endorse the idea of the system's 'margin of perfectibility' that was advanced a few years ago by the economist Jean-Charles Asselain.[201]

It is obvious that Lavigne's global analysis is both necessary and useful. It is a pity, though, that she does not cast aside her caution and commit to print her personal views on the nature of the Soviet political system. Nevertheless, Lavigne's subjective viewpoint on this important topic is reasonably transparent in her writings. For instance, to write without challenging the underlying assumption that the finality of the socialist economy is the 'welfare of all members of the society' is not a value-free statement.[202] In reality, one may find in her writing statements of a similar nature that may suggest a true sympathy with the subject of her scholarly investigation. At times Lavigne shows more than sympathy. For instance, her conception of the political nature of Soviet social relations closely follows the Soviet arguments. In this way, her unspoken political views seep through the fabric of an apparently non-ideological 'economism'.

3 Totalitarianism and Ideology

TOTALITARIANISM AND RELATED TOPICS

In French Sovietology the place occupied by writings using the concept of totalitarianism to interpret Soviet politics can be regarded as marginal. In this respect the contrast with Anglo-American Sovietology is striking. Any student of the latter will discover that the totalitarian model became prominent in the 1950s, only to begin to fall into disrepute during the 1960s.[1] The model, even at the height of its popularity among scholars when it was generating numerous articles and books in Anglo-American Sovietology, remained essentially untapped and disregarded in France. However, it should not be inferred that the idea of totalitarianism was a kind of *terra incognita* in France.

Indeed, one ought to bear in mind that the word totalitarianism, as observed by A. Brown, was first used in the 1920s and began to gain a certain currency in the 1930s.[2] Thus, it would have been unlikely that France would turn a blind eye to such a theoretical novelty: '"totalitarian", *selon le mot à la mode*' is the adjective applied to the new Soviet mystique by Jean Marquès-Rivière, in his 1935 book *L'URSS dans le Monde – L'expansion soviétique de 1918 à 1935*.[3] Of course some writings merely make use of the word, but there are a number of early instances where authors have gone further than a simple reference and sought, as in Jules Monnerot's book *Sociologie du communisme* published in 1949,[4] to develop a definition of totalitarianism or to examine at length some of the elements considered as intimately connected with the concept. An illustration of this attitude is best provided by Thierry Maulnier, in his 1951 book *La face de méduse du communisme*.[5] Basically, Maulnier set out to explore the dependence of Communism upon a state of permanent terror, embodied in a police apparatus and concentration camps. He sought more particularly to isolate the specific function attached to such a state of terror. Having rejected the explanation advocating an *ad hoc* utilitarian function, Maulnier then asserted that the whole question could not be examined in a proper manner without keeping in mind the ultimate objective pursued in a totalitarian society by a Communist power:

> The ultimate aim of the terrorist apparatus is the total confiscation of the individual for the benefit of the society by those who have taken possession of this society. The Terror is indispensable to the totalitarian society, because only the Terror . . . can make mankind accept . . . the renunciation of individuality . . .[6] It is the very powerful means whereby the individual is forced, in the totalitarian society, to adhere without reservations to the ideology on which the power is based.[7]

In retrospect it stands to reason that this kind of crusading anti-Communist literature inflicted serious long-term damage upon the idea of totalitarianism, which became characterised – as mentioned in an earlier chapter – as a ploy aimed at diverting minds from attacking the real target, namely the capitalist, imperialist system. In truth, any explanation seeking to elucidate the absence of a substantial body of French writings on totalitarianism has to strike at the heart of the issue – that is that totalitarianism was long perceived as an 'unsavoury' concept within advanced French intellectual circles. Of course this inevitably points to the important and pervasive hold upon them once enjoyed by Marxism. In short, such an influence helped shape and feed a negative or, at most, detached attitude towards the very concept of totalitarianism, which then became excluded for a long period from the sphere of serious debate. In *Les orangers du Lac Balaton*, a book published in 1980, the political scientist Maurice Duverger captured the full significance of this influence: 'The Marxists consider the concept of the totalitarian system to be *a weapon*, one that tends to relate the Eastern bloc countries to the ignominy of the Nazis' heinous crimes'.[8] Duverger adds that the concept is denied any scientific value by the Marxists because it is intrinsically tied to the idea of power, and thus relegates the key notions of productive forces and relations of production to the background.

The idea underlined by Duverger would not displease Claude Lefort, who recently propounded interesting insights into the non-Communist Left's uneasiness in the face of the concept of totalitarianism. Why, Lefort wonders, has this important segment of the French Left so obviously failed to grasp the concept? The answer he offers is both sharp and critical: 'At first, we answered: because it has been invented by the Right. But, as we also asked ourselves, why has it [the Left] not preceded its opponents? We would now say: because this concept is *political* and the Left does not think in terms of politics.'[9] In his opinion, the non-Communist Left has long been wedded to a vision of a State as a powerful agent of social transformations, and as a repository of measures capable of dealing with the numerous centrifugal forces and trends at work in our contemporary societies. Lefort criticises this statist vision, as it helps to generate a formidable bureaucratic expansion to the detriment of the society. Therefore, as he puts it:

> the Socialist Left is unaware of the fact that . . . it precipitates the process of formation of a stratum of bureaucrats that . . . breaks away from the rest of the population. As a result, the totalitarian phenomenon escapes it again, because it [the phenomenon] is essentially linked to the idea of a State that seeks to be omnipresent through its bureaucratic network.[10]

Paradoxically, Lefort wrote these lines at a time when the 'Solzhenitsyn effect' was already in full swing, opening up a period highlighted by a number of vociferous denunciations of the totalitarian phenomenon by young disillusioned intellectuals. Lefort's attitude vis-à-vis these voices, widely known as the 'new philosophers', is worth noting, since he himself dared to write about totalitarianism in the Soviet Union as far back as the 1950s. At that time, as he once put it, 'to speak of totalitarianism in relation to the Soviet Union was scandalous'.[11] The Preface to his 1979 book, *Eléments d'une critique de la bureaucratie*, shows Lefort giving some credit to these intellectuals for their attacks on the totalitarian phenomenon. On the other hand, Lefort appears quick to blame them for not matching these attacks with a serious attempt to reflect upon the phenomenon and to pin down its very essence.[12]

In spite of these reservations, it cannot be disputed that a whole new reality has emerged on the French intellectual scene. Since the mid-1970s (and especially since the publication in French in 1974 of Solzhenitsyn's *The Gulag Archipelago*), totalitarianism has become a popular item on the intellectual agenda. As recently pointed out by the political scientist Pierre Hassner, there is no doubt that the concept of totalitarianism has been rediscovered and reintroduced in public debate.[13] Such a new interest in totalitarianism has already had, in Hassner's view, several significant consequences. For instance, he relates the French intelligentsia's deep lack of enthusiasm for pacifism to 'the realisation among our intellectuals of what totalitarianism is'.[14]

This new interest has naturally been translated into the discovery of some of the classics on totalitarianism. This may be illustrated by a special issue of *Esprit* in June 1980 dedicated to an examination of Hannah Arendt's writings. In this publication, after recalling and deploring the degree to which the French intelligentsia was for decades very much oblivious to this thinker's work, Olivier Mongin felt somewhat obliged to qualify his affirmation by mentioning a notable exception, namely 'once again, R. Aron who introduced her work during his Sorbonne lectures . . .'.[15]

As underlined by Mongin, Aron was undoubtedly an early reader of Arendt's reflections. In a 1954 issue of *Critique* Aron undertook a review of *The Origins of Totalitarianism*, in which he expressed polite reservations with respect to Arendt's method of trying to establish the essence of the totalitarian phenomenon.[16] Several years later Aron insisted upon the issue in a more critical fashion, wondering openly 'whether the "essence" has not simply been created by theorists like Miss Arendt on the strength of certain historically-observed and historically-explicable phenomena'.[17] Aron went as far as to judge Arendt's interpretation dangerous: in his opinion her insistence on a kind of 'essence' of totalitarianism tended to leave out the most important consideration of all, namely the possible future evolution of the Soviet regime under the influence of circumstances different from those which had led to the emergence of a totalitarian regime. For Aron, it appeared 'illogical to exclude dogmatically a softening up' or even the disappearance of Soviet totalitarianism.[18] This said, one must add that Aron held Arendt in great respect, editing some of her writings in the 1960s in order to make them more accessible to the French public.

The question of totalitarianism came to Aron's attention well before the 1950s. Indeed, traces of such a precocious interest can be found in a lecture entitled *Etats démocratiques et Etats totalitaires*, which Aron gave in June 1939 before the Société française de philosophie.[19] On the occasion of the publication of Aron's *Mémoires* at the end of 1983, the historian François Furet, former President of the Ecole des Hautes Etudes en Sciences sociales, paid tribute to the role of precursor performed by the late Aron:

A tireless critic of the totalitarian temptation that has taken root in diverse circumstances . . . Raymond Aron has analyzed it in all its forms and masks. If the intelligentsia has finally become well vaccinated against its dangers, to whom does it owe its greatest debt, if not to him? Solzhenitsyn has widened the furrow, but it is Aron who has ploughed it.[20]

Démocratie et totalitarisme is one of the works which opened up this 'furrow'.[21] Based on a series of lectures delivered by Aron at the Sorbonne in 1957–8, this book reminds many French intellectuals that they owe Aron an intellectual debt. In this book Aron, the sociologist, chooses to define an ideal-type of totalitarianism which displays five essential features:

1. The totalitarian phenomenon occurs in a regime which gives to one party the monopoly of political activity.

2. The . . . party is animated or armed with an ideology on which it confers absolute authority and which consequently becomes the official truth of the state.

3. To impose this official truth, the state reserves for itself . . . the monopoly of the means of coercion and those of the means of persuasion.

4. Most economic and professional activities are subject to the state and become, in a way, part of the state itself.

5. As all activity is state activity and subject to ideology an error in economic or professional activity is by the same token an ideological fault. Thus at the very root . . . an ideological transfiguration of all the possible crimes of individuals and in the end police and ideological terrorism.[22]

Having pointed out that the Soviet Union fully met these five elements during two periods of time, namely 1934–8 and 1948–52, Aron moves on to address three questions deemed in his opinion to be of fundamental importance. In the first place, he differentiates totalitarianism from more classic political phenomena such as despotism. Aron admits that the bureaucratic absolutism observable in the Soviet Union is highly reminiscent of other bureaucratic despotisms which have dotted human history, such as the Asiatic one. Aron's assertion in his 1977 book *Plaidoyer pour l'Europe décadente* that the Soviet regime 'is a lineal descendant of Asiatic despotism'[23] is consistent with his scholarly discourse at the Sorbonne. This being said, Aron, in *Démocratie et totalitarisme*, states his case for the originality of the Soviet regime. His argument revolves around two elements, namely the revolutionary inspiration and the proclaimed rationalist ideology of the regime. Aron has quite often returned to this particular question. His viewpoint has remained fairly constant over time, though the emphasis has come to be laid almost exclusively on the ideological factor. Aron's Foreword to his friend Alain Besançon's *Court traité de soviétologie à l'usage des autorités civiles, militaires et religieuses*,[24] illustrates this shift: 'Which specific feature differentiates the Soviet Union from the classic despotism or tyranny? . . . One word provides, not the answer, but the principle of the research: *ideology*'.[25]

When discussing the question of the originality of the Soviet regime, Aron indeed acknowledges the importance of the means of action at the disposal of a modern industrial society. As he writes, 'the modern industrial society has given to the Soviet regime means of action such as no despotism in the past disposed of'.[26] Related views were expressed by Jules Monnerot in an article published in *La Nef* in April 1948,[27] and in his book *Sociologie du communisme*. A staunch opponent of Communism, Monnerot calls totalitarianism the 'Twentieth-century absolutism',[28] defining it as a global confusion of all powers, political, economic and spiritual. The Soviet totalitarian state whose ultimate objective, writes Monnerot, is to establish the most absolute sway over mankind ever achieved in history, is thoroughly condemned as it essentially treats the governed purely as objects.

The tyrants and despots of the past, as Monnerot interestingly remarks, 'could not be totalitarian in more than intention',[29] since they completely lacked the means or, as it were, the 'equipment' necessary to gain total control of the governed's thoughts and actions. It follows that, in this author's mind, totalitarianism owes its rise to the organisational means and mechanisms which have accompanied the emergence of the industrial, post-capitalist society. In such a line of reasoning, then, the key-word is organisation. Thus, Monnerot explains:

Totalitarianism has inherited the organisational techniques of capitalism, but the high degree of organisation made available to it by capitalist development is used for different ends. The progress and triumphs of capitalism are turned to controlling, with maximum efficiency, the movements of men and the circulation of goods, and also to repressive and police techniques, and terror, and the 'conditioning of minds'.[30] . . . post-capitalist tyranny . . . is called totalitarian because the capitalist era has revealed that it is possible to organise and rationalise *everything*.[31]

In Monnerot's analysis the idea of total state control over the means of communication is of great weight as it permits the steady instillation of mental stereotypes upon the whole of the Soviet population, in accordance with 'the totalitarian ambition [which] is to totally infiltrate each man's psychological life'.[32] Hence the advent, claims Monnerot, of an *homo totalitaris*, the necessary product of what he perceives as a system designed to train the 'human animal almost from birth',[33] from which derive tragic consequences:

> Exposed to the pressure of unremitting suggestion by the obsessive technique of press and wireless, 'totalitarian man', as an *individual*, begins to experience and to accommodate himself to affective states which properly belong to the *mass* . . .[34]

Thus, for Monnerot, the Soviet individual is, as it were, '*contaminated* by the mass'.[35] Monnerot, not surprisingly, writes that *homo totalitaris* loses any capacity to question, oppose or go against any current or trend. Conformism reigns supreme. As observed by Monnerot, this tragic atrophy of the personal will 'follows totalitarianism as colitis follows dysentery'.[36]

These quotations exemplify how the theoretical posture of Monnerot and others of similar disposition alienated French intellectual circles, impregnated as these circles then were with Marxism and prevented, by their idealised image of the Soviet Union, from entertaining the very idea of totalitarianism.

An important question raised by Aron was that of the possible causal link between a regime boasting a single political party and totalitarianism. With his usual caution, Aron takes the view that it would be theoretically improper to assume any sort of automatic relationship. He suggests rather that to opt for a single-party regime increases the risk of totalitarianism.[37] This is in line with the view expressed some years before the Sorbonne lectures, according to which the achievement of a political monopoly by a single party constitutes a necessary but insufficient condition for the establishment of totalitarianism.[38] In Aron's eyes the crucial condition which sets totalitarianism into motion resides in ideology. As he explains: 'The regimes did not become totalitarian through a kind of gradual impulse, but through an original intention – the will to transform fundamentally the existing order by means of an ideology'.[39]

As indicated by Aron, this *sine qua non* factor fulfilled its role in both Soviet and Nazi totalitarianism. Indeed, Aron's analysis would not shy away from comparing these instances. Taking stock of various similarities, the judgement handed down by Aron considers the ideological matrix as the decisive differential factor:

> it can be taken as a starting point that between these two phenomena the difference is essential, no matter what similarities there may be. The difference is essential because of the idea which inspires the two undertakings; in one case the final outcome is the labour camp and in the other it is the gas chamber. In one case, it is the will to construct a new regime and perhaps a new man, regardless of means; in the other the truly daemonic will to destruction of a pseudo-race.[40]

Needless to say, Aron was concerned with the immense, irreducible gulf between humanitarian ideals and Soviet historical achievements, noting that Communist power did not shrink from any coercive means to shape the society according to its ideology: 'for the Soviet undertaking, I would recall the well-known formula: he who would create an angel creates a beast'.[41]

From all these arguments one easily realises that the very notion of ideology represents a cornerstone in Aron's reflections. This is well beyond dispute. In his brief discussion of Aron's ideal-type, Besançon points to Aron's awareness that ideology seems to have priority even over totalitarianism as far as the analysis of the Soviet Union is concerned: 'it appears – *and Raymond Aron is fully aware of this* – that totalitarianism . . . is second in relation to the ideology'.[42] At one point in *Démocratie et totalitarisme* Aron, it is worth noting, calls the Soviet Union an 'ideological regime'.[43] Such a perception was to become very much a part of Aron's analysis, as the emphasis laid upon the characterisation of the Soviet Union as an 'ideocracy' in his later writings amply demonstrates.[44] The Soviet regime, according to Aron, is ideocratic as 'it defines and justifies itself, it proclaims its universal mission by reference to Marxism–Leninism'.[45] One should not be surprised to discover that Aron's way of broaching totalitarianism and, to a lesser extent Monnerot's, have reverberations in published writings decades later. There is, for example, a particular chapter on totalitarian socialism in Duverger's book *Les orangers du Lac Balaton* which basically employs the same 'thématique'. For instance, Duverger takes an interest in the relationship between Communism and Fascism. In his mind it would be too simplistic to plead for a pure assimilation of what he calls the socialist and capitalist incarnations of totalitarianism; one of the reasons he advances makes reference to different objectives overtly pursued in either case. At this point, one may sense a lingering Aronian influence in Duverger's explanation:

> We cannot consider fascist regimes and communist regimes to be on an equal footing. The former are based upon inequality between men and races, and on the permanent incapability of all men to govern themselves . . . The latter are based, in theory, on the equality of all men . . . [and on] the advent of a total and authentic democracy . . .[46]

Aron, in *Démocratie et totalitarisme*, had wondered whether Communism and Fascism could represent 'two species of the same kind?'.[47] Duverger later uses much the same words and concludes that there are 'two distinct species within the same kind . . . They are as similar as the fox and the wolf'.[48] Duverger, as much as Aron, regards the socialist variant as the most developed form of the totalitarian state in each of its key features, such as the existence of an ideology suppressing any dissidence, as well as of a monolithic party.

Finally, Duverger also addresses the question connected with the novelty of the totalitarian state. On this score he writes that 'the totalitarian State is not a modern invention. the XXth century has clothed a very ancient system in new forms.'[49] He then points to the medieval theocracy as an illustration. Duverger is very much aware that the present century has witnessed two crucial changes, which have given governments the capacity to assume control over the population and have made possible the advent of, as it were, 'a total totalitarianism'.[50] In this context Duverger strongly stresses two modern features, being the immense technical progress (more particularly in communication systems) as well as the ideological phenomenon.[51]

To write about Aron and Duverger in succession begs a short examination of an interesting and specific question on which both scholars were always at great odds – the theory of convergence of industrial societies. Duverger has long been a supporter of this idea, as an article in a June 1956 issue of *Le Monde* reminds us.[52] In his classic *Introduction à la politique*, first published in 1964, Duverger makes the point that the Soviet Union and advanced Western countries are bound to evolve into a regime of democratic socialism:

> The USSR and the popular democracies will never become capitalist; the USA and Western Europe will never become communist. But both parties seem to be heading towards socialism by a twofold movement: liberalization in the East, socialization in the West. It is likely that such movement will come up against enormous obstacles and take a very long time . . . But it seems irresistible.[53]

The 1970s did not see any theoretical turnaround on the part of Duverger, who kept on advocating the validity of the idea of convergence. Yet his conviction has begun to show a noticeable degree of circumspection with regard to the speed of the evolution. In 1972, in his book *Janus, les deux faces de l'Occident*, Duverger affirms that although the idea of convergence of the systems has gone out of fashion, it none the less remains 'valid in a global perspective of which we can pinpoint neither the rhythm nor the end'.[54]

To Aron, such an affirmation is highly objectionable and nothing more than a kind of prophecy. Within the framework of the concept of industrial society discussed at length in his book *Dix-huit leçons sur la société industrielle*,[55] Aron has always been very conscious of the basic economic realities and tendencies generally common to the Soviet Union and advanced Western countries. However, he has persistently rejected the theory of convergence, although, as he remarks, some of his ideas expressed in the 1950s and 1960s may have given rise to another impression.[56] Aron's recent *Mémoires* bring the whole point home in a clear fashion:

> The comparison between the Soviet regime and the Western regimes did not in the least imply their *convergence* to use a word which summarises a theory that was once popular. In spite of fables, I have never subscribed to this thesis. A few passages in *18 Lectures* could be misleading: the Soviet planners would, in the future, resort more to market mechanisms; . . . the State-owned

sector of the productive apparatus would be broadened in the West
. . . I did not infer from such structural evolutions the likelihood
or inevitability of convergence . . . I stated that such possible
economic rapprochements (that, moreover, have not as yet taken
place) would hardly lessen the distance between two types of
society which are essentially different.[57]

In all Aron's reflections on the theory of convergence, a number
of points seem to be particularly relevant. Aron always discarded as
being unfounded the idea that industrial societies must move towards
one correct form of political superstructure, as if some kind of innate
nature were given and operating. As he once put it an 'industrial
society . . . has no immanent finality',[58] hence his affirmation that 'it
is possible to imagine broad industrial civilizations with different
political systems'.[59] This explains why Aron, for instance, found the
assumption that 'a multi-party system is the only rational policy which
can be imposed on an industrial economy' very debatable.[60] Finally,
mention ought to be made of Aron's steady condemnation of the
advocacy of a necessary link between political evolution in the Soviet
Union and economic progress and/or rationalisation. Condemning
this idea as a by-product of a primitive Marxism, Aron considers as
very naive, if not absurd, the supposition that democracy will make
progress in the Soviet Union at the same pace as the index of
consumption or industrial output.[61] In essence, Aron has long
objected to what he once labelled as 'the theory of "autodestruction"
of the one-party regime, in this industrial age, under the mere
influence of welfare'.[62]

There are 'two types of society essentially different', writes Aron
in the excerpt from his *Mémoires* cited above. For Aron *the* principle
differentiating the opposing variants of industrial society lies entirely
within the realm '*de la politique*'.[63] He defines its essence as revolving
around the method of selecting those who govern and the method
by which authority is exercised.[64] Such a position is unambiguously
bound to one of the constants which run through the whole of the
Aronian analysis – what Aron calls the 'primacy of politics'[65] in
human society where power, by nature, is shared and exercised by a
small number of men. One can hardly find a better illustration of the
influence attached to this primacy of politics than in Aron's discussion
of the question of classes in Soviet society. In his mind such a specific
problem cannot be dealt with without paying due heed to the political
regime itself. Aron has made this very plain:

It is the political regime, that is the constitution of power and the idea that those who govern have of their authority, which decides the existence or nonexistence of classes and above all their self-awareness.[66]

In his book *La lutte de classes – nouvelles leçons sur les sociétés industrielles*,[67] Aron embraces the opinion that the social strata sociologically observable in the Soviet Union are not equivalent to the social classes existing in the industrialised Western world. To a certain extent Aron views Soviet society as a classless society. The key point conveyed here bears on the difficulty encountered by these strata in attaining the necessary state of consciousness or cohesion to constitute classes, a difficulty essentially attributable to the sheer political negation in the Soviet Union of the freedoms of discussion and association. In Aron's mind social classes presuppose the existence of a degree, albeit limited, of political and social freedom. As he puts it:

> We see a profound difficulty in finding the equivalent to classes as they exist in the West. If one defines a class as the organisation of a sub-group within the global society – a homogeneous community being aware of its existence and opposition to others – it is probable that there exists, despite economic inequalities, objective discriminations and social distance, no such reality in the Soviet Union. The formation of coherent groups is difficult because the power, by its very nature, does not accept the constitution and organisation [of such groups] . . .[68]

So, in his comparison of the two variants of industrial society, Aron logically deems as key the fact that 'in a Soviet-type society, no pressure group has the right to exist'.[69]

Such an interesting viewpoint does not mean that Aron has remained aloof from the general conclusions reached by a number of specialists concerned with the study of interest groups in the Soviet Union and Eastern Europe.[70] Though Aron acknowledges a limited degree of influence wielded by groups and important social categories existing outside the party's institutional structure, but none the less belonging to the Soviet élite, he held serious doubts (as he made very clear in an interview with this author in 1982) about the validity of the application of interest group analysis to the Soviet polity.[71] As mentioned above, what strikes Aron is the absence of organisational independence or autonomy in the Soviet Union. Essentially politically motivated, this situation results from the very nature of the Soviet regime which, writes Aron, is to display a 'façade of unanimity',[72] a fact which, in his mind, not only runs counter to a fundamental feature germane to human and social nature (that is, divergence and conflict), but which also overtly contradicts the heterogeneity inherent in any modern industrial society. Finally, as he points out, the Soviet regime, unlike its Western counterpart, tends to 'reestablish the confusion of state with society, while modernity has been creating or emphasising the distinction [between state and society] by differentiating political functions, by tolerating organisations independent from one another and legitimately rivals'.[73]

This last point raised by Aron concerning the confusion of state with society was noted long ago by Lefort. As mentioned earlier, Lefort developed an early interest in the question of totalitarianism. On the heels of the CPSU's XXth Congress he contributed to *Socialisme ou Barbarie* an essay entitled *Le Totalitarisme sans Staline*.[74] At a later stage his reflections on totalitarianism would yield two books which bear a clear philosophical imprint – *Un homme en trop – Réflexion sur l'Archipel du Goulag*[75] and *L'Invention démocratique – les limites de la domination totalitaire*.[76] Published respectively in 1976 and 1981, these books coincide with a shift in Lefort's global analytical direction which saw him lay greater stress on the analysis of the relationship of totalitarianism to democracy.[77]

As a kind of preliminary, Lefort claims that any conceptualisation of totalitarianism ought to go beyond the simple consideration of the features associated with dictatorship. In his 1956 essay, Lefort interestingly writes that totalitarianism is not a form of political regime, and goes on to differentiate the concept from a theoretical standpoint which insists on the idea of dictatorship:

Totalitarianism is not a dictatorial regime, as it appears when we speak summarily of it as a type of absolute domination in which the separation of powers is abolished. More precisely, it isn't a political regime: it is a type of society – that form in which all activities are immediately tied to each other, deliberately presented as modalities of a single universe in which a system of values predominates absolutely, such that all individual and collective activities must necessarily find in that system their coefficient of reality, in which, finally, the dominant model exercises a total constraint at once physical and spiritual on the behavior of the particular individuals.[78]

Lefort identifies two moments in the totalitarian enterprise which he regards as really inseparable. In his eyes the first principle resides in the regime's affirmation of a '"consubstantiality" of State with civil society'.[79] Secondly, he underlines the proclaimed abolition of the social division, in the sense that a totalitarian society is supposed to render impossible the emergence of groups or classes whose interests would be based upon antagonism. In the last analysis, Lefort holds firm to the view that 'it is the very notion of social heterogeneity which is impugned'.[80]

Any totalitarian system, in Lefort's opinion, is grounded in a triptych of crucial images which, in reality, makes up its ideological matrix. In the first place there is 'the image of the People-as-One', whereby social division in all its forms is denied,[81] which combines with 'the image of the Power-as-One', which Lefort defines as a 'power concentrated within the limits of the ruling organ and, ultimately, in a single individual who incarnates the unity and will of the people'.[82] Finally there is 'the Other' image, which symbolises the permanent enemy of the People-as-One. This last image is of particular importance in Lefort's analysis; in proportion to the unfolding of the negation of the social division, this 'Other' becomes necessary to the totalitarian state. In other words, it is the very nature of such a state to continually forge an enemy.[83] Lefort's idea may be related to a recent point made by M. Heller, that the history of the Soviet Union 'could be symbolised by a list of words designating the enemy that have in steady succession appeared and disappeared . . . perpetrators of acts of sabotage, kulaks . . . Trotskyists . . . cosmopolitans . . .',[84] and more recently, Zionists and dissidents.

At this point, a few words concerning the origin of totalitarianism are in order. Lefort's theoretical efforts rest upon a particular conception of democracy. In his view, democracy means 'a *form of society*, a symbolic constitution' where political power is a *res nullius* and where the nature of the society remains wholly indeterminate and conflictual.[85] In *L'Invention démocratique – Les limites de la domination totalitaire*, Lefort summarises his ideas as follows:

The modern democratic revolution is best recognised in this mutation: there is no power linked to a body. Power appears as an empty space and all those who exercise it . . . occupy it temporarily . . . there exists no law . . . whose clauses cannot be challenged, whose foundations are not susceptible of being questioned; finally, there is no image of a centre and of the contours of society: the unity cannot obliterate social division.[86]

Lefort explains that the indeterminate quality intrinsic to democracy naturally tends to desire and seek its own abolition. In this context, totalitarianism constitutes the answer to the democratic ambiguities, as it aims to establish total unity and ban this indetermination which haunts the democratic experience. Hence, as one will understand, the phantasmagorical images of the People-as-One and Power-as-One.

At the centre of the totalitarian enterprise lies an unprecedented type of political entity, the party, the analysis of which, it must be said, is implanted deep in Lefort's thought. Going back to the cited essay, one finds him characterising the party as 'the fundamental institution of totalitarianism'[87] and expatiating upon its very nature:

it is something other than a coercive apparatus, something other than a caste of bureaucrats, something other than an ideological movement aimed at proclaiming the sacred historical mission of the state although it connotes all these traits. It is the essential agent of modern totalitarianism.[88]

In Lefort's mind the party penetrates the state entirely, 'so far as . . . to use it as a mere façade of political power . . .'.[89] But, most importantly, it also creates hundreds of social micro-organisations which are designed to help it in its unrelenting efforts to achieve both elements of the totalitarian enterprise. Such a network of micro-organisations represents an absolutely essential component of Soviet totalitarianism, as it allows the tracking down and destruction of any manifestation of social autonomy: 'Anyone who would not pay attention to the vast apparatus erected to dissolve . . . the subject into a "we", to agglomerate, to melt these "we" into the big Communist "we" and to produce the People-as-One, would not understand how the totalitarian logic works'.[90]

The party, argues Lefort, does not rest upon a popular consensus.[91] Indeed, in spite of all its endeavours to camouflage itself behind this network of micro-organisations, the party cannot avoid being perceived by the Soviet populace as an entirely foreign body reigning through coercion above the proclaimed homogeneous society. This reality, as pointed out in a short article published in a 1977 issue of

Esprit, is said to be the 'fundamental contradiction of totalitarianism',[92] and is all the more dangerous as it is artificially restrained. Indeed, Lefort is prone to rebut the suggestions made by those who tend to regard the Soviet regime as being somehow invincible. On the contrary, he claims that Soviet totalitarianism suffers from an 'exceptional vulnerability'.[93] The Soviet regime, adds Lefort, shows signs of erosion and appears continually to be exposed to the threat of a 'violent return of all the signs of division'.[94] Finally, he supposes that a political crisis in the Soviet Union would bring about 'a massive revolt in which would join all oppositions nowadays latent and crushed, but the finality of which would be beyond doubt'.[95]

Finally, a word should be said about Edgar Morin's essay, *De la Nature de l'URSS – Complexe totalitaire et Nouvel Empire*.[96] Morin is a well-established sociologist, whose name can be found in any comprehensive study of the post-1945 French Left. He was one of the founders of the Arguments group. Comprised essentially of philosophers and sociologists who had either quit or, like Morin, been expelled by the PCF, Arguments published from late 1956 to 1962 a theoretical journal of the same name that became the flourishing focal point of revisionism in France.[97]

In his essay published in early 1983, Morin basically attempts to show that Soviet totalitarianism is, as he puts it, a 'multidimensional complex'.[98] It is nothing less than a synthesis transcending all of its necessary and complementary constituents, such as the Party, the State, the Nomenklatura, the Ideology, the Gulag, the Police and so on. Morin declines to mention his main sources of inspiration. Among the very few French writers to whom he openly refers one notes Lefort, whose analytical approach is praised by Morin. Morin's essay is in fact a very imaginative and well-presented patchwork of ideas and conceptions, essentially emanating from a number of specialists and writers such as Carrère d'Encausse, Aron, Voslensky and Besançon.[99] Morin has a particular leaning towards a kind of intellectual jargon; his definition of the notion of totalitarianism, which is tantamount to mere tautology, suffices as an example. In Morin's mind, this notion literally means '*the enclosure of the social totality by a total power through the scanning of the whole from a centre enjoying this total power*'.[100]

Morin's long-term interest in the Soviet Union and Eastern Europe is beyond question.[101] It is of interest that, inspired by the intellectual *Zeitgeist* brought about by Solzhenitsyn, he could not refrain from jumping onto the rolling band-wagon of totalitarianism.

Totalitarianism remains, in our view, an important element in the discussion of the Soviet Union, if one accepts as a premise P. Hassner's position that 'there exists no totalitarianism *per se*, but only totalitarian behaviours, tendencies, logics, objectives and residues'.[102] The acknowledgement of its relevance has, indeed, nothing to do with the idea of a grand totalitarian conceptualisation of the Soviet Union. That would be a simplistic ideological reading of the Soviet system for, clearly, the Soviet Union is not, to use the words of G. Nivat, 'a non-place where everything has been levelled off by an Orwellian totalitarianism'.[103]

The Soviet Union may not be Orwellian, but it is a land ruled by a single political entity which has long been allergic to any serious questioning of the official ideology, and whose ambitions to rule over every sphere of Soviet life remain basically unchanged 70 years after the Revolution. Article 6 of the Soviet Constitution, adopted in 1977, provides the student of Soviet politics with an unambiguous reiteration of such totalitarian ambitions. Historically, need we say, the degree of success of these ambitions has never been total and has varied *vis-à-vis* the different spheres of Soviet life and society. It stands to reason that the party's control of political life and behaviour in the Soviet Union has been more successful than, for instance, its control over the Soviet economy. In this respect, as the economist Zaleski once very aptly observed, 'the claim of commanding production as one commands men is mere illusion'.[104] But, however illusory it may be, this particular claim to control and plan the entire economic life, which is paradoxically at the heart of the extreme anarchy prevailing in the Soviet economy, has been an enduring one.

The Soviet Union is also a country where a true civil society based on the recognition of an unfettered social 'horizontality', capable of asserting itself and choosing its autonomous organisational structures, forms of action and discourses, has been denied the right to exist. It remains a nation where pluralism has been basically outlawed. The Soviet regime has long felt, to refer to Monnerot's words of 1948, 'repugnance to any pluralism'.[105] Acknowledgement of this historical fact does not exclude the eventuality that such deep repugnance be whittled down, or even significantly weakened, by the party. History, need we add, does not stand still.

IDEOLOGICAL REGIME: FROM AN 'IDEOCRACY' TO A 'LOGOCRACY'

A historian who for a certain time during the 1960s was strongly attracted to the application of psychoanalytical methodology to historic investigation, Alain Besançon holds the position of Directeur d'études at the Ecole des Hautes Etudes en Sciences sociales. Besançon is also currently one of the columnists of the magazine *L'Express*. In his approach to Sovietology, Besançon recognises that his expertise lies primarily in the area of Russian culture. He is at the forefront of that current referred to in Chapter 1 as 'the "right-wing" tendency in modern French Sovietology'. It is impossible to dissociate Besançon's present analysis of the Soviet Union from the Communist experience to which he so enthusiastically subscribed during his early student days at the Institut d'études politiques in Paris. The total disintegration of the Communist system of reference, which occurred in 1956, and the brutal eruption of reality in what he refers to as 'our delirium of certitudes'[106] were the first, though indispensable, agents which determined the direction his future analysis would take. It may be justly considered that the year 1956 saw the moment of truth which caused Besançon to suddenly seek out the reasons for his intellectual wanderings:

> In the course of three months, I woke up as from a dream . . . How can one enter into this closed system that has an answer for everything . . . and where no objection can be heard? How can one make such a bad mistake . . . since it turned us into unconscious accomplices of innumerable crimes? This is the problem with ideology.[107]

Besançon believes that the Soviet system is very simple to understand, to the extent that it is unnecessary, in his opinion, to have acquired 'a first-hand physical experience of the Soviet reality'.[108] In other words, to spend time in the Soviet Union could be a meaningless experience. Besançon maintains that the problem which confronts the Sovietologist is not that of keeping abreast of new developments in his field as is the case with other disciplines. Rather, understanding of the Soviet system stems from a global intuition. He seems to believe that such an understanding is indeed very rare and that without it, as he recently put it, 'the "experts", however learned or pedantic they may be, are infallibly mistaken'.[109]

One can spend one's life studying Soviet documentary sources, analysing *Pravda* . . . and understand nothing, since Sovietology also requires shrewdness of mind. . . . one must be capable of entering into a very specific way of thinking and giving up one's usual methods of reasoning. It seems that it is difficult.[110]

At this point, Besançon postulates that the major difficulty in understanding the Soviet system is a result of the normal intellectual tendency to draw a conceptually symmetrical comparison between it and a Western-style system. Besançon observes that every time a General-Secretary dies it causes this intellectual propensity to surge in an irrestible fashion.[111] But, in his view, comparisons between the two systems must hinge on a basic dissymmetry. Indeed, it is only by 'resolutely forgoing the "comparatist" approach that one may hope to comprehend the Soviet phenomenon'.[112] Taking this stance on comparative analysis, Besançon goes on to caution against the equivocal results to be derived from using the concepts of economy and society in the analysis of the Soviet Union:

There are two concepts . . . that we cannot use with regard to the Soviet Union without vitiating the very basis of the reasoning. These are the concepts of *society* and *economy*, understood . . . as 'self-regulated systems' that do not require the intervention of an 'extra-social' or 'extra-economic' force in order to function.[113]

It is interesting to note that this particular aspect of Besançon's analysis bears some similarity to passages contained in Jules Monnerot's *Sociologie du communisme*. Monnerot, whose writings influenced Besançon to some degree, stated in 1949 that Western historians and sociologists had a tendency to view the Communist phenomenon according to 'their familiar categories',[114] which in his view fail to capture the originality of the phenomenon. Furthermore, it comes as no surprise to learn of Besançon's belief that the Soviet regime clearly cannot be reduced to the categories of government defined by traditional political philosophy. In other words, the notions of tyranny and oligarchy are regarded by Besançon as inadequate.[115]

At the same time, Besançon considers totalitarianism to be a less than ideal notion for dealing with the Soviet phenomenon. In his view totalitarianism is the political consequence, the embodiment on a social scale, of an ideology which, logically, predates its own manifestation. He objects to a characterisation of a phenomenon through its effects rather than through its causes and principles. Thus, Besançon views the Soviet regime as an ideological regime, the historical originality of which he holds to be absolutely unquestionable. As he puts it, 'This is a new beast.'[116] Besançon indeed sees little need to grasp or learn pre-revolutionary Russian history, since it may only serve to buttress what he regards as the dangerous theory that the Soviet Union is the mere continuation of the old and traditional Russia.[117] Rather, its originality is entirely attributable to the position occupied by Soviet ideology, which Besançon considers as 'the only legitimacy of the power and of the very existence of the party'.[118]

But how exactly does Besançon view Soviet ideology? Firstly, he believes it cannot be simplified into a straightforward system of ideas and therefore cannot be grasped by mere reference to the propositions of which it is comprised. Secondly, he is quick to warn against the most grievous of errors, which would be to consider the ideology as a philosophy. As he claims, 'you cannot enter into a philosophical discussion with the ideology, even to refute it, because it is foreign to philosophy, and cannot be refuted by it'.[119] At the same time, although Besançon is aware of possible analogies, he holds that the ideology is not a religion. Although both have in common the need for salvation sought by man, Besançon feels that 'it is not enough to establish a legitimate descent'.[120]

It is interesting to note in this connection that the notion of Soviet Communism having a religious character has been given credence by French writers on numerous occasions since the late 1920s. For example, Jean Marquès-Rivière spoke, in 1935, of Bolshevism as a new religion having 'its rites, its prophets . . . its canons, its excommunications, its faith . . . its icons and its mystique: the Dynamo and the Plan'.[121] Later, the conjunction of a subjugated Russian people and a secular religion, namely Communism, led Monnerot to put forward the idea of an 'Islam of the twentieth-century'.[122] Monnerot believes that the Party and the State simply assume the functions of a universal Church. Finally, the sociologist Kerblay reiterates the idea that Marxism–Leninism has become a secular religion whose message, like that of all great religions, was meant to be universal in nature.[123] In particular he observes that the consensus surrounding the party has become a substitute for communion and that, moreover, the members of the Central Committee form an 'oligarchy of a clerical nature'.[124] Writing as recently as 1985, Kerblay underlines the existence of analogies with the institutionalised religions, such as the deference accorded to sacred books and the 'sacralization' of 'everything that relates to Lenin'.[125]

In order to understand why Besançon has rejected such reasoning, one may refer to his work *Les Origines intellectuelles du léninisme*. Here he supposes that a formal trait, that is the structure of the act of faith, is conclusive in separating ideology from religion. In his view:

> At the basis of religions of faith, there is a conscious *unknown*. Abraham, Saint John, Muhammed know that they do not know. They know that they believe. When Lenin declares that the materialist interpretation of history is not a hypothesis, but a scientifically demonstrated doctrine, it is doubtless a belief, but a belief he imagines proven, and based in experience.[126]

Besançon adapts a statement made by Monnerot, regarding the Communist religionist, reversing the phrasing, when he claims that the ideologue, like Lenin, 'does not know that he believes. He believes that he knows.'[127]

Further to this idea, Besançon writes that the history of religions provides a degree of precedent for the ideology and that we are dealing with gnosis, which he considers as 'an imperfect model of ideological thinking'.[128] He cautions against taking the comparison too far: ideology is comparable to gnosis although the former cannot be found in the tradition of the latter because, unlike gnosis, ideology is founded on a totally new type of certainty – scientific certainty. According to Besançon, ideology could not have appeared on the scene before the birth of modern science.

Stemming from a corruption of both religion and science, Soviet ideology is based on a global science which has successfully decoded the fundamental laws of the world and its evolution. All knowledge is imparted at once to the ideologue, with the result that his cognitive relationship with the world is given a definite structure. In short, as Besançon puts it, 'the intellectual effort is complete, the discovery of the truth is accomplished. There remains only the practical task of implementing such truth.'[129] Being essentially political *praxis*, ideology, as was demonstrated above, has no predetermined limitation: it can have no other objective than to reshape the world. It is on the basis of this predestined universality that Besançon considers Soviet power unable to forgo the exporting of the revolution, even if it wanted to do so.[130] In this regard, Besançon mentions the dissident Vladimir Bukovsky's idea that the Soviet state is, in its essence, a base of universal subversion, a 'centre of gradual crystallization of the planet on the model of the initial crystalline germ'.[131] This is, according to Besançon, the essential project which underpins the conduct of the Soviet Union in the world.

In Besançon's mind the party was entirely aware of what would occur after the rise to power in November 1917, that is, the implementation of socialism. For Besançon, socialism has always been and always will be a chimera.[132] In setting up an 'ideocracy', the party attempted to bring society into line with what ideology deemed and dictated it should be. To use the words of Dominique Colas, 'it is a matter of bending the world to the idea'.[133] However, the effect of this direct attack was to provoke the strongest form of social resistance. According to Besançon, 'the only spontaneity shown by the historical raw material has been to resist . . . and follow with obstinacy a course opposed to the expected one'.[134] It was thus that, after November 1917, nothing proceeded according to plan in the Land of the Soviets. Besançon explains that there rapidly appeared a breach between 'real' reality and 'ideological' reality. This resulted in an ever-broadening gap between the party's vision of the world and that of the Russian people. The party has unceasingly attempted to bridge this fundamental hiatus, which has always seriously threatened the legitimacy of Communist power which, as Besançon sees it, depends entirely upon the substantiation of the scientific nature and correctness of its theory.

In dealing with this threat, the party has adopted two distinct approaches. First of all, Besançon believes, the regime has always tried 'to build socialism', to seize every opportunity, within the limits of its capability, to smelt the social matter down and pour it 'into the mould prepared for it'.[135] He reduces the synthesis of the regime's history to the relationship between two models of political action – 'war communism' and the New Economic Policy (NEP). These models relate to the early years of the regime. But, according to Besançon, they have reappeared in later circumstances. The meaning of this idea may be better perceived in the light of his explanation that 'these models do not exist in their pure state: they are analytical tools for interpreting concrete situations'.[136] The first model refers to the effort aimed at destroying everything within society which resists party action. This is essentially based on coercive intervention by the state. In pursuing demented and illusory goals through logical means, the state, as perceived by Besançon, attempts to break down the resistance of the 'real' and to absorb Soviet civil society. The second model relates to a retreat of ideological power, and is characterised by a margin of independence granted to society. This model will appear when the regime perceives that it is threatened through its own excesses.

If, as described by Besançon, 'the inherent principle of ideology is to pursue its postulations to their limits',[137] it is none the less true that if it goes too far, it imperils the very power which embodies it. This sheds light on his definition of NEP: 'The compromise of ideology . . . with "externality" in order to survive and grow stronger under its mode of power'.[138] It is worth noting that Besançon compares the Brezhnev years to an apparently successful NEP, characterised by the strengthening of both ideological power and civil society.

Secondly, Besançon stipulates that the party devotes its energy not only to building socialism, but also to gaining full recognition by the Soviet people of the fiction of its existence and the idea that socialism is functioning effectively. Thus it is not a matter of coercing the population into agreement on the establishment of socialism, nor gaining its approval of the excellence of the socialist ideal being pursued. It is rather a question of the population showing enthusiasm for results that are deemed to have been obtained and of thus confirming the ideological 'surreality' while denying reality.[139] This observation led Besançon, as well as Aron before him, to characterise the Soviet regime as one in which lies are held to be reality. This regime, according to Aron, is fundamentally perverse, in that it encourages, imposes and 'permanently fosters the lie'.[140]

At this stage, Besançon's analysis revolves around the important notion of bridging the irremediable gap through the magic of language. In his view any rise to power of an ideology is necessarily accompanied by a language, whose meaning changes at this point: 'After the seizure of power . . . It becomes the fundamental pillar of surreality'.[141] He perceives it as a melding of the languages of liturgy and science and describes its role as follows:

> its function is to *evoke*, in the magical meaning of the word, that is, to suggest the non-existent reality. It is formulary, because its power is linked to the letter, and it is incantatory. Dedicated to suggesting through words an illusory reality, side by side with and transcending real reality, it is the medium for that reality's necessary transfiguration.[142]

Besançon is therefore of the opinion that the party can only act upon 'real' reality through the language of 'ideological' reality, and that the subsequent transformation of the former can only be described using the fundamentally inadequate terms of the latter. On a practical level, this will translate into an inordinate proliferation of ideological speech. He explains that all propaganda and public speech is aimed not at convincing but at conditioning the population, and is especially concerned 'to make manifest the fact of the power of the ideology'.[143] This language is to be obeyed and such obedience, in Besançon's view, is a simple matter: 'It must be *spoken*, because language is a social institution and that particular language is the institution of the society which is supposed to exist'.[144]

Given that the original ideas retain only verbal substance, Besançon posits that the Soviet regime has become a veritable 'logocracy' in which there is publicly acknowledged devotion to the ideological 'langue de bois' (wooden tongue), and to a system of action and behaviour whose prime objective is to safeguard its monopoly. This is what he refers to as 'the social contract of the Soviet regime'.[145] The 'logocracy' thus implies 'the disconnection of the individual subjectivity',[146] meaning the withdrawal of individuals into private, and especially family, life, where normal and free speech, with its dire anarchic implications for the regime, is given free rein.

It is worth mentioning here that the sociologist Kerblay concludes a study entitled *Les Problèmes de la socialisation dans le milieu rural soviétique* with an observation he believes to be applicable to the entire Soviet social system. He confirms that the family enclave 'remains one of the few privileged areas where the individual can forget the double language and fully be his own self'.[147] It may be mentioned, moreover, that in Kerblay's view the permanent dichotomy between the radiant ideological world and the real world is in itself a valid explanation of the problems encountered in attempting to socialise the Soviet individual. Such a dichotomy means, for the Soviet citizen, a dual or split personality which, argues the sociologist, represents 'the commonest form of their social integration'.[148]

It is interesting to observe that Besançon refers to a Soviet social contract, although he calls the regime 'terrorist' because of its continuing imposition of the notion that the 'surreality' is already a matter of fact. Paradoxically, this utterance does not prevent him from claiming that the 'Soviet regime rules peacefully'.[149] Besançon states that one would be mistaken in believing that for the citizen of the USSR the Soviet regime is more difficult to live with than a non-socialist regime. Besançon reveals an awareness of the arguments recently put forward by Zinoviev when he opines that Soviet subjects draw pleasure and satisfaction from their regime.[150] In the following extract Besançon makes particular reference to an idea of Marx's son-in-law, Paul Lafargue:

> Nevertheless, for the first time in the history of the world, the ancient curse of work has been lifted, not under the reign of abundance, as hoped by the founders of socialism, but under the reign of laziness and irresponsibility.[151]

In referring once again to the notion of the 'langue de bois', it must be recognised that this notion is among those used by Besançon which have, according to the historian Emmanuel LeRoy Ladurie, 'become . . . part of the vulgate'.[152] Besançon is making use of a notion which originated in Polish intellectual circles in the mid-1950s. As noted by the sociologist Morin in 1963, 'the wooden tongue, to use the expression coined by the Poles in 1955 . . .'[153] was meant to describe the litany-like ritual and repetitive nature of the official language used by the Communist authorities. As pointed out by G. Nivat, the expression 'has been prospering for some time among French political analysts'.[154]

Among the recent French writings on this particular topic is an interesting article published in the periodical *Commentaire* by Louis Martinez, Professor of Russian Literature at the University of Provence. One finds here an attempt to outline in theory the ins and outs of this phenomenon. In view of its purpose to occupy and saturate all available public space, the 'langue de bois' is described by Martinez as a total, repetitive, unanimist and impersonal discourse, whose prolixity is all the more striking in that the subject is entirely predictable, inescapable and unreal. The explicit finality of the 'langue de bois' is perceived by Martinez as being 'the "exclamatic" or discursive designation of an asymptotic finality of the history of mankind . . .: communism'.[155] The author obviously considers the 'langue de bois' as being radically indifferent to the communication of true information, any empirical fact or phenomenon being generally presented as the sign of a transcending construction. Martinez concedes, however, that the amorphous body of printed matter might bear orders and directives. He none the less sees as ludicrous the work undertaken by Sovietologists in an attempt to extract the true message from Soviet printed matter. Martinez concurs with Besançon, whose influence shows through in the following excerpt:

> This 'tracking down' (*dépistage*) means the absorption of thousands of futile pages . . . and this entails a kind of intellectual disarmament in face of the fable, an . . . overestimation of the rare positive elements . . . and an irreparable deformation of judgement. Thus, the *langue de bois* brutalizes and subdues the majority of Sovietologists more surely than it surprises the Soviet readers who keep a natural suspicion towards the printed word.[156]

Martinez concludes by saying that the 'langue de bois' is 'doubly mutilating'[157] in that it prevents and imposes speech. Such a statement recalls the postulations of Besançon, for whom linguistic conformity is the prime indication of allegiance to the regime.[158]

This idea has recently been taken up by Charles Bettelheim, though it must be noted that he rejects the ideocratic interpretation of the Soviet Union which, in his view, conceals the reality of the system of economic exploitation existing in the Soviet Union.[159] It is Bettelheim's contention that the pervasive 'langue de bois' is in fact a '*code of allegiance*',[160] whose role is that of an 'instrument of social submission'.[161] He believes that any Soviet citizen who employs it, in open submission to that to which he is subjectively opposed, is pronouncing an act of allegiance to Communist power. It may be said in conclusion that this reasoning is in agreement with the opinion expressed by Claude Orsini, for whom the 'langue de bois' possesses 'functions of *pure* socio-political *control* . . . it *delimits* the field of authorised discourse and . . . makes it easier to spot any attempt at independent discourse'.[162]

It may be easily understood that to speak the 'langue de bois' is not a neutral gesture. Whenever the Soviet subject uses it, either through 'a reflex of basic self-preservation'[163] or to ensure the survival of that society which is hidden under the socialist pseudo-society, then a sort of acknowledgement that the more powerful 'surreality' is triumphant manifests itself. In Besançon's words, 'hardly has one spoken it . . . than one can see it take shape'.[164] Interestingly, this general point can probably be made with respect to Soviet rites. Participation in various ceremonies and observance of the numerous rites are not neutral or anodyne phenomena, since they constitute, as rightly noted by M. Heller, 'a sign of allegiance . . . the mark of an indefeasible link with the State, the fatherland, the Party . . .'.[165]

They induce, to use Lubomir Sochor's words, a certain 'political belief' in all participants.[166] It is worth remarking that in his analysis of relations between the Soviet government and Western countries, Besançon emphasises the fact that the ideological regime once again strives to obtain that which it needs the most – formal recognition of its legitimacy. Besançon adds that the regime will seek to obtain this legitimacy through the negotiation of treaties which will subsequently be put to use in an attempt to gain sanction of 'the legitimacy of the imaginary and the recognition of the nonexistent'.[167] He provides a golden rule for negotiating with such a regime: 'to treat with the reality and not with the surreality'.[168] In simple terms, this means never to negotiate on the basis of the 'noble' socialist vocabulary (for example, social progress, racial equality) and never to make any verbal concessions for, as Monnerot stated more than 35 years ago, 'to accept the terms in which communists present the problems of our time . . . is to accept terms which are necessarily false . . . and it amounts to an unconscious endorsement of the communist Campaign'.[169]

At this point the question is raised concerning the relationship between Soviet leaders and the ideology which they support. Besançon is of the view that the leaders' conditioning is strict, 70 years after the Revolution. They believe what they say: when Chernenko stated that freedom reigns in his homeland he was not lying because, as we are already aware, he was referring to the 'surreality' in which words take on a new and very precise meaning. Besançon believes that the 'langue de bois' is their natural language, 'the one they even speak at home'.[170] Given that political power is entirely enslaved by ideology, 'it can only act according to the scheme which the ideology imposes, which is unrealisable, but which cannot be changed'.[171] Soviet leaders implement whatever ideology prescribes, regardless of the dire consequences it may have on reality. Besançon regards Soviet leaders, who are selected for their ability to endure the notion that fictitious reality is not fictitious, as merely the interchangeable tools of ideology. For him these leaders are nothing more than 'the impersonal managers of the party line'.[172] He invokes an aspect of psychoanalysis when he writes that ideology, having replaced the self with knowledge, has no need for the person.[173] Brezhnev, Andropov, Chernenko and Gorbachev: the leader makes no difference at all.

In his essay entitled *La Chute finale – essai sur la décomposition de la sphère soviétique*, Emmanuel Todd disagrees with this part of Besançon's analysis. Todd suggests that Soviet leaders are ideologically and psychologically liberated, though they are 'prisoners of a system they did not want, in which they do not believe, but from which they cannot disentangle themselves'.[174] For this young Frenchman, who is a graduate of Cambridge University, the Soviet ruling class is conscious, lucid and very cynical. The Soviet oligarchs are not paralysed by ideology. On the contrary, argues Todd, they make a fairly proper and objective analysis of their own social system. The inability of the leaders to be rid of the myths and litany of Marxism–Leninism is essentially a result of the regime's need to prevent the Soviet populace from achieving a state of awareness, which would inevitably reveal the true totalitarian nature of the regime and possibly lead to a widespread collective release.

It must be underlined that the question of cynicism raised by Todd is to be found in Besançon's theorisation. Its omission would have been surprising, to say the least. Besançon perceives cynicism (that is, the tendency to be internally detached from ideology and to use it as a means to gain power and privileges) as being one of the two ills which undermine the party: 'Cynicism is the illness of ideological parties that have come to maturity'.[175] As we know, Besançon rejects the idea that cynicism has taken root in the higher spheres of the political apparatus, although he firmly believes that it is to be increasingly found among subordinates. Thus, he is of the opinion that we are witnessing an invasion of the party by the cynical attitude, a situation in which he denotes a long-term threat to the party legitimacy.

Corruption is the second ill detected by Besançon. He recognises at the outset that corruption enables the regime to function and survive.[176] He states, in fact, that without those goods and services which are not officially planned for, the official economy would quickly founder. He characterises the black market economy as 'a kind of survival raft used to cross, without perishing, the turbulent waters of socialism under construction'.[177] However, corruption endangers the regime in that one may detect in it a strong rebirth of the civil society: 'the very figure of the trafficker is a victory for the individual'.[178] Furthermore, Besançon views clandestine commerce as having a corrosive effect on the 'langue de bois'. Yet the party is much tempted to get deeply involved in the black market economy, which has developed spontaneously beyond its reach. However, its propensity for entering into self-interested relations with 'real' society may undermine the party's morals. Party members use their influence to sway political decisions taken in upper party spheres, in favour of particular groups in which they have an interest. For Besançon, such behaviour calls into question the true nature of the party, a fact which the corrupt *apparatchiki* are well aware of, if one may judge their efforts to conceal their wealth. In Besançon's view, '*The Party cannot amalgamate itself with an entrepreneurial class in the making without modifying its nature and vanishing.*'[179]

> The Party, then, tends to turn into a privileged class, whereas its nature is to be neither a caste, nor a class but rather a kind of sect or order which, while present in the society, remains strictly separated from it and is without any organic link to it.[180]

Only if the party relinquished ideology, writes Besançon, would it then become a privileged class. Until such a condition obtains, the CPSU has to be regarded as a sect existing outside of Soviet society. In this context, one is led to examine whether the party can, in the face of the numerous tensions which internally plague the Soviet Union (such as the national problem) relinquish ideology altogether. For Besançon there is very little doubt that such an occurrence could relieve the entire Soviet population of a terrible burden, as it would be the end of the 'exercise of obligatory hallucination'[181] which debases every Soviet citizen. It would also bring obvious advantages to the party itself, which would then stop pursuing its socialist chimera and start using rational means in order to reform the whole of the Soviet economy, which has fallen into decay. As Besançon observes, the party, using rational procedures, 'could then handle reality as it is'.[182] The armament industry, he adds, would benefit from such a change, in that it would no longer rest on a chaotic economic infrastructure. Such a global evolution which, thinks Besançon, seems to be contemplated by a segment of the party's membership, would indeed have very profound consequences. More particularly, this would signify a drastic change in the regime's sources of legitimacy. As we know, Besançon does not view the Soviet ideology as an ornament or as a mere superstructure, but rather as being the regime itself. So, as he explains:

> Can it renounce ideology? This would be a change of legitimacy that would not take place without bringing in its train a power vacuum. Tensions are such that everything could then decompose. Once the ideological magic is destroyed, the new national-Bolshevik

State would have to face other legitimacies, among which, of course, none would be more formidable than the national oppositions.[183]

Sensing such a potential danger of decomposition, the party's leadership cannot but keep clinging to what Besançon calls 'the paralysing legitimacy of the nonsense'[184] and straightforwardly dispose of any possibility of abandoning the Soviet ideology.

Finally, Besançon argues that as long as the party's leadership remains united and avoids splintering over the political line to follow, it is almost impossible to conceive of a collapse of the Soviet regime. On this particular question Besançon sounds very much like Aron, who expounded quite a similar proposition many years ago. Thus, repeating in 1977 an old idea of his, Aron does not hesitate to recognise the durability of the Soviet regime which, as he points out, is, from an historical perspective, 'one of the most durable and stable political forms, *as long as the ruling class remains coherent and the mass continues to be aware of its powerlessness*'.[185]

Besançon, whose style, as G. Nivat puts it, is close to that of an ironist in its ferocity,[186] offers an analysis of the Soviet Union which, despite its deplorable underlying anti-Soviet violence, is not devoid of seduction. It is unquestionable that some of his ideas have found their way into circles of the French intelligentsia. Indeed, Besançon's analysis makes many good and intellectually challenging points. Due heed must be paid, for instance, to the notion of 'logocracy' and to the dangers connected with the methodological bias towards conceptual symmetry.

None the less, Besançon's line of reasoning seems to be too abstract. For instance, it disregards the interplay between ideology and the social, economic and political phenomena which, from an historical perspective, have accompanied the very development of the Soviet Union. It overlooks the fact that Soviet realities have been, to some extent, a factor in the shaping of the Soviet ideology.[187] But, perhaps more importantly in our opinion, Besançon's line of reasoning is needlessly extremist. A fitting example of such extremism concerns Besançon's treatment of the relationship between ideology and political leadership.

This is clearly a question that cannot receive a black and white answer. Acceptance by the Soviet leaders of the reality of Western statistics on the state of the Soviet economy does not obscure the fact that Marxist–Leninist dogmas still influence these leaders in a number of spheres. For instance, ideology has long been, and still is to some degree, one of the factors playing a part in preventing the development of a more efficient Soviet agriculture.[188] In the international sphere there is also little doubt, as rightly noted by Aron in a posthumously published text, that 'the leaders of the Soviet empire remain sufficiently Marxist–Leninist to nourish illimited ambitions and to exclude the eventuality of a peaceful coexistence that would be prolonged indefinitely'.[189] Indeed, such acknowledgement does not imply any 'overestimating' of the role of ideology in the shaping of Soviet foreign policy. In this respect it seems proper to regard such a policy as being at one and the same time pragmatic as well as ideological.[190]

It can safely be argued that the Soviet political leadership and apparatus have long internalised or, as it were, fallen victim to central dogmatic images of the ideology in which they operate, such as the absolutely sacred image of the party as 'the leading and guiding force of Soviet society'. Images of this kind undoubtedly shape the leadership's vision of the world, and also provide it with some prefabricated explanations for various difficulties encountered on the long road to Communism. However, none of these facts warrant the proposition advanced by Besançon of an absolute enslavement of the Soviet political leadership to ideology: this is merely simplistic caricature.

Besançon's extremism, it is fair to say, derives from the fact that he is himself an ideologue. The idea of a global intuition in relation to the comprehension of the Soviet Union reveals, in our opinion, a pretension to belong to some 'enlightened happy few'. Indeed, Besançon's unconcealed and mocking disrespect with regard to Western Sovietology must be condemned. By having fallen into what J. M. Vincent has called 'the trap of overestimating ideology',[191] Besançon has openly impinged upon one of the essential teachings put forward by Aron in his Sorbonne lectures. The late sociologist once wisely taught his students that any theorisation bearing on the Soviet Union must necessarily be complex, as 'its different aspects cannot be explained by a single scheme or a single cause'.[192]

4 Institutional Analyses

Hélène Carrère d'Encausse, whose analysis of the Soviet political system we shall discuss in a moment (to be followed by Castoriadis's latest interpretation), once observed that 'with regard to . . . the institutions . . . the studies in this field have been basically descriptive and the essential dynamics of the system have eluded the researcher'.[1] In this particular respect it would be fair to say that French scholarly writings on Soviet political institutions appear, on the whole, to have confined themselves to a knowledgeable description and discussion of these structures. Descriptions of the mechanisms of the Soviet system (party, state organs, and so on), often set against an historical backdrop, have not generally been purely formalistic. None the less, the overwhelming impression which many works in this class of writing leaves is one of dryness; the treatment of the functioning of the political system and of the real decision-making process has remained at an unsatisfactory level.

Patrice Gélard, Dean of the Faculté de Droit et des Sciences Economiques of the University of Rouen–Haute-Normandie, is a specialist in Soviet law and institutions. In the last fifteen years, in addition to several articles, he has published some valuable books such as, in 1972, *L'administration locale en U.R.S.S.*[2] and, three years later, *Les systèmes politiques des Etats socialistes*.[3] The relevance of Gélard's work in the present context lies as much in his position on the Communist Party of the Soviet Union as in his somewhat controversial general conclusions.

Acknowledging the leading role of the party as one of four essential components constituting a socialist political system (together with Marxist–Leninist ideology, a planned economy and international relations built upon the idea of proletarian internationalism), Gélard then observes that this 'leading and guiding role' is not merely bowed to by the Soviet population, but desired. The party's role, in his view, is not simply an imposition from above. As Gélard makes clear, the party's direction 'is not entirely imposed. It is accepted and *desired*, and is considered, by the vast majority of Soviet citizens, as the only possible means to ensure the political development of the system.'[4]

It would appear almost superfluous to add that the Soviet political system is now, in Gélard's eyes, perfectly legitimate, being firmly grounded in a broad consensus originating in, as he argues, the struggle against the Nazi invader. Thus, the 1977 Constitution is described by Gélard as the clearest manifestation of 'the maintenance of this consensus inherited from Stalin and from the war and reconstruction efforts'.[5] His belief that there is no serious threat to the political leadership and the Soviet regime as such is a logical consequence of this position. Gélard's treatment of this general question of consensus remains unsatisfactory and includes a number of truisms, such as the remark that 'one must not naively believe that, following the results of each election, Soviet society is unanimously behind its rulers . . .'.[6]

Concluding his analysis of Soviet institutions, Gélard openly wonders whether the Soviet Union can be properly equated with a new model of democracy, different from the one which is prevalent in the West. As he points out:

> Then, [is] the Soviet Union a new model of democracy? Yes! but, more specifically, the Soviet Union is building, day by day, a new model of democracy. It took France more than a century after 1789 to find its own democratic model . . .[7]

Such an affirmation has to be seen against Gélard's belief that democracy is compatible, provided some conditions are met, with a single party system. Gélard deplores what he perceives to be a lack of genuine interest in this important theoretical issue on the part of Western political thought. In his opinion, the fundamental question to be answered is whether the party is, as he puts it, 'truly the spokesman of popular aspirations . . . if its functioning is democratic'.[8]

The first of the elements Gélard mentions concerns the necessity of opening up and consolidating channels of communication between party and masses for the growth of democracy. In a 1975 publication Gélard propounds the view that there exists in the Soviet Union a singularly original system of political communication, by which the Soviet system has been able to filter popular demands with notable efficiency.[9] In this context Gélard underlines the importance of some organs of communication – the soviets and, especially, the social organisations. The latter are described as being in charge of explaining the party's political line, conveying the demands emanating from below while fostering political integration and socialisation. It is worth noting that the view expressed to the effect that the system of political communication is 'at the moment constantly improving'[10] has since been revised by Gélard. Thus, writing in 1978, he introduces a different prognosis about a *blocage* 'regarding the communication between the rulers and the ruled',[11] indicating the unsatisfactory functioning of some of these key intermediaries. Suffering from a lack of autonomy *vis-à-vis* the party, they are unable to fulfil their role which is essential to the establishment of Soviet democracy: namely, to convey popular aspirations.

On another plane, it is abundantly evident from Gélard's writings that democracy in the Soviet Union is directly proportional to the degree of democracy which is achieved within the party. In an article published on the advent of the 1977 Constitution, Gélard repeats a theoretical position previously fully explained:

> if the party complies more with the rules of centralism, if it maintains secrecy on its . . . methods of recruiting, if it rules more than it orients, if it complies more with its internal exigencies than with those of the population . . . then . . . in spite of the consensus . . . the Soviet Union will only be a democracy in the making.[12]

In another contribution on the same topic he describes the party as being 'above the Constitution',[13] as being in reality everything which, in his eyes, it ought not to be. (That is, a very secretive body where there is little discussion, a carefully co-opted élite, etc.) At this point the student of Gélard faces the task of reconciling this highly negative depiction of the party with a view expressed in 1975, that since the XXth Congress, at the cost of great effort, 'it is . . . sure that democracy within the Party has not ceased developing . . .'.[14]

It is also worth noting Gélard's grand conclusion that the Soviet socialist system is neither unjust (the pertinence and substance of such a judgement could be questioned) nor inefficient (interestingly enough, Gélard once wrote of the Soviet bureaucracy's management of the society as being, despite its problems, 'indisputably efficient').[15] A constant in Gélard's writing has been his opinion that the Soviet system is well able to change and adapt itself to evolving circumstances. Wholly subscribing to the general conclusion reached by M. Lesage in his 1971 book *Les régimes politiques de l'U.R.S.S. et de l'Europe de l'Est*,[16] Gélard believes that the Soviet Union, as well as all other socialist states, 'will make efforts to . . . adapt their structures to the economic and social necessities without fundamentally transforming the system'.[17]

The general impression one may derive from reading Gélard is that his analysis lacks a definite sense of direction. In all likelihood, the basic problem stems from Gélard's overriding concern not to show the smallest hint of bias in his analysis. In his case, what would otherwise be a laudable attitude yields positions which are not only questionable but which, more importantly for Gélard, seem to run perversely counter to his basic concern with objectivity. For instance, to write about a 'new model of democracy' or a 'democracy in the making' in the Soviet Union (and in Brezhnev's Soviet Union at that!) is objectionable. Moreover, perhaps even more significantly, it is reminiscent of the Communist Sovietology *à la Cohen* (the later Cohen, that is). This is somewhat surprising and paradoxical since Cohen, unlike Gélard, does not and cannot anchor his analytical musings on the basis of scholarly objectivity. Yet there exists a strange impression of similarity between their writings, which at times unfortunately cannot be dispelled.

Having said that, we should be aware that some traces of democracy (as the latter concept is generally understood in Western political culture) may be superficially detected in the Soviet Union. There are discussions in the Soviet Union, to be sure. Debates, at times lively, periodically appear in journals of an academic nature. There are also consultations and discussions on a much greater scale. The nationwide popular discussion on the draft of the Constitution of 1977 exemplifies this particular point, but also clearly shows that the voice of the Soviet masses is, at the very best, merely 'deliberative'.[18] To be sure, there is also the well-known and much vaunted 'readers' corner' in the Soviet newspapers, although one must recognise that such phenomenon is certainly not devoid of serious ambiguity since, as noted by C. Revuz in her book *Ivan Ivanovitch écrit à 'la Pravda'*, it amounts neither to a stream of spontaneous democracy nor to a cold manipulation from above.[19]

The hard reality is that whatever traces of democracy in the Soviet Union one may locate and patiently dissect, such elements remain extremely limited in their scope and rather illusory in the face of the severe overt and unconscious constraints which bear upon each Soviet man and woman. One must constantly bear in mind that Soviet society is permeated by the absolute omnipresence of political considerations, and a society in which the life of each citizen, as recently argued by Strmiska, is unequivocally 'conditioned by his political status which follows each individual like his shadow'.[20] This question of democracy reminds us of a perspicacious remark by M. Duverger, who wrote in 1948 that there exists in the Soviet Union a 'démocratie dans le détail', or a democracy where 'one can criticise the manufacturing of tractors' brakes, but not the last speech of foreign policy made by Mr. Molotov'.[21] Almost 40 years later, it seems that the substance of Duverger's words holds good and, indeed, the name of Shevardnadze can safely be substituted to that of the late Molotov.

A more interesting analysis than Gélard's is the one tentatively expounded at the end of the 1970s by the sociologist Thomas Lowit. Paying due regard to the *de facto* and *de jure* permanent, institutionalised and universal supremacy of party over state, Lowit puts forward the simple idea that the classical notion of the state no longer has any relevance in the context of a discussion of a Soviet-type regime. In short, Lowit argues that the state in the Soviet Union has been transformed or, rather, entirely absorbed by the party. Thus, 'the State has not been maintained, let alone strengthened'.[22] Logically, Lowit thinks that the very word 'state' ought to be eliminated from any theoretical discussion bearing upon Eastern Europe, as it is a real source of confusion. Also worth noting in this connection is Lowit's suggestion that it would be quite in order to revise a number of current notions, such as state property and state capitalism. Indeed, Lowit claims that another power structure has duly replaced the state. He suggests a new concept, the 'polymorphous party', which he explains in the following terms:

> contrary to the current affirmations (and to appearances), the Party is the only institution of such regimes. All other existing bodies (or 'apparatuses'), to wit the State, the trade unions, the social organisations . . . must be considered as integral elements of the Party itself. In this perspective, the multiplicity of institutions in Eastern Europe is merely apparent . . . This specific system . . . enables the Party not only to appear, but especially to act simultaneously under various forms *i.e.* to multiply, from a single centre, the means of . . . action and control. Hence, the choice of the term 'polymorphous party' to designate this type of regime.[23]

Thus, what appears to be a plurality of institutions is nothing more than a mere plurality of denominations. The party in the Soviet Union is the only institution whose defining feature is located in its very diversification. The state, writes Lowit, must not be regarded as an instrument of the party, but as one of its branches or segments.[24]

According to Lowit, the actual functioning of the polymorphous party depends upon three key principles: (1) the branches' organisational autonomy which, in practice, signifies that each branch enjoys its own hierarchical structure; (2) a particular division of labour among branches within the framework of an identity of goals; (3) the complementarity of the branches. To maintain the polymorphous party's unity and to ensure its correct functioning, all branches are brought under the permanent direction and control of the party apparatus.

In view of its own nature – its systematic ramification – the party can be subject to significant centrifugal tendencies. The formulation of programmes by the directorates of individual branches, which diverge from the general orientations laid down by the party leadership, is the system's most serious dysfunction. One observes that for Lowit the partial economic reforms of the mid-1960s and 1970s have been the leadership's response to the centrifugal trends which have persistently agitated the party's economic branch. On the other hand, these economic reforms exemplify a point made by Lowit, that the system of the polymorphous party is not 'a system that is set once and for all'.[25]

A second dysfunction consists in a tendency to ' "mix" the roles and the duties, *i.e.* the tendency to substitute an apparatus for another apparatus'.[26] This feature highlights the degree to which the party apparatus tends to intervene and take the place of its branches, thereby encroaching upon the principle of complementarity cited above.[27] In order to cope with these negative features the party has resorted to a number of methods, two of which are stressed by Lowit. The first concerns the Nomenklatura, by virtue of which all branches' cadres 'carry out their duties on behalf of the party and are ultimately "accountable" to it'.[28] The second is based both on a policy of fostering continual movement of cadres from the party apparatus to its branches and vice versa, and on the phenomenon of plurality of offices. This is regarded by Lowit as probably the central mechanism of the polymorphous party: 'This makes it very difficult to obtain a precise determination of the status and real power of each "leader" within the whole established system'.[29]

Since 1980 Lowit does not seem to have carried his reflections about the polymorphous party any further. This is unfortunate. None the less, the thrust of his analysis has attracted some attention. For instance, P. Hassner has called Lowit's analysis 'seminal'.[30] More recently, in 1985, B. Kerblay explicitly referred to the notion of the polymorphous party, which in his view is that a plurality of names is used to conceal what is the ramification of the CPSU, considered to be the unique centre of power in the Soviet Union.[31] Less positively, C. Bekelheim has taken the view that Lowit's description does not lead to the conclusion that there has been a 'disappearance of the state' but, rather, to there being an 'exercise of state power' by the party present in all state apparatuses.[32]

At any rate, Lowit's merit lies in reminding the student of Soviet politics of the pervasive and real supremacy of the party over the *totality* of the public and social life in the Soviet Union (evinced by the fact that no governmental decision of any importance can be taken without the party's direct and decisive involvement). Obviously, the phenomenon of the subordination of the state to the party has to be regarded as a structural characteristic of a Soviet-type system. In this context, it is worth bearing in mind, as recently pointed out by Strmiska (and others before him), that analyses looking at the nature of the relationship between party and state in this kind of system often lose their interest if they use the notions of party and state constructed for the study of other political systems without re-interpreting their meaning.[33]

CPSU'S ADMINISTRATIVE DICTATORSHIP

Hélène Carrère d'Encausse, Professor at the Sorbonne and Secretary of the Institut français des relations internationales, is generally regarded, inside and outside France, as the most prominent French specialist on Soviet politics. Carrère d'Encausse's interest in the Soviet Union originally sprang from a desire to understand the country from which, as pointed out by Fred Kupferman, 'she was uprooted by the Bolshevik revolution'.[34] Born in France and daughter of a Georgian philosopher who, like many other *émigrés*, turned taxi-driver in Paris in the 1920s, Carrère d'Encausse apparently felt it necessary to devote herself to the study of the society which had witnessed the expulsion of so many members of the intelligentsia and nobility. In our opinion she has done so with perseverance and intelligence, always shying away from ideological fashions. In addition it is clear that, despite her personal link to her subject, she has not allowed 'emotionalism' to seep through the thoughts expressed in her various academic writings.[35]

Carrère d'Encausse has been writing about the Soviet Union since the 1950s. However, her renown is not restricted to the academic community alone. Benefiting at the end of the 1970s from a sudden and sharp surge of interest in the Soviet Union by the French public, she then acquired, thanks to the French mass media, a large audience. Carrère d'Encausse's arrestingly titled book *L'empire éclaté – la révolte des nations en U.R.S.S.*, published at this time of aroused interest in the Soviet Union, became a bestseller.[36]

While we shall refer to this work later in the chapter, our present and primary concern is with a more recent publication, *Le pouvoir confisqué – gouvernants et gouvernés en U.R.S.S.*, published in 1980.[37] As in a number of her other works, this book illustrates an unusual degree of integration for a French writer with mainstream Anglo-American Sovietology. Carrère d'Encausse places at the centre of her analysis the notion of power which, as she has recently observed, does not only cover political institutions but 'also all the spheres which contribute to the organisation of social life'.[38] More generally, she seeks to shed light on the nature of Soviet power, as well as on the question of legitimacy. In addition to explaining the structure of the political system, she also examines the relationship between the power-holders and society.

Carrère d'Encausse's analysis rests upon the basic premise of an unequivocal confiscation by the Bolshevik Party of the power which the revolutionary masses had seized in February 1917, which they sought to organise and use in their own interests, as exemplified by the activities undertaken by many of the soviets throughout the Spring of 1917. In the course of the rapid emergence of a political system 'confiscated from the forces "from below"' and dominating society,[39] three features were of fundamental importance: the suppression of the Constituent Assembly; the establishment of an overall Bolshevik control over the media; and the creation of a police apparatus to enforce such decisions.

A number of remarks relating to the question of confiscation of revolutionary power are relevant here. A. Nove has expressed reservations about the propriety of the book's title – a polite way to cast serious doubts upon Carrère d'Encausse's entire premise. Regarding the title as misleading, he writes: 'It is consistent with the notion of a workers' state that had somehow degenerated, as if the masses *did* rule and the party apparatus usurped power.'[40] A. Kriegel, in a review contributed to *Le Figaro*, has objected on philosophical grounds. As she rather laconically put it: 'From whom . . . according to the writer, would it have been "confiscated"? From the revolutionary masses. In this case, it is not a deadly sin, since this reality which is at best ephemeral – the masses – is naturally condemned to have its power confiscated.'[41]

None the less, Carrère d'Encausse lays great stress on the idea that more than 65 years after the October Revolution the nature of power in the Soviet Union remained absolutely unaltered. In her view this power is foreign to society. As she writes: 'The Party has jealously held on to the power it confiscated from society in the aftermath of the revolution; there is no doubt about that.'[42] This specific trait – the unchanging nature of Soviet power – has to be considered as being intrinsically connected with the type of legitimacy espoused by Lenin and his successors. As the true and only incarnation of the proletariat's consciousness, the Bolsheviks justified their power by their certainty that history was on their side. Endowed with infallibility, in pursuing its historical mission of building Communism, Bolshevik power could not be limited by society. Thus, Carrère d'Encausse rightly determines the crucial consequences for the organisation of the Soviet political system which have flowed from this source of legitimacy of a fideistic nature:

> This initial choice . . . has involved specific constricting consequences for the Soviet system. It must be, and must remain, an ideological system; and a system with a monopoly on ideology, because admitting the existence of other ideologies would amount to accepting a challenge to the 'truth' underlying the system. It must also be a system directed by a single political organization, because the existence of competing organizations would have as a corollary the competition among different kinds of truth. . . . From Lenin's initial choice . . . flowed the entire Soviet system as it came to be organized: a single monolithic party, and an ideology in possession of a monopoly on the truth. From this choice also came the fact that the Soviet system might change its methods or choices, but the mono-organizational and mono-ideological system remained inviolable, for this inviolability was the source of its legitimacy and invulnerability.[43]

According to Carrère d'Encausse, the condemnation of Stalin's calamitous activities and crimes by Khrushchev at the XXth Congress inevitably, though unintentionally, inflicted lethal damage on the infallibility dogma, thus stripping Communist power of its original legitimacy. Bereft of its dogma, the party has consequently emerged as just a mere machinery of power which, in her opinion, enjoys no other justification for its continued existence than the mere capacity to continue imposing its rule on society by means of the state. Lacking genuine legitimacy, the King is naked: 'What legitimates power now is simply the fact that it exists and perpetuates itself'.[44] The party, invoking its revolutionary nature and its historical mission, can hardly accept a state of affairs in which the sheer weight of tradition assures the legitimising function. An awareness of this discrepancy appears to have led the party to embark on a course which centres on a type of legitimacy essentially rooted in a dynamic and expansionist foreign policy. Thus, she suggests, Soviet power which extends beyond national boundaries serves, in reality, to legitimise the Soviet political system domestically.[45]

Such a development in the party's constant quest for new legitimacy cannot be ignored. In this connection, Carrère d'Encausse observes that the progress of the Soviet Union on the international scene has not had the effect of mobilising society into a patriotic outburst. In her view, international success cannot divert society's attention. It is far too sensitive to more immediate problems. Moreover, she argues, Soviet patriotism has been russified, thus becoming for the non-Russian population of the Soviet Union a mere symbol of domination.

In Carrère d'Encausse's opinion the Soviet political system essentially amounts to the administrative dictatorship of an oligarchy. The power of this oligarchy rests upon several key features. First and foremost, there is the establishment and maintenance at the highest level – that is, the Politburo, regarded as being the true government of the Soviet Union – of a coherent and steady coalition of interests determined to perpetuate its power by eliminating any possible political alternative. This Soviet reality, the product of a readiness among Khrushchev's successors to regulate relations among themselves according to principles and rules and, above all, to settle once and for all the problem of personal power, can be encapsulated in two words: collegiality and consensus.[46] It is in this context that Carrère d'Encausse assesses the real position attained by the late General-Secretary L. I. Brezhnev. Despite the important functions he held and the official cult surrounding him, Brezhnev is seen by Carrère d'Encausse as having been no more than the true incarnation of the coalition's consensus.[47]

The institutionalisation process initiated by Khrushchev's successors was aimed not only at the relationships prevailing within the highest political body, but also at the system in its entirety. The second feature of Soviet oligarchical power (to which we referred above) consists of the significant degree of interest representation within the organs of real power, which has been gradually ensured by the most important Soviet groups (the party bureaucracy, other institutions, the major regions). Qualification for membership of the Central Committee, Secretariat and Politburo pivots on the grounds of interest representation to the exclusion of any other significant consideration.

Although admitting that the various Soviet bureaucracies may exert some kind of influence on the central political decision-making process, Carrère d'Encausse is none the less prone to dismiss the recently debated idea that the phenomenon may be equated with institutional pluralism. In this respect Carrère d'Encausse joins a fairly important number of French specialists, such as B. Kerblay, M. Ferro and A. Smolar, who have considered as improper the use of the theory of institutional pluralism in the context of the Soviet Union.[48] As Carrère d'Encausse explains: 'In this system, the Party remains the integrating element. It is inside the Party, and first of all in the Politburo, that the different bureaucracies reach the sphere of power. The Politburo is the arbitrator among bureaucratic interests, but the Party exercises this arbitration.'[49] Carrère d'Encausse is in no doubt of the subordination of the bureaucratic apparatuses to the party. Thus for her the pre-eminence of the party hierarchy *vis-à-vis* all other institutions is unquestionable. She adds that such pre-eminence has been particularly stressed since 1976, as shown by the 1977 Constitution which unambiguously asserts the leading role of the party. In this connection it is worth citing a comment in *Le Monde diplomatique*, in which Carrère d'Encausse maintains that the new Soviet fundamental law 'sets up the supreme rationality, political rationality, in opposition to a possible "pluralisation" of the Soviet system'.[50]

The expression in the 1977 Constitution of such a supreme rationality may be examined in the context of the somewhat classical question concerning the respective position achieved within the party by, on the one hand, the practitioners of pure politics and, on the other, the specialists (assumed by Carrère d'Encausse to look favourably upon a rationalised and 'de-ideologised' system). In an article published in 1978 she underlines the clear predominance of political power which remains 'as yet only a potential technocratic power'.[51] However, she suggests that republican or regional party organisations *are* capable of fostering changes more rapidly than the central organisation, and these may display a degree of cooperation between the political and technocratic components of the party, thereby weakening the predominance of *political* power and its objectives.[52] None the less, the renewed insistence on the primacy of *partiynost'* (party-mindedness) that she notes cannot but have an effect on this evolution. At any rate, it carries decisive weight for the party's cadres policy, in the sense that the party essentially trusts the individuals who spend their careers in the apparatus.

The third feature of Soviet oligarchical power resides in the recognition by the coalition of the major aspirations voiced by the bureaucratic élites during the Khrushchev years. These élites, at least at the time when Carrère d'Encausse was writing *Le pouvoir confisqué* (i.e. pre-Gorbachev), enjoyed a real sense of security, job stability and full restoration of the various privileges which had been threatened by Khrushchev. Indeed, the stability which so marked the Brezhnev era has lent impetus to the emergence of strong and confident élites who support the coalition, because they are indebted to it for their own share of power and privileged status. However, continuation of such support is conditional on these élites remaining sheltered from any change or initiative which could jeopardise their power and privileges, as well as their capacity to reproduce themselves.

In Carrère d'Encausse's view, the increasing stability enjoyed by regional cadres within the Russian Socialist Federated Soviet Republic (RSFSR) has been conducive to the development of political clientelism. She regards this phenomenon as an important characteristic of the party under Brezhnev's reign. In addition, she underlines that political stability has helped strengthen the power of the regional party organs, through the Nomenklatura system, in the realm of personnel selection.

Our reference here to the Nomenklatura raises the interesting problem of how Carrère d'Encausse defines the parameters of the Soviet ruling class. In *Le pouvoir confisqué*, she specifically focuses on the system of party Nomenklatura which, she affirms, 'outlines the contours of a political, economic, and cultural ruling class'.[53] In our view, Carrère d'Encausse's definition of the ruling class remains at an unsatisfactory level, if only because of its vague and overly broad character.

For Carrère d'Encausse it is incontestable that profound repercussions have resulted from that overall political stability which, as we have noted, has proved so favourable towards the evolution of bureaucratic representation at the highest levels of power. As choices and policies must coincide with the interests of bureaucracies, the coalition finds itself in the position of having to avoid proposing options or raising issues which could either represent a threat to some particular interests, or prove damaging to the general consensus.[54] In her view such immobility wholly frustrates the demands generated in Soviet society since Stalin's death. Any answer to the problems which confront the leadership (in the economic sphere) would need to strike at their very roots. That is, the answer must engage with the issue of the enormous degree of centralisation which marks the whole of the Soviet system. This would indeed have to be translated into an actual granting of 'some degree of initiative and power to the entire social body'.[55] Such a course would impair the Soviet ruling class's privileges, but would also run counter to the party's fundamental *ab origine* logic to exclude society from power, from the sphere of decision-making.

Carrère d'Encausse thinks that such a dichotomy between power and society is attenuated when one descends to the local level. In her opinion, this particular level is the privileged point of contact between power and society. Here, she suggests, there is a greater possibility of the system being adapted to meet society's demands and frustrations.

At this stage of her analysis Carrère d'Encausse devotes much attention to the question of participation.[56] Participation is regarded by the party leadership as an essential element of the Soviet political system. It depends upon the development of the role of the local soviets and on increasing voluntary activities 'hand in hand with power', though she emphasises the party's exploitative and opportunistic relationship with social organisations and the soviets. More significant for her argument is the point that such 'societal activism' allows the party to perfect the political socialisation of the mass of the people, to obtain their adherence to the system. More generally, by calling for sustained participation and by adopting a policy stressing involvement of the individual in local and civic activities, the party has achieved certain well-defined and coherent goals: 'the authorities attempted simultaneously to gain permanent knowledge of the aspirations and reactions of the rank and file, to include as many of these as possible in their decisions, and *to restrain and control social movements*'.[57]

Carrère d'Encausse expands the idea of containment and control in terms of the party's obsessive anxiety that a more educated and sophisticated society (one no longer haunted by the spectre of terror, one less subject to an ideological monopoly, and one more individualistic – even to the extent of showing evidence·of an entirely new culture alongside the Soviet official culture) may be on the verge of embarking on a course leading ultimately to that society's autonomy from the party. To avoid any possibility of such a development – that is, social groupings or organisations falling outside its control – the party, as Carrère d'Encausse remarks, 'by organizing it, occupies the totality of social space . . .'.[58] There is no doubt that the widespread participation advocated by the party on its own terms represents the surest means of preventing the emergence of a genuine civil society in the Soviet Union. In this connection, Carrère d'Encausse is entirely right, in our opinion, to argue that such participation can only serve to create 'false citizens'.

The existence of a social consensus cannot, she believes, be denied. Owing little to the official political culture, such consensus is considered to be 'acquired by the power in exchange for a generalised laxity that enables the citizen to disregard absolutely the exigencies of the common good'.[59] Thus, Soviet society seems to adapt itself to a political system which has precluded its right to exist as a civil society. However, in spite of years of relative passivity, more recently there have been signs of an embryonic civil society. Carrère d'Encausse underlines the rise of a 'social consciousness' which, albeit weak and fragmented, 'recognises' that nothing can be gained from official forms of participation whose end, as we have said, is one of permanent control. Consequently, this consciousness 'realises' that it has to find what she calls its own 'organisational structures' ('structures de rassemblement')[60] in order to attain the sphere of power and bring its weight to bear upon it. The difficulties of developing such forms are formidable. Given the considerable means of pressure and coercion at the party's disposal, Carrère d'Encausse believes that, for the foreseeable future, a *rassemblement* that would escape the notice of the system is '*unthinkable* in the Soviet Union'.[61] In other words, society has therefore to organise itself within the framework of the existing political system. At this juncture, Carrère d'Encausse turns to the nation.

The image she attempts to convey is of a society which tends to think that 'the best way to organise itself is to integrate itself into the national framework'.[62] This framework is provided by the federal nature of the Soviet state. The reiteration by the Constitution of 1977 of the principle of federalism – despite considerable weakening of the federal organisation[63] being as she says 'in a state of reprieve' ('en sursis')[64] – has been seen by Carrère d'Encausse as constituting an important decision. It maintains a framework within which national aspirations can be legally expressed, even developed at times, against the all-Union global interest. Soviet power, as she writes, 'by maintaining the national status . . . enables the various nationalisms to affirm themselves and to grow'.[65] One of the claims shared by all the national communities consists in the search for a more balanced economic life, one which is more autonomous and less subject to a narrow division of labour. None the less, it must be borne in mind that national communities, however vigorous their nationalism may be, do not act according to a plan threatening the Soviet system. In Carrère d'Encausse's view, the strict application of federalism – real autonomy of power within each republic and access to federal decision-making on an equal basis by each of the republics – is the goal sought by each national community.

'Nation', it is worth noting, does not have the same meaning for Soviet Muslims. They identify with a much larger community, that of Islam. Soviet Muslims sense that they belong, first and foremost, to the '*Muslim nation* . . . and only afterwards to the Uzbek or Tatar nation'.[66] The question of the national identity of the Soviet Muslims has long occupied A. Bennigsen, to whose work we now briefly turn. This writer, a specialist on Islam in the Soviet Union, has distinguished three levels of Muslim consciousness: subnational, national and supranational. The first level is that of the persisting sense of clannish or tribal identity evident in several nations and influencing some aspects of the cultural and political life of these Muslim nations.[67] As for the purely national consciousness, Bennigsen acknowledges that it is a difficult problem. In his mind the nations of Central Asia have emerged as administrative, economic and bureaucratic realities, but they still remain wholly artificial from a cultural perspective. Finally, there is the supranational religious (Islamic) or ethnic (Turkic) consciousness which is described by Bennigsen as follows:

The supranational consciousness is mainly, but not only, religious. It corresponds to the feeling of belonging to a 'community of believers' (*Umma*) and to the 'Muslim nation' (*Millet*) from which are excluded neither the unbelievers, nor even the atheists but only . . . the rare Russified Muslims living outside their national territories. Within these two traditional notions, the concepts of nation and religion are 'indissolubly' merged and their members always feel like they inhabit the *Dar ul-Islam* (the land of Islam) . . . which is opposed to the *Dar ul-Harb* (the land of war) in which Muslims are only a foreign minority . . . This supranational consciousness of belonging to a Turkic or Islamic 'Commonwealth' is justified by the strong similarity of social customs, and by the existence of common folklore and epic literature . . .[68]

Bennigsen adopts the view that the vitality of both subnational and supranational consciousness is stronger than that of the national consciousness.[69] In his opinion, these levels of consciousness

in the future . . . are likely to define the nature of Central Asia's ethnic identity. This identity would then cut across Soviet-imposed national divisions, thus contributing to the growth of Central Asian unity. Sub-national and supra-national levels of consciousness therefore constitute a potentially important long-term threat to Moscow's control of Central Asia.[70]

The growing pan-Islamic and pan-Turkic sense of brotherhood which prevails within the proud and well-educated Asian intelligentsia has not been accompanied by overt dissent, or by the establishment of a Muslim nationalist movement. In fact, remarks Bennigsen, Muslims cooperate with the regime.[71] He goes as far as to claim that Muslims 'are probably more at ease in the Communist Party system than the Russians themselves. The Muslims accommodate themselves very easily to Communism.'[72] This is reminiscent of Carrère d'Encausse's observation that Muslim dignitaries explicitly affirm the compatibility of Islam with Communism.[73] Also, as she points out, the *homo islamicus* is not an opponent to the Soviet system 'which he does not even criticise'.[74]

Despite this 'peaceful' attitude, Bennigsen argues that the final dream of the overwhelming majority of the Muslim intellectuals and political leaders revolves around the ideas of independence, full sovereignty and liberation from Russian control.[75] As for their political inspiration, Bennigsen notes that Muslim intellectuals are passionately interested in the non-Soviet Muslim world. In their political reflections ('search for eventual models'),[76] they appear prepared ultimately to adopt options ranging from religious traditionalism to revolutionary radicalism. As recently noted by Bennigsen, 'particularly worrisome to the authorities must be the increase in the number of youths and intellectuals showing political interest in the various revolutionary "neo-Islamic" movements of Iran, Algeria, and Libya'.[77]

The Muslim-Turkic élite, unlike the Russian intellectual élite, displays optimism: 'the Muslim élites feel that time works for them'.[78] The demographic dynamism which has been a characteristic of the Soviet Asian world is one factor contributing to this optimism. Another factor resides in the close links binding the Muslim intelligentsia and the masses.[79] Such a factor provides the intelligentsia with a sense of security. Therefore, knowing that the future belongs to them, the Muslim political leaders, argues Bennigsen, do not foresee themselves engaging in any provocative action against their 'Russian masters' for fear that it might imperil this future.[80] They favour forms of subtle and indirect resistance.[81] They acknowledge that their 'masters' possess power of such an overwhelming kind as to render any action of this nature clearly premature. Thus, the current status quo will be maintained for as long as possible. But, as Bennigsen openly wonders, 'the final, inescapable, violent crisis will be delayed, but for how long?'.[82]

Returning to Carrère d'Encausse, it is worth noting her viewpoint that the national problem is also of direct concern to the Russian people. She claims that Russians profoundly feel the mounting hatred expressed by many nationalities towards their nation. As she points out, the Russian people find this 'hatred' unjustifiable, if only 'because it feels that it has made the greatest sacrifices in the course of Soviet history for the general development of other peoples'.[83]

Finally, what conclusion does Carrère d'Encausse derive from her analysis of a political system which, in her opinion, is scarcely intelligible in terms of the categories current within Western political science? 'In the end,' she writes, 'what comes out of an analysis of the Soviet system is its anachronism and its contradictions'.[84] She also writes of an absurd gulf separating a 'living society determined to live'[85] and a petrified power preoccupied with its own reproduction, unable to adapt to a new social environment.

It is worth observing that Carrère d'Encausse has never suggested, as M. Tatu has done, that the Soviet military, on the occasion of a succession crisis, could constitute 'the remedy'[86] to unblock the system. According to this view, the military, having intervened and subsequently consolidated its grip on power, would then put an end to such a state of systemic paralysis and launch the Soviet system on a more modern and efficient course. On the contrary, says Carrère d'Encausse, the domination of the party over the military is unquestionable.[87] In addition, the contemporary Soviet political culture can be characterised by a wide agreement between party and military on 'the objectives of the Party's activity, the legitimacy of its power, and the importance of the mission the Party has given to the army'.[88] Taken together with these two considerations, a historical argument should not be overlooked: Russian history reveals no tradition of military government.[89]

In her contribution to the recently published voluminous *Traité de science politique*, Carrère d'Encausse puts forward the view that the Soviet system, as during Lenin's day, seeks to achieve *'rationality within a total power'*.[90] According to her, the essential features of the totalitarian system, as they were defined by theoreticians like Friedrich or Aron, are still present in the Soviet system. Some of these features, such as ideology and repression, have been either transformed or attenuated. She views as remarkable the fact that totalitarianism, which was born in a period of severe economic and moral devastation, seems able to perpetuate itself at a time when the educated Soviet society is capable of confronting the utopia. While fully observing that the Soviet reality has weighed on the overall behaviour of the Soviet political system, she also emphasises that any concession made to such reality can at all times be removed or questioned by the party. More importantly, Carrère d'Encausse writes that the Soviet system is entirely able to evolve 'from a state of virtual totalitarianism to a state of total totalitarianism'.[91]

Carrère d'Encausse's recent views would appear to provide the student of her writing with a logical answer to the question left open in her conclusions in *Le pouvoir confisqué*. That is, whether the new generation of 'politicians' destined to succeed the Brezhnevian central gerontocratic élite would institute changes in the Soviet organisation of power. One is not surprised to find that Carrère d'Encausse assesses with caution the situation created by the arrival of a new top party leadership. A short article, contributed to *Le Nouvel Observateur* after a visit to the Soviet Union where she travelled in July 1986 as a member of President Mitterrand's entourage, appears to reveal, although perhaps in a sketchy form, the basic thrust of her thoughts on this subject. After stressing the opposition between the new generation's growing individualistic values and the collective and disciplinarian values advocated by the party, Carrère d'Encausse, as in her 1981 book, openly wonders about the eventual victor of this confrontation. *Kto Kogo* (Who will win?): the Soviet society or, as she puts it in *Le Nouvel Observateur*, *'the rulers . . . who are unremittingly bent on breathing life into the old utopia that triumphed in Russia three quarters of a century ago?'*.[92] Indeed, Carrère d'Encausse is critical of the Western leaders' keenness to celebrate what they regard as 'the innovative spirit'[93] of the Soviet rulers. Thus, it can be said that her voice may be added to those which have already expressed pessimism with respect to what may be expected to emerge from the new Gorbachev period.

Such pessimism is understandable. Suffice it to say that Gorbachev is the representative of a new generation of leaders who 'believe in their power, and regard it as their inalienable property'.[94] More generally, we have never lent serious credence to the idea that a generational change in the party leadership would, in a mechanical way, bring about substantial changes in the Soviet system. Gorbachev has been carefully chosen by a system whose selection criteria merge into one paramount requirement – total political conformity or unconditional devotion to the party. Gorbachev, as the direct successor of Lenin, is now guardian to the sovereign power of the party in all spheres of life in the Soviet Union. As pointed out by M. Heller, 'Gorbachov spent 30 years getting to the top, and for 30 years the Party worked on him, shaped him. There is no doubt that he will consider his major duty to be the strengthening, broadening and consolidation of the Party's power.'[95]

This fact must be borne in mind when assessing the various developments which have taken place in the Soviet Union since Gorbachev's accession to the post of Secretary-General. These developments, which include the undeniable policy of *glasnost'* (openness) as well as the visible relaxation occurring in the cultural arena, clearly demand of Sovietologists analytic caution and avoidance of conjectural constructions. These measures of liberalisation may be signs of more significant changes to come. It has been argued by leading Sovietologists that Gorbachev is not reluctant to propose some measures of political reform.[96] Indeed his surprising proposal put forward at the January 1987 Plenum of the Central Committee, that party officials at the republic, region, city and district levels be elected by secret ballot with a choice of Communist candidates, supports this view.[97] However, it must be noted that this specific proposal, the future of which is uncertain given its omission from the resolution adopted by the Central Committee, does not undermine the key Leninist principle of democratic centralism and leaves the party's grip on power intact. One of the likely effects of this proposal, if implemented *in toto* in the near future, would be to bring about a subtle removal of conservative middle-ranking *apparatchiki* distrustful of the idea of economic reform.

Much has already been written in relation to the subject of economic reform in the Soviet Union under Gorbachev. It is widely assumed that he and some important elements in the party leadership are disposed towards making the changes needed to tackle the problems plaguing the Soviet economy. But the crucial question concerns the nature of the intended changes. Any economic reform in the Soviet Union worthy of the name could only be a *radical* one. In our view, any minor reform favouring a degree of economic decentralisation is bound to be either rejected like an alien graft or neutralised by the old system. A radical reform would implement measures to sever 'the umbilical cord with the command economy'[98] and cause the party to impose some structural–social reforms in various fields such as Soviet agriculture.

An essential factor weighing against the radical course remains the innate political conservatism of the Soviet leadership. To embark on a radical course would pose a threat of unknown dimensions to the sacrosanct sovereignty and indivisibility of the party's power. Why would the party wilfully stoop, to use Castoriadis's words, to a process of 'self-mutilation'? The very idea that the Soviet economic sphere could be officially separated from the political one runs counter to the 'psychological fabric' of the party, which has hitherto meant that the party has been suspicious and opposed, almost in a visceral way, to the basic ideas of self-regulation, spontaneity and autonomy, be it economic or social. The free market, as once noted by the economist P. Kende, basically remains an institution 'foreign to the body of the system'.[99]

To be sure, there are other well-known factors of great political or sociological magnitude coalescing against the idea of radical reform. For instance, there is not the slightest doubt that the ministerial–administrative apparatus represents a formidable stumbling block. A second factor relates to the widespread and deep reluctance within large segments of the Soviet population to accept the idea of economic reform. The average, poorly qualified Soviet worker, unlike perhaps his more specialised counterpart, does not seem inclined to reject, as rightly noted by W. Brus, 'the familiar cushions of absolute job security, overmanning and take-it-easy attitudes' in return for eventual rewards in a reformed economic system.[100] More fundamentally, the historical experience of totalitarianism has meant not only the emergence of a phenomenon of social passivity on an unprecedented scale, but has also shown that the vast majority of Soviet people have, as pointed out by P. Lorrain, 'adapted to the system in which they live . . . and can hardly think of other living conditions'.[101] Such passivity is a formidable obstacle to any reform, and it will take much more than the limited revival of the elective principle in the party and soviets to effect the great psychological change.

The future, conditioned by such factors, will probably show that Gorbachev's much vaunted propensity to reform will be reduced to bold but limited initiatives, as well as extensive tinkering with the central economic mechanism. In this regard, one may perhaps surmise that organisational restructuring will begin to dominate Gorbachev's words and deeds. Such restructuring, as L. Sochor noted, replaces 'reforms and produces the purely fictitious appearance of movement'.[102]

However, one may wonder, could Gorbachev, against all ideological and sociological odds, emerge as the truly bold innovator determined to take drastic action to break all the vested and entrenched interests opposed to systemic economic reform? Economist G. Sokoloff, for one, alluded to such a hypothesis when writing that Gorbachev could eventually 'search for his salvation in a vast choice of solutions, ranging from imitating Stalin to plagiarising Deng'.[103] E. Morin, rightly or wrongly, once asserted that Soviet history has been marked by the occurrence of the 'improbable'. Could Gorbachev embody this 'improbable'?

'STRATOCRATIC REGIME'

In the aftermath of the invasion of Afghanistan Castoriadis published a book entitled *Devant la guerre – Les réalités*, in which he emphasises the threat posed by the increasing Soviet military might. He argues that Russia is entirely devoted to seeking world domination and is preparing for war on the grounds that it cannot, and knows not how to, do otherwise. Unlike his first characterisation of the Soviet Union, which had to remain a number of years in a state of quasi-intellectual limbo before being 'discovered', Castoriadis's 'stratocracy' rapidly erupted into the limelight as soon as it was propounded in this more recent work. Such a scathing assessment of Soviet intentions apparently touched a sensitive chord, especially in intellectual circles. More generally, Castoriadis's thesis reverberated in an environment where the majority of the non-Communist French public had already shed an image of the Soviet Union that was particularly strong at the peak of East–West detente, that of a country sincerely devoted to peace.[104]

According to Castoriadis we have been witnessing the emergence of what he calls a 'new historical type of society'[105] – that is, a 'stratocratic society'. In his opinion the well-entrenched view of Soviet society as one dominated by a totalitarian Party-State unfortunately ignores the Soviet regime's evolution and is, therefore, in need of thorough revision. Castoriadis puts forward the thesis that the Army has taken the place of the Party-State as the 'heart and soul' of the power in the Soviet Union;[106] the concept of power being propounded here is essentially that of the capacity of a group or entity to influence the evolution and determine the central 'orientation' of a given society.[107] As he writes, 'to what degree is Russian society . . . not already, or in the process of becoming, a stratocracy (*stratos* = army), the army as social body assuming, by the intermediary of the upper echelons, the direction and orientation of society?'.[108]

How does Castoriadis explain the concept of the 'army as social body'?[109] In the first place, he refers to a bureaucratic, technical and industrial apparatus of very considerable proportions, whose innumerable activities and complexity necessitate constant coordination. Secondly, such a 'multi-trust' constitutes a *separate* society. This particularly provocative idea directly relates to the sociological meaning which Castoriadis attaches to the qualitative cleavage which is so striking in the Soviet Union, between military production and non-military production. The fact that a society which provides its population with insufficient supplies of goods and public services of, on the whole, mediocre quality, but turns out highly sophisticated and apparently effective military or spatial hardware, raises a decisive question.[110] The answer, in Castoriadis's eyes, cannot be merely put down to the quantity or amount of resources allocated to military production. For him, the *only* possible answer is that 'there is not *one* Russian society, industry and economy – there are two. There is the non-military society, industry and economy – and there is the other one.'[111]

This military society, whose population is estimated by Castoriadis at about 25 millions, reveals, unlike the other society, an economic life which, in his eyes, does not experience anarchy, chronic waste and passive but efficient opposition from its workers. Indeed, its *own* labour force is said to be differently motivated towards its work, especially in the secret 'closed enterprises' on which Castoriadis lays great stress.[112] He is in no doubt that this military society systematically skims the cream off the other society in all domains, thus contributing to the latter's permanent state of decay. Importantly, the military society, in his view, has extricated itself from the party's hold and crippling interference.

Castoriadis considers the party to be an absolutely petrified entity. As for the party's role in the 'stratocratic society', he observes:

> Its main role increasingly becomes, on the one hand, to manage and sub-contract the 'non-military' society in the margins left by the army's demands, and on the other, to be the internal, but above all external *Propagandastaffel* of the General Headquarters of the Russian army.[113]

The process which has led to the institution of the 'army as social body' and to its 'autonomization' in relation to the party, mainly rests upon a combination of two conditions. Firstly, as opposed to the party's failure to modernise a society where nothing works but repression, there has been the reality of modernity and functional efficiency imposed upon the army by the obviously growing 'technicization' of contemporary warfare. On the other hand, the putrefaction of the party's Marxist–Leninist ideology has allowed the army to become the sole entity in the Soviet Union able not only to organically incarnate, but also to sustain, an ideal which is referred to by Castoriadis as 'the nationalist-imperial imaginary'.[114] This idea, writes Castoriadis, has been espoused by the party. Perched on the ruins of its ideology, the party, this 'historical cadaver',[115] has totally identified itself with this specific 'imaginary' to assure continuation of its existence. As he puts it:

> Since the ousting of Khruschev, who was the last 'illusioned' illusionist, the Party has nothing to say, nor to propose to society. Neither to realise heaven on earth, nor even to 'surpass capitalism' . . . The only ideology which can still be proposed to the population – or rather the only surviving imaginary – is nationalism, which is incarnated by the military; the ambition of power, of world domination, under cover, of course, of the 'triumph of socialism'.[116]

How Castoriadis defines this 'nationalist imaginary' is of prime importance, if one is to grasp the absolute historical originality of the Soviet phenomenon. Castoriadis takes the view that there is no longer a Russian 'national consciousness'. After more than 65 years of 'real socialism', Russian values, *Weltanschauung*, traditions and culture have been destroyed (with the exception of the survival of some of the most typical Russian traits, such as servility to the state) with the concomitant establishment of an absolutely pervasive cynicism. Devoid of any substance this 'nationalist imaginary', notes Castoriadis, is nothing more than an 'empty form'.[117] But, as far as the army is concerned, it is pointed out that such 'imaginary' has acquired a content which is linked to the very tangibility of the impressive nuclear and conventional Russian weaponry. Thus, as he explains:

> Empty nationalism fulfils itself by resorting to brute Force; it cannot fulfil itself otherwise. It can then function as the animating principle for the personified representative of this Force, that is the Army and the military society.[118]

On the basis of this theoretical point he moves on to assert that, for the first time in human history, a society has unfolded in which religion and other belief systems have been replaced by a single *raison d'être* previously unheard of. That is, adoration of 'brute Force' for the sake of 'brute Force'. Central to Castoriadis's interpretation is the idea that the development in the last two decades of the military society, and what he regards as the relentless military build-up at the expense of the civilian economy, constitutes a structural feature of the Russian regime. He insists that such a marked development has not sprung from a 'decision' made at a particular conjuncture, which would be subject to modifications or reversal. As he has observed:

> There is not, and has never been, a completely free choice that the regime could make between . . . military might and economic 'prosperity'. Almost from the start, however, each successive step drew it closer to the former, merely because it made pursuit of the latter increasingly difficult. Even when it was far from pursuing military strength *per se*, the regime, by persisting in achieving the pseudo-'industrialisation' of the country by the only means of violence and bureaucratic hypercontrol . . . created and continually consolidated a situation that made impossible any 'development' of another kind and any substantial reform of a huge edifice that was rotting even as it was being built.[119]

As for the Russian regime's evolution, Castoriadis, convinced of the impossibility of its reforming itself, argues that there can be only two possible courses. Either it keeps on proceeding according to its own internal and irreversible dynamic, or it explodes. Such a possibility of explosion, which we have previously noted, relates to Castoriadis's perception of the 'stratocratic regime' as being a regime of great fragility.[120] This state of fragility is said to be rooted in both the strong contradictions and the phenomenon of social degradation which exist in the Soviet Union. In Castoriadis's mind, the mass of the people hold the key to the regime's evolution. In this regard, the essential question concerns the extent to which the regime has been successful in transforming the population into what he calls 'Zinovian' people,[121] or alternatively, whether the dissidents are 'the representatives of a race in the process of disappearing'.[122] In the view of Castoriadis the die has not yet been cast; no answer can be given to this critical question.

We should not conclude this chapter without briefly noting some of the criticisms which have been levelled at Castoriadis's recent characterisation. For E. Morin the 'stratocratic hypothesis' is not acceptable, as it manifestly underestimates the power of the party in the Soviet 'totalitarian system'. To his mind, the notable efficiency of the military has been rendered possible by the unabated impulse given to it by the party, acting in accordance with the principal objective pursued by such a system (that is, 'the Power of Empire').[123] Having said that, Morin then acknowledges Castoriadis's merit in having drawn attention to what he sees as a key element in the context of contemporary analysis of the Soviet Union – the growing place being carved out by the army within the Soviet system. In this sense Morin has no hesitation in characterising Castoriadis's hypothesis as a 'promising hypothesis'.[124]

The mildness of Morin's critical remarks is in contrast to the systematic and firm rebuttal of Castoriadis's ideas by C. Ost and G. Lourmel. Especially noteworthy here is their clear rejection of Castoriadis's thesis relating to the partition of the Soviet Union into two different societies. By visualising the Soviet Army essentially as a military 'multi-trust', and overlooking its narrower meaning (that is, its human and social aspect), Castoriadis, claim his critics, has erred. His theoretical stance may be regarded as amounting to, as they put it, 'denying any reciprocal permeability between army and civilian society, and failing to take into account the social stratification of the former'.[125] Far from being a distinct and closed society, the

Soviet army is seen by Ost and Lourmel as having 'close' links with the Soviet population. (In this connection, they point to, for instance, the existence and activities of the Voluntary Society for Cooperation with the Army, Aviation and the Navy: DOSAAF.)

Finally, one comes across the view of M. Heller, who also rejects the thesis of two distinct societies in the Soviet Union. Commenting upon the less than brilliant behaviour of the Soviet army on Afghan soil, he then observes that 'the army cannot be better than society. Despite the views expressed by some philosophers, there is no military society separate from the civilian society. The military officers are Soviet men and the weaponry is mediocre, *à la soviétique* . . .'.[126]

It is unquestionable that there is in the Soviet Union an astounding contrast between the formidable military build-up and the society of scarcity in which the vast majority of the Soviet citizenry live. There is little doubt that Soviet society has shown in various ways disquieting signs of growing militarisation, that the Soviet military has enjoyed and enjoys priority over the allocation of material as well as human resources, that the Soviet military voice is sought after by the party leadership and is likely to weigh heavily in the realms of defence and foreign policies. But to claim that the Soviet military has replaced the party at the helm of the Soviet Union constitutes a bold intellectual extrapolation which is not borne out by the evidence.

In Chapter 2 of this book Castoriadis's thinking was portrayed by a student of his writings as being marked by 'a certain dynamic quality that constantly pushes analysis forward'. Faced with the theoretical endeavours developed in *Devant la guerre*, it is difficult to resist the conclusion that Castoriadis has somewhat overdone it this time. One finds a brilliant intellectual and a long-standing observer of things Soviet succumbing to the always tantalising temptation to infer, merely on the basis of one or two features, the 'true' nature of the Soviet regime. Such an approach, need we say, is somewhat mystifying and indeed improper, even when the features on which he relies are the accumulation of a massive arsenal and the lamentable state of under-development of the civilian sector of the Soviet economy.

The choice of the accumulation of arms has essentially been political. That is to say, it has been made and overseen by the party. T. Maulnier wrote in 1957 that Soviet rulers deliberately built an economy 'specialised in the accumulation of means of power'.[127] This is supported by E. Zaleski, who recently concluded that Stalinist central planning was essentially a propaganda exercise designed to mobilise the Soviet populace around an economic policy. It promised a better future but was, in reality, a policy of selective growth aimed at creating a vast infrastructure of heavy industry, favouring the emergence of a powerful military. More recently J. Sapir underlined, and rightly in our view, that the Soviet ruling class has historically been willing to pay the price for an arsenal which it has basically seen as a source of its power.[128] Indeed, such opinions are reminiscent of the idea that the *raison d'être* of the Soviet system has been and still is to nourish the power of the state and ultimately the power of the party. For Sapir the Soviet military has adapted to a situation which, from an historical perspective, it did not choose nor provoke but which has provided it with 'indisputable advantages'.[129] The adaptation evoked by Sapir has meant more fundamentally the full acceptance by the Soviet military of its mission and of the objectives pursued by the party.

Castoriadis announced in his 1981 book that a second volume would follow, in which he would discuss the theoretical and political questions raised by his new analysis. This second volume has yet to appear, and one would be justified in speculating that the non-publication of the projected book is a telling sign of the inherent weakness of his recent polemical efforts.

5 Conclusions

Jean Bonamour recently wrote that the necessity for growth in Soviet and East European studies in France would eventually 'lead to the realization that the organizational problems are of decisive importance'.[1] At this final stage, we turn our attention briefly to a question which has been surfacing intermittently in the recent past, namely the question of setting up an important centre for research on the Soviet Union and Eastern Europe. A centre of this kind would ideally be endowed with substantial financial and technical resources. It would also assemble a 'critical mass' of French specialists of the first rank, as well as young and lesser-known researchers. Such a centre would promote interdisciplinary research, and would seek to establish durable and fruitful relations with some of the key research centres located outside France. However, the realisation of the idea, in spite of its undeniable merits, has yet to materialise. In this connection, it may be noted that the newly created IMSECO has little to do with such an 'ideal' centre. As mentioned to us by its director Marc Ferro, this new institute clearly does not have the ambition to centralise French research on the Soviet Union, but rather, to use Ferro's words, to give 'more visibility' to Soviet studies conducted in France.[2]

It seems unlikely that an 'ideal' centre will come into being in the foreseeable future. The difficulties are severe. The main reason is essentially one which we have already identified in a previous chapter – the existence of 'ideologico-methodological coteries'. This point scarcely brooks any dispute. Most French specialists acknowledge such a reality. Besançon has rightly observed that 'to the extent that intellectual life is polarised by ideology, I do not see how, barring a certain homogeneity in the approach to Communism and to the U.S.S.R., an Institute of Sovietology could work'.[3] Carrère d'Encausse shares Besançon's opinion. Thus, speaking about the most important French specialists, she made it clear to us that 'it is difficult to gather these individuals together and to build an Institute. It would not be a blissful and happy marriage.'[4] The problem, it would appear, is compounded by serious personal rivalries.

A few years ago J.-P. Chevènement, then Minister responsible for scientific research in P. Mauroy's first government, began to be 'worried about the weakness of Soviet studies in France'.[5] He asked a few French scholars to launch a serious examination into the possibility of creating what Lilly Marcou, one of these scholars, has called an 'Institut de soviétologie de gauche'.[6] As Marcou explained to us, one of the first steps consisted in trying to link up this proposed institution to the Fondation Nationale des Sciences Politiques. The FNSP met this preliminary demand by inviting these scholars to associate Carrère d'Encausse with the development of the project. This particular insistence on the part of FNSP caused the rapid abandonment of this project. It is reasonable to suggest that, had this Institute envisaged by Chevènement been created, research conducted under its auspices would have aimed at providing us (especially in the field of political studies) with a portrayal of the Soviet Union different from the one which, in the last decade, has become prevalent in many specialised writings and which resorts to tones, terms and concepts which, as Pierre Hassner notes, must seem to an American social scientist 'disturbingly reminiscent of both the prescientific and the Cold War eras'.[7]

When one attempts to determine what has been responsible for this prevalence, a number of factors spring to mind. First and foremost, as we noted earlier, there is the tremendous impact in France of the writings and experiences of Solzhenitsyn, and other important figures of the dissident movement. The decisive character of this specific influence can be assessed, for instance, when one looks at a phenomenon discussed in a previous chapter – the French rediscovery, in the 1970s, of the concept of totalitarianism. This tendency owes something to East European as well as to Russian developments and, more specifically, to the political thought of the East European opposition. As Jacques Rupnik has shown, the failure of the Prague Spring sparked an original attempt, in Eastern Europe, to reflect on the concept of totalitarianism, that is, to understand not only its essence but also its necessary mechanisms of social control.[8] Another factor which must be noted is the Soviet invasion of Afghanistan.

Some of the most interesting French interpretations, which have sought to formulate a definition of the 'true' nature of the Soviet system, are often marked by a display of acrid rhetoric and moral pronouncements about Communism, as well as by a relatively high degree of abstraction. And yet, the critical remarks which scientifically oriented Sovietological quarters may level at these features ought not obscure the intellectually stimulating character of some of the interpretations. They ought not to discredit a number of propositions or ideas of theoretical significance which are being expounded or generated.

A timely illustration of this character is provided by M. Heller's latest book, *La machine et les rouages – la formation de l'homme soviétique*. It may be argued that Heller somewhat errs on the side of caricature when he puts forth the thesis that the whole of the history of the Soviet Union is plainly reducible to the history of the creation of the *homo sovieticus*. Yet Heller produces many interesting comments, ideas and perceptive insights about the Soviet system which it would clearly be wrong to belittle because of his somewhat aggressive tone and 'reductionistic' approach. Indeed, it would be a mistake to underestimate or overlook what Heller has to say about, for instance, the Soviet political mythology and the important phenomenon of mental conditioning that has resulted from nearly 70 years of permanent ideological pressure.

In our view, the abstract and philosophical tradition which is manifest in French Sovietology must be regarded, so long as the pitfalls of an excessive jargon are avoided, not as some idle intellectual speculation, but as an asset, since it can throw light on important dimensions of the Soviet system. This last point is not at issue for P. Hassner, who has commented critically on American Sovietology:

> Is it not striking that it is from great literary works and philosophical meanderings that one realises every so often that something simply escapes all conceptualisations and empirical research in the social sciences applied to Sovietology, and that this something is related to totalitarianism?[9]

There is some truth in this suggestion. Totalitarianism, despite its shortcomings, remains, as we previously indicated, a relevant element in the discussion of the Soviet Union. As a matter of fact, the generalised absence of the concept in Anglo-American Sovietology may help to explain why the vast majority of those who come from the Soviet and East European world can hardly recognise their own experience in the erudite or 'passionless' Anglo-American specialised writings. We believe that Anglo-American scholars should reflect upon this particular point. The acknowledgement of the relevance of totalitarianism has, it should be emphasised, nothing to do with the idea of a grand conceptualisation of the Soviet Union. More generally, as Archie Brown has reminded us, the complexities of the Soviet system and society make it impossible to encapsulate 'in a word or a phrase'.[10] The temptation to try to come up with what could become the right word or phrase has long preoccupied specialists, and our study of French Sovietology bears further witness to that fact. We cannot but stress again the principle, once underlined by the late Aron, that 'any theory about the Soviet regime is bound to be a complex one; its different aspects cannot be explained by a single scheme or a single cause'.[11]

French Sovietology, as noted earlier, has long been described as suffering from a chronic state of under-development. We can hardly deny that, in comparative terms, avenues explored by Anglo-American Sovietology have remained, by and large, untrodden by French specialists. This particular Sovietology, need we repeat, has made extremely limited inroads in France. It is not unreasonable to suggest, though, that the rising generation of French Sovietologists, some of whom have pursued postgraduate studies in American universities, will contribute to altering this situation to some limited extent.

Our detailed research has revealed a specialised literature which is valuable and useful, on account of its diversity of theoretical perspectives, its specific foci of interest, its sensitivity to the ideas and theories advanced by East European and Soviet *émigrés* as well as its intellectual lustre. It has been excessively underestimated or ignored in the English-language scholarly literature. We are convinced that French Sovietology has made, in its own way, a worthy contribution to a better understanding of the Soviet Union. It surely deserves more from the Anglo-American specialists than the occasional nod.

Notes and References

Preface

1. Joseph LaPalombara, 'Monoliths or Plural Systems: Through Conceptual Lenses Darkly', *Studies in Comparative Communism*, vol. VIII, no. 3 (Autumn 1975) p. 305.
2. A. H. Brown, *Soviet Politics and Political Science* (London: Macmillan, 1974).
3. H. Carrère d'Encausse's introduction to L. Marcou, *L'Union Soviétique* (Paris: Armand Colin, 1971) p. 15. Throughout this book, translations are my own, except where the title of the book or article is given in English. All emphases are in the original, except when indicated otherwise in the Notes and References section.

1 The Development and Orientation of French Sovietology

1. Conseil de direction, 'Notre programme', *Le Monde slave*, no. 1 (November 1924) p. 7.
2. André Mazon, 'Slavonic studies in France', *The Slavonic and East European Review*, vol. XXV, no. 64 (November 1946) p. 210.
3. J. Bonamour, 'Soviet and East European Studies in France', in A. Buchholz (ed.), *Soviet and East European Studies in the International Framework – Organization, Financing and Political Relevance* (New York: Transnational Publishers, 1982) p. 51.
4. The reasons why Denis felt so strongly about ending the publication of his periodical were summarised as follows by Eisenmann and his collaborators: 'it is out of decency . . . out of fear of undermining a just cause by continuing to plead it when circumstances play so strongly against it. Such a defence would not only be bound to be inefficient, but would also appear as an act of awkward provocation. Freed from the domination of the new masters of Russia, German armies are preparing for the final assault on France; would it have been the right time in France . . . to demonstrate the necessity and benefits of the French–Slavic solidarity?' See Conseil de direction, *Le Monde slave*, no. 1 (November 1924) p. 3.
5. Alfred Fichelle, 'Origines et développement de l'Institut d'études slaves (1919–1949)', *Revue des études slaves*, vol. 27 (1951) p. 96.
6. Louis Eisenmann, 'Slavonic Studies in France', *The Slavonic Review*, vol. I, no. 2 (December 1922) p. 299.
7. Conseil de direction, *Le Monde slave*, no. 1 (November 1924) p. 9.
8. Ibid., p. 16.
9. Ibid., p. 6.
10. Ibid., pp. 17–18.

124

11. Marcel Mauss, 'Socialisme et bolchévisme', *Le Monde slave*, no. 2 (February 1925) pp. 201–22.
12. André Pierre, 'Le XIVᵉ Congrès du parti communiste russe', *Le Monde slave*, 3ᵉᵐᵉ Année, no. 2 (February 1926) pp. 274–93.
13. Jules Legras, 'La politique de nationalités du gouvernement soviétique en Ukraine', *Le Monde slave*, 3ᵉᵐᵉ Année, no. 11 (November 1926) pp. 317–19.
14. G. Méquet and André Pierre, 'La femme en Russie soviétique', *Le Monde slave*, 4ᵉᵐᵉ Année, nos. 11–12 (November–December 1927) pp. 419–41.
15. André Pierre, 'En U.R.S.S. – La vie politique, économique et intellectuelle (janvier–février 1929)', *Le Monde slave* (March 1929) pp. 457–80; 'La vie politique, économique et intellectuelle en U.R.S.S.', *Le Monde slave* (April 1929) pp. 145–60; (May 1929) pp. 302–20; (July 1929) pp. 135–60; (August 1929) pp. 303–20; (September 1929) pp. 441–53; (October 1929) pp. 103–121; (November 1929) pp. 271–284; (December 1929) pp. 450–466.
16. Paul Olberg, 'Le Komsomol', *Le Monde slave*, 8ᵉᵐᵉ Année (Tome II) no. 2 (May 1931) pp. 280–8.
17. 'La politique de Stalin', *Le Monde slave*, 7ᵉᵐᵉ Année (Tome I) no. 1 (January 1930) pp. 1–15.
18. Paul Olberg, 'La seconde révolution agraire russe', *Le Monde slave*, 8ᵉᵐᵉ Année (Tome III) no. 2 (August 1931) pp. 304–16.
19. André Pierre, 'La presse de l'U.R.S.S. en 1932', *Le Monde slave*, 9ᵉᵐᵉ Année (Tome III) no. 7 (July 1932) pp. 115–29.
20. André Pierre, 'L'Académie des Sciences de l'U.R.S.S.', *Le Monde slave*, 10ᵉᵐᵉAnnée (Tome III) no. 7 (July 1933) pp. 90–104.
21. B.X., 'La récolte en U.R.S.S. en 1933', *Le Monde slave*, 10ᵉᵐᵉ Année (Tome III) no. 7 (July 1933) pp. 104–14.
22. For instance, in sociologist Emile Sicard's view, '[Between 1920 and 1945], our sociological writings devote no more than three or four lines to such socio-economic phenomena as the *Mir* and the *Kolkhoz*'. See Emile Sicard, 'Réflexions sur les études françaises de Sociologie des peuples slaves', *Sociologie et Droit Slaves*, no. 1 (December 1945) pp. 16 and 7.
23. Richard Szawloski, review of *Annuaire de l'URSS. Droit-Economie-Sociologie-Politique-Culture*. Volumes for 1965, 1966 and 1967. (Paris: Editions du Centre National de la Recherche Scientifique, 1966–1967–1968) in *Soviet Studies*, vol. XXI, no. 2 (October 1969) p. 260.
24. Mme Françoise Héritier-Augé, of the Collège de France, noted that, prior to the 1930s (with the exception of naturalists), there was a strange lack of interest in African matters among French scholars. See M. K., 'L'Afrique, enfin', *Le Monde*, 1 March 1983, p. 1.
25. A. Leroy-Beaulieu published, at the turn of the last century, *L'Empire des Tsars et Les Russes*. This book has often been hailed as an important contribution of French scholarship on Russia.
26. Richard Szawlowski and Hanna Terlecka, 'Western Research on Russia until 1939: 1. Developments up to 1914', *Canadian Slavonic Papers*, vol. IX, no. 2 (1967) p. 167. Unsurprisingly, our survey of the contents

from 1906 to 1936 of the *Revue des Sciences Politiques*, a periodical published with the collaboration of the Ecole's professors and former students, has revealed only a handful of articles relating to Tsarist Russia or the Soviet Union.

27. S. Hoffman, W. Leontieff and H. Tajfel, *Social Sciences Policy – France – Examiners' Report* (Paris: OECD, 1975) p. 195.

28. M. Pollak, *Social Sciences Policy – France-Background Report* (Paris: OECD, 1975) p. 55.

29. Boris Souvarine (one of the founders of the PCF) was for three years a member of the Secretariat and Presidium of the Communist International, from which he was expelled in 1924 on grounds of indiscipline. His years in Moscow taught him much about the nature of the emerging Soviet regime and, in effect, instigated a process which caused him to radically alter his thinking about Communism. As Claude Roy has recently written, 'His Russian years, his familiarity with Lenin and Trotsky, as well as his friendship with Kollontai, Riazanov . . . enabled him to get a thorough knowledge and understanding of the new Russian society, the new dominant Soviet class and of the emerging regime of arbitrariness, intimidation and oppression'. See Claude Roy, 'Le premier homme', *Le Nouvel Observateur*, no. 994 (25 November 1983) p. 55. Souvarine died in 1984. For a brief biographical profile of Souvarine see Michel Heller, 'Boris Souvarine 1895–1984', *Survey*, vol. 28, no. 4 (1984) pp. 198–204.

30. B. Souvarine, *Staline – Aperçu historique du bolchevisme* (Paris: Plon, 1935). An interesting book had been published a few years earlier by Souvarine under the signature of Panaït Istrati. See P. Istrati, *Vers l'autre flamme. La Russie nue* (Paris: Ed. Rieder, 1929).

31. Yves Delahaye, review of H. Chambre, *Le Marxisme en Union soviétique Idéologie et institutions Leur évolution de 1917 à nos jours* (Paris: Seuil, 1955) in *Revue française de science politique*, vol. vi, no. 1 (January–March 1956) p. 201.

32. Mazon, 'Slavonic studies in France', p. 210.

33. Emile Sicard, '1. Réflexions sur l'Information scientifique, juridique et sociologique, concernant les pays et les peuples slaves', *Sociologie et Droit Slaves*, no. 2 (March–April–May, 1946) p. 102.

34. Ibid., p. 108.

35. Y. Delahaye, review of H. Chambre, pp. 201–2.

36. Basile Kerblay, 'Soviet studies in Western Europe: France', *Survey*, no. 50 (January 1964) p. 98. One of such publications was the *Cahiers de l'économie soviétique*. Published from mid-1945 until 1949 under the aegis of the Institut d'Etude de l'Economie Soviétique run by Alfred Sauvy, this periodical was unquestionably pro-Soviet. The tone was set by the very first issue in July 1945, which contained articles written by arch-Communist French scholars Pierre George and Jean Bruhat, and also by a Soviet scholar from Moscow. As a matter of fact, Soviet scholars contributed a few articles to this publication. The highly respected Sovietologist Kerblay, who had one article in the April–June 1947 issue ('Le régime juridique des brevets d'invention en U.R.S.S.', *Cahiers de l'économie soviétique*, no. 8 (April–June 1947) pp. 3–10) must

look back with some amusement on having been published among such singular company.

37. Richard Szawloski, *Soviet Studies*, vol. xxi, no. 2 (October 1969) p. 262.
38. M. Lesage, *Les régimes politiques de l'U.R.S.S. et de l'Europe de l'Est* (Paris: Presses Universitaires de France, 1971) p. 7.
39. Georges H. Mond, review of M. Lesage, ibid., in *Revue de l'Est*, vol. 2, no. 3 (July 1971) p. 183.
40. H. Carrère d'Encausse's introduction to L. Marcou, *L'Union Soviétique*, p. 23.
41. Gérard Wild, review of H. Carrère d'Encausse, *L'empire éclaté – la révolte des nations en U.R.S.S.* (Paris: Flammarion, 1978) in *Le Courrier des Pays de l'Est*, no. 225 (January 1979) p. 47.
42. See Eisenmann, 'Slavonic Studies in France', p. 302.
43. One finds a further illustration of the problem caused by the divorce existing between language studies and social sciences in a short article by N. Davies about the organisation and methods of Polish studies in France. See N. Davies, 'Study visit in France: a short Report', *International Newsletter* – International Committee for Soviet and East European Studies, 15 (July 1982) p. 46.
44. Michel Lesage, 'Les études soviétiques et est-européennes en France', *Canadian Slavonic Papers*, vol. xi, no. 3 (Fall 1969) pp. 295–96.
45. Bonamour, 'Soviet and East European Studies in France', p. 51.
46. Kerblay, 'Soviet studies in Western Europe: France', p. 105.
47. Jean Train, 'L'étude du Russe en France', *Cahiers du Monde Russe et Soviétique*, vol. 1, no. 1 (May 1959) p. 183.
48. Kerblay, 'Soviet studies in Western Europe: France', p. 105.
49. The same comment may be made as to the action of the DGRST (Direction générale de la Recherche scientifique et technique). See Bonamour, 'Soviet and East European Studies in France', p. 52.
50. Ibid., pp. 51–2.
51. In an interview given in Paris on 22 March 1983, Jean Bonamour, former director of the INES, made it very clear that, due to a chronic lack of financial resources, the INES was then on the brink of disappearance. He also made clear that more financial resources constitute an absolute priority if some efforts towards coordinating and organising the research are to see the light of day and yield results.
52. The IMSECO is a joint unit CNRS/University of Paris IV–Sorbonne.
53. H. Carrère d'Encausse did not hesitate to underline the minimal collaboration among French Sovietologists. Interview with H. Carrère d'Encausse in Paris, 5 November 1982.
54. S. Hoffman, W. Leontieff and H. Tajfel, *Social Sciences Policy – France – Examiners' Report*, p. 262.
55. Jacques Lautman has recently drawn attention to this danger, when he writes about these 'few talented authors working in auspicious fields who become prominent, thus running the risk of being swallowed up by success and becoming imperceptibly entangled in the promotion of the product . . .'. See Jacques Lautman, 'Les sciences sociales et le C.N.R.S., entre la culture et la demande bureaucratique', *Commentaire*, vol. 6, no. 21 (Spring 1983) p. 196.

56. According to another French specialist on Soviet politics, Michel Tatu of *Le Monde*, it is no secret that Sovietological research in France revolves around a number of 'small fiefs, small units'. Interview with M. Tatu in Paris, 8 November 1982.

57. Interview in Paris with Jean Bonamour, 22 March 1983 and with Jean-Guy Collignon, 24 March 1983.

58. P. Sorlin, *La société soviétique 1917–1964* (Paris: Armand Colin, 1964) p. 5. In this regard one reads with great interest the brief preliminary remarks to a series of articles focusing on the Soviet Union, which appeared in a 1956 issue of *Les Cahiers de la République*: 'Suddenly the communist world presents itself as an enigma. We see it as a land of turmoil: what does this turmoil hide? The three articles published here are free of passion. We believe that, in France, serious discussions of these problems have been rare . . . We also believe that our readers will not regret the absence of claptrap and uncontrolled passion that this subject generally brings about.' See 'Le Monde communiste', *Les Cahiers de la République*, 4 (December 1956) p. 41.

59. Conseil de direction, *Le Monde slave*, no. 1 (November 1924) p. 6.

60. As pointed out by J. Lyon, 'It is nowadays unwise to address Russian issues without taking precautions and without clearly identifying the objective pursued. Apology or indictment are out of place here. We have deliberately attempted to examine Soviet Russia as a fact . . . the impact and future of which are impossible to assess if one does not examine it coldly as one would in a laboratory experiment aimed at understanding and describing.' See J. Lyon, *La Russie Soviétique* (Paris: Librairie Félix Alcan, 1927) p. 1.

61. Emile Sicard, 'I. Sociologie et Histoire des peuples et des Etats slaves', *Sociologie et Droit Slaves*, no. 1 (1947) p. 10.

62. F. Bourricaud, *Le bricolage idéologique – Essai sur les intellectuels et les passions démocratiques* (Paris: Presses Universitaires de France, 1980) p. 162. In view of its backwardness on the material, technological and scientific planes when compared to America, many in France saw Marxism and the Socialist utopia in terms of a return, as suggested by M. Crozier, to the 'avant-garde'. France could regain, as he noted, 'the advantage on the level that counted most, that of working out the future society'. See Michel Crozier, 'The Cultural Revolution – Notes on the Changes in the Intellectual Climate of France', *Daedalus*, vol. 93, no. 1 (Winter 1964) p. 532.

63. Jean-Marie Domenach, 'L'intelligentsia française et la perception de l'Est communiste', *Cadmos*, 4ème Année, no. 13 (Spring 1981) p. 21. As for the ideological bankruptcy of the French Right, Bourricaud writes: 'The French Right's involvement in the ignominious bankruptcy of European fascism caused its ideology to be temporarily deprived of any legitimacy . . . dismissed because of its complicity, the ideological Right left a vacuum that a new generation of Marxist–Existentialist ideologues could fill without facing competition.' Ibid., pp. 141–2 and 143.

64. G. Martinet, '1956 et le renouvellement de la gauche française', in P. Kende and K. Pomian (eds), *1956 Varsovie Budapest – La deuxième révolution d'Octobre* (Paris: Seuil, 1978) p. 149.

65. Domenach, 'L'intelligentsia française et la perception de l'Est communiste', p. 19.
66. M. Poster, *Existential Marxism in Postwar France – From Sartre to Althusser* (Princeton: Princeton University Press, 1977) p. 38.
67. C. Lefort, *L'Invention démocratique – Les limites de la domination totalitaire* (Paris: Fayard, 1981) p. 9.
68. Claude Lefort, 'Kravchenko et le problème de l'U.R.S.S.', *Les Temps modernes*, 29 (February 1948) reprinted in C. Lefort, *Eléments d'une critique de la bureaucratie* (Paris: Gallimard, 1979) pp. 117–18.
69. G. Lavau, *A quoi sert le parti communiste français?* (Paris: Fayard, 1981) p. 369. For a survey of the general policy followed by the PCF towards the Soviet Union until 1980, see chapter IX – 'L'URSS au-dessus de tout soupçon'.
70. A. Touraine, *Un désir d'Histoire* (Paris: Stock, 1977) p. 71.
71. Alain Drouard, 'Réflexions sur une chronologie: Le développement des sciences sociales en France de 1945 à la fin des années soixante', *Revue française de sociologie*, vol. XXIII, 1 (January–March 1982) p. 70.
72. C. Lefort, *L'Invention démocratique*, p. 86.
73. Yves Hardy and Pascal Gabai, 'La gauche française et les contestataires soviétiques', *Le Monde diplomatique*, December 1977, p. 12.
74. This approach was suggested to us by Georges Lavau, a prominent French political scientist, in an interview in Oxford on 26 February 1983. He resorted to Bourdieu's terminology and thought that 'during this period, the field of French Sovietology was entirely "parasitized" by the PCF'. On the idea of 'field', see Pierre Bourdieu, 'Le champ scientifique', *Actes de la recherche en sciences sociales*, no. 2–3 (June 1976) pp. 89–104 and 'La représentation politique – Eléments pour une théorie du champ politique', *Actes de la recherche en sciences sociales*, no. 36–7 (February–March 1981) pp. 3–24.
75. Raymond Aron, 'Fascinés par l'Union Soviétique', *La Nef*, vol. 13, no. 12 (March 1956) p. 214.
76. Kerblay, 'Soviet studies in Western Europe: France', p. 103.
77. A. Besançon, *Présent soviétique et passé russe* (Paris: Librairie Générale Française, 1980) p. 10.
78. 'Memento de la "guerre froide"', *Bulletin d'études et d'informations politiques internationales*, 16–30 November 1951, p. 13.
79. Kerblay, 'Soviet studies in Western Europe: France', p. 103.
80. M. Winock, 'La gauche non communiste en France: la coupure de 1956', in P. Kende and K. Pomian (eds), *1956 Varsovie-Budapest – La deuxième révolution d'Octobre*, p. 145.
81. Bourricaud, *Le bricolage idéologique*, p. 178.
82. Martinet, '1956 et le renouvellement de la gauche française', pp. 150–1.
83. Christian Descamps, 'Claude Lefort le peuple et le pouvoir' (interview with C. Lefort), *Le Monde Dimanche* (7 November 1982) p. IX.
84. For a brief explanation of this French phenomenon, see Hélène Carrère d'Encausse, 'Paris–Moscou L'U.R.S.S. au purgatoire?', *Le Débat*, no. 36 (September 1985) pp. 166–7.
85. In the 1920s books written by exiled Russian socialists and bearing upon the Cheka and the existence of camps were translated and published in

France. On this general question, see Jean Rabaut, 'Le goulag et la France', *Le Monde Dimanche* (17 October 1982) pp. x–xi. For the sociologist Raymond Boudon, apart from the ideological aspects, the surprisingly late discovery of the Gulag by the French intelligentsia has something to do with the French literary spirit, seen as 'the main source of the relative indifference of French intellectuals to reality . . .'. See R. Boudon, 'L'intellectuel et ses publics: les singularités françaises', in J.-D. Reynaud and Y. Grafmeyer (eds), *Français, qui êtes-vous? – des essais et des chiffres* (Paris: La Documentation française, 1981) p. 479.

86. See C. Jelen, *L'aveuglement – les socialistes et la naissance du mythe soviétique* (Paris: Flammarion, 1984) and J. Sapir, *Pays de l'Est vers la crise généralisée?* (Lyon: Fédérop, 1980) p. 10.

87. Pierre Hassner, 'Western European Perceptions of the Soviet Union', *Daedalus*, vol. 108, no. 1 (Winter 1979) p. 130.

88. Interview with Michel Heller in Paris, 5 November 1982.

89. Sorlin, *La société soviétique 1917–1964*, p. 5.

90. Roger Kanet, review of H. Carrère d'Encausse, *Le pouvoir confisqué – gouvernants et gouvernés en U.R.S.S.* (Paris: Flammarion, 1980) in *Slavic Review*, vol. 40, no. 2 (Summer 1981) p. 294.

91. Rudolf L. Tökés, 'Comparative Communism: The Elusive Target', *Studies in Comparative Communism*, vol. viii, no. 3 (Autumn 1975) p. 222.

92. Pierre Favre, 'La science politique en France depuis 1945', *International Political Science Review*, vol. 2, no. 1 (1981) pp. 111–12.

93. Jean Leca, 'La science politique dans le champ intellectuel français', *Revue française de science politique*, vol. 32, no. 4–5 (August–October 1982) pp. 658–9.

94. J. Viet, *Les sciences de l'homme en France – tendances et organisation de la recherche* (Paris: Mouton, 1966) p. 50.

95. G. Burdeau, *Méthode de la science politique* (Paris: Dalloz, 1959) p. 43.

96. Leca, 'La science politique dans le champ intellectuel français', p. 664.

97. It is worth noting that numerous professors of constitutional law nowadays consider political science as annexed to their own speciality. They dispute political science's autonomy. In their opinion, the political science one comes across is not really serious, since it has lost sight of the main problem, namely the study of political institutions. See Pierre Favre, 'Regards sur la science politique française', paper delivered to the Association française de science politique, 19 June 1981.

98. C. Morrisson has written about the difficulty facing many researchers in social sciences, that is, to get acquainted with a methodology different from the one germane to their original discipline (a difficulty felt especially during the period 1950–68). The gradual movement of researchers towards the social sciences has not come about without serious difficulties. Thus, as noted by Morrisson, 'the methodology, the role of experimentation, the use of mathematics . . . are not the same in social sciences as in the fields of literature, philosophy or history. Hence, the adaptation of the researcher to the methodology of social sciences has been impeded by his initial training'. See Christian Morrisson,

'Les moyens des sciences sociales en France', *Revue Economique*, vol. XXVI, no. 6 (1975) p. 1010.

99. Alfred Grosser, 'I. Recherche et enseignement', *Tendances* (December 1960) p. 473. (my emphasis)

100. Jean-Guy Collignon, 'De l'isolationnisme au comparatisme – méthodes et approches anglo-saxonnes pour l'analyse du système politique soviétique', *Revue française de science politique*, vol. 26, no. 3 (June 1976) pp. 445–82.

101. Daniel Tarschys, 'The Soviet political system: Three models', *European Journal of Political Research*, vol. 5, no. 3 (September 1977) pp. 287–320.

102. Kerblay, 'Soviet studies in Western Europe: France', p. 105.

103. H. Carrère d'Encausse's introduction to L. Marcou, *L'Union Soviétique*, p. 27.

104. R. Charvin, *Les Etats socialistes européens – Institutions et vie politique* (Toulouse: Dalloz, 1975) pp. 2–3.

105. Interview with H. Carrère d'Encausse in Paris, 5 November 1982.

106. Kanet, review of H. Carrère d'Encausse, p. 294. More strictly, Kanet might have spoken of English-language writing on the Soviet Union, for British and Australian scholars – as well as Americans – are often cited in her work.

107. Favre, 'La science politique en France depuis 1945', p. 117.

2 Analyses in the Marxist Tradition

1. Brown, *Soviet Politics and Political Science*, p. 22.

2. Paying tribute to Laurat who died in 1973, Souvarine recalls the circumstances of their meeting and how they became friends. See Boris Souvarine, 'Un demi-siècle d'amitié', *Est et Ouest*, vol. 25, no. 515 (16–30 September 1973) pp. 1–4.

3. Boris Souvarine, 'Octobre noir', *Le Bulletin communiste*, nos. 22–3 (1927) p. 346. On this point, see Jeannine Verdès-Leroux, 'Souvarine le premier', *Esprit*, no. 89 (May 1984) p. 27.

4. L. Laurat, *L'économie soviétique. Sa dynamique. Son mécanisme* (Paris: Librairie Valois, 1931) p. 163. Laurat loathed the Soviet regime. In a later book published in 1955, he depicted the regime as a slavemaster *vis-à-vis* its employees and as a feudal lord *vis-à-vis* the peasants working on collective farms. See L. Laurat, *Problèmes actuels du Socialisme* (Paris: Les Iles d'Or, 1955) p. 97. Interestingly, Emmanuel Todd, more than 20 years later, propounded a theoretical viewpoint which strangely resembles that of Laurat. See E. Todd, *La chute finale – Essai sur la décomposition de la sphère soviétique* (Paris: Robert Laffont, 1976) p. 116.

5. Frank died in 1984. For a brief biographical profile of Frank see Peter Burnett, 'Pierre Frank', *The Journal of Communist Studies*, vol. 1, no. 1 (March 1985) p. 90.

6. P. Frank, '"Novateurs" et "Conservateurs" dans la question de l'U.R.S.S.', Supplément-Bulletin intérieur du Secrétariat international,

juillet 1947, reprinted in P. Frank, *Le stalinisme* (Paris: Maspéro, 1977) pp. 171–219.

7. P. Frank, 'La nature de classe de l'Union soviétique à la lumière de ses crises', in *Entstalinisierung* (Frankfurt a.M.: Editions Suhrkamp, 1977) reprinted in Frank, ibid., p. 73.

8. P. Frank, 'La théorie du stalinisme de Trotsky', in *Sowjet Gesellschaft und stalinistiche Diktatur* (oeuvres choisies de Trotsky, tome II) (Cologne: Europaische Verlagsanstalt, 1974) reprinted in Frank, ibid., p. 53.

9. The idea that the revolutionary process, interrupted many decades ago, may be reactivated or, as it were, picked up again is rather simplistic. It totally leaves out numerous political features which have accumulated throughout 65 years of 'victorious socialism'. On this point, see more particularly J.-M. Vincent, 'Trotsky et l'analyse de l'URSS', in L. Marcou (ed.), *L'U.R.S.S. vue de gauche* (Paris: Presses Universitaires de France, 1982) pp. 58–9.

10. Frank, 'La théorie du stalinisme de Trotsky', (in *Le stalinisme*) p. 55.

11. J. Elleinstein, *L'U.R.S.S. contemporaine – histoire de l'U.R.S.S.* (tome IV) (Paris: Editions Sociales, 1975) and *Histoire du phénomène stalinien* (Paris: Grasset, 1975), published in English translation as *The Stalin phenomenon* (London: Lawrence and Wishart, 1976).

12. G. Lavau, 'L'URSS et eux . . . (le Parti communiste français et le socialisme existant, 1964–1981)', in L. Marcou (ed.), *L'U.R.S.S. vue de gauche*, p. 196.

13. J. Elleinstein, *The Stalin phenomenon*, p. 93 note 9.

14. J. Elleinstein's foreword to M. Voslensky, *La Nomenklatura – Les privilégiés en URSS* (Paris: Belfond, 1980) p. 21.

15. Ibid., p. 18.

16. Ibid., p. 17.

17. A. Adler, F. Cohen, M. Decaillot, C. Frioux and L. Robel, *L'URSS et Nous* (Paris: Editions Sociales, 1978) p. 25.

18. Lavau, *A quoi sert le parti communiste français?*, p. 390.

19. For instance, in a review of the book, a member of the PCF's Bureau politique had nothing but praise and concluded by writing: 'Each page invites us to reflect, to research and to discuss. The book deserves, within our ranks, and far beyond, the attention of numerous readers.' See Guy Besse, '"L'URSS et Nous"', *Cahiers du Communisme*, 54 ème Année, no. 10 (October 1978) p. 101. This critical book has to be considered in the context of what V. Wright has described as the PCF's 'policy of de-Sovietization'. See V. Wright, 'The French Communist Party during the Fifth Republic: the troubled path', in H. Machin (ed.), *National Communism in Western Europe: a third way to socialism?* (London and New York: Methuen, 1983) p. 95. See also Jean Baudouin, 'Le P.C.F.: retour à l'archaïsme?', *Revue politique et parlementaire*, 82e Année, no. 889 (November–December 1980) pp. 30–40 and Julius W. Friend, 'Soviet Behavior and National Responses: The Puzzling Case of the French Communist Party', *Studies in Comparative Communism*, vol. xv, no. 3 (Autumn 1982) pp. 212–35.

20. E. Ambartsumov, F. Burlatsky, Y. Krasin and E. Pletnyov, 'Against distortion of the experience of real, existing socialism', *New Times*, 52 (December 1978) p. 18.

As mentioned, the same condemnation was also published in the December 1978 issue of *Kommunist*.

Some French writers have seen, not without irony, a link between the condemnation in Moscow and the subsequent curbs put by the PCF leadership on the circulation of the book. See J. Kéhayan, *Le tabouret de Piotr* (Paris: Seuil, 1980) p. 141.

21. Ibid., p. 21.
22. Ibid., p. 19.
23. In an interview given to us in Paris on 5 November 1983, Cohen, while discussing his work, came up at one point with the expression 'Communist Sovietology'.
24. By 'worshipping' Stalin (whom he once called 'the greatest scientist of our times' – Francis Cohen, 'La supériorité de la civilisation socialiste', *Cahiers du Communisme*, 26ème Année, no. 11 (November 1949) p. 1361), Cohen was indeed just reflecting the attitude prevalent within Communist intellectual circles. In this connection, see 'Les intellectuels communistes et le culte de Staline', *Est–Ouest* (Supplément), 273 (16–28 February 1962) pp. 1–57. As the authors point out, this supplement is not 'an anthology of the Stalinist cult – in its French version – . . .' but rather 'a mere sampling of a *delirious literature*' (p. 3) (my emphasis).
25. Ibid., p. 1366.
26. F. Cohen, *L'U.R.S.S. en mouvement* (Paris: Editions Sociales, 1963) p. 161.
27. Ibid., p. 157.
28. Ibid., p. 160.
29. Francis Cohen, 'L'URSS et le monde – Réflexions', *Cahiers du Communisme*, 41ème Année, no. 12 (December 1965) p. 57.
30. F. Cohen, *Les Soviétiques – Classes et société en U.R.S.S.* (Paris: Editions Sociales, 1974) p. 289.
31. Francis Cohen, 'Démocratie et réalités sociales dans l'Europe socialiste', *La Pensée*, 217–18 (January–February 1981) p. 112.
32. Francis Cohen, 'Mutations sociales et contradictions', *Recherches internationales*, no. 9 (July–August–September 1983) p. 84.
33. Francis Cohen, 'La révolution socialiste d'octobre soixante ans après', *Cahiers du Communisme*, 53ème Année, no. 10 (October 1977) p. 89.
34. Adler, Cohen, Decaillot, Frioux and Robel, *L'URSS et Nous*, p. 216.
35. Francis Cohen, 'Connaissance des pays socialistes', *Cahiers du Communisme*, 59ème Année, no. 7–8 (July–August 1983) p. 94.
36. Cohen, 'Mutations sociales et contradictions', p. 85.
37. Cohen, 'Connaissance des pays socialistes', p. 94.
38. Francis Cohen, 'Structure sociale, classes et différenciations dans le socialisme existant (notes préliminaires)', *La Pensée*, 225 (January–February 1982) p. 99.
39. Cohen, 'Connaissance des pays socialistes', p. 94. See also Dominique Vidal, 'Les pays socialistes et nous – 1976/1984 – Entretien avec Francis Cohen', *Révolution*, no. 246 (16 November 1984) p. 58.
40. Cohen, 'Démocratie et réalités sociales dans l'Europe socialiste', p. 104.
41. Ibid., p. 105.
42. Dick Howard, 'Introduction to Castoriadis', *Telos*, no. 23 (Spring 1975) p. 118.

43. Ibid.
44. Anti-mythes, 'An interview with Claude Lefort', *Telos*, no. 30 (Winter 1976–7) p. 175.
45. Christian Descamps, 'Claude Lefort le peuple et le pouvoir' (interview with C. Lefort), *Le Monde Dimanche* (7 November 1982) p. IX.
46. Anti-mythes, 'An interview with Claude Lefort', p. 174.
47. C. Castoriadis, 'Sur le régime et contre la défense de l'U.R.S.S.', *Bulletin Intérieur du P.C.I.*, no. 31 (August 1946) and 'Sur la question de l'URSS et du stalinisme mondial', *Bulletin Intérieur du P.C.I.*, no. 41 (August 1947), reprinted in C. Castoriadis, *La société bureaucratique 1: Les rapports de production en Russie* (Paris: Union Générale d'Editions, 1973). Numerous pertinent articles by Castoriadis in *Socialisme ou Barbarie* have also been reprinted in *La société bureaucratique 2: La révolution contre la bureaucratie* (Paris: Union Générale d'Editions, 1973).
48. Brian Singer, 'The early Castoriadis: Socialism, Barbarism and the bureaucratic thread', *Canadian Journal of Political and Social Theory*, vol. 3, no. 3 (Fall 1979) p. 35. Singer completed his examination of Castoriadis's thought in a second article dealing with the recent and more philosophical reflections: 'The later Castoriadis: Institution under interrogation', *Canadian Journal of Political and Social Theory*, vol. 4, no. 1 (Winter 1980) pp. 75–101.
49. Cornelius Castoriadis, 'The social regime in Russia', trans. by David J. Parent, *Telos*, no. 38 (Winter 1978–9) pp. 32–47. This article originally appeared in *Esprit*, no. 7–8 (July–August 1978) pp. 6–23.
50. C. Castoriadis, *Devant la guerre – Les réalités* (Paris: Fayard, 1981).
51. Marcel Gauchet, 'La logique du politique', *Critique*, vol. 30, no. 329 (October 1974) p. 908 note 2. A similar comment was expressed by Olivier Mongin in 1977: 'just a few years ago . . . only a small minority sensed the importance and the originality of your articles in *Socialisme ou Barbarie*'. See Olivier Mongin, Paul Thibaud and Pierre Rosanvallon, 'L'exigence révolutionnaire – Entretien avec Cornelius Castoriadis', *Esprit* no. 2 (February 1977) p. 201.
52. As Socialisme ou Barbarie began advocating a revolution aiming at transforming the totality of everyday life in the 1960s, its message was being carefully studied by young universitaires at Nanterre. In this respect, Socialisme ou Barbarie cannot be denied an influence on the events of May 1968. See D. Cohn-Bendit and G. Cohn-Bendit, *Obsolete Communism. The Left-Wing Alternative* (London: André Deutsch, 1968) p. 18.
53. Lefort, *Eléments d'une critique de la bureaucratie*, p. 9.
54. René Lourau, 'La bureaucratie comme classe dominante', *L'Homme et la Société*, no. 21 (July–August–September 1971) p. 261.
55. Poster, *Existential Marxism in Postwar France – From Sartre to Althusser*, p. 205.
56. Castoriadis once admitted that the notion of a 'degenerate workers' state' could have been, at one point in time, a possibly valid interpretation, as long as the economic foundations of the bureaucratic domination

remained limited to the nationalised segment of the industry and as long as some capitalist tendencies survived. That interpretation, in his opinion, suffered a powerful blow as the 'Grand tournant' was being planned and imposed upon the Soviet economy and society.

57. Castoriadis, *La société bureaucratique 1*, p. 17.
58. Paul Cardan, 'Socialisme ou Barbarie', *The Review*, vol. 2, no. 6 (October 1960) p. 97.
59. Pierre Chaulieu, 'Les rapports de production en Russie', *Socialisme ou Barbarie*, 1ère Année, no. 2 (May–June 1949) pp. 1–66.
60. Cardan, 'Socialisme ou Barbarie', p. 97. (my emphasis)
61. Chaulieu, 'Les rapports de production en Russie', p. 17.
62. Ibid., p. 10.
63. Ibid., p. 26.
64. In the 1978 article published in *Telos*, Castoriadis uses the notion of 'producers' (defined as 'workers, peasants and "service" employees') rather than the term proletariat. His early persistent use of the latter may well be related to his Marxist background. However, this emphasis did not mean that he overlooked the Russian peasantry. In the October 1949 issue of *Socialisme ou Barbarie* he considered the extensive exploitation of the peasantry by an agricultural bureaucracy. See Pierre Chaulieu, 'L'exploitation des paysans sous le capitalisme bureaucratique', *Socialisme ou Barbarie*, 1ère Année, no. 4 (October–November 1949) pp. 19–44.
65. Castoriadis, 'The social regime in Russia', p. 32.
66. Claude Lefort, 'What is Bureaucracy?', trans. by Jean L. Cohen, *Telos*, no. 22 (Winter 1974–5) p. 49. This article originally appeared in *Arguments*, no. 17 (1960).
67. 'Socialisme ou Barbarie', *Socialisme ou Barbarie*, 1ère Année, no. 1 (March–April 1949) p. 11.
68. Lefort, 'What is Bureaucracy?', pp. 53–4.
69. Castoriadis, 'The social regime in Russia', p. 33.
70. Ibid.
71. Castoriadis, *La société bureaucratique 1*, p. 21.
72. Castoriadis, 'The social regime in Russia', p. 32.
73. Ibid., p. 38.
74. 'Let us give the name of *social regime* to a given type of institution of society that applies to more than one individual society'. Ibid.
75. Singer, 'The early Castoriadis: Socialism, Barbarism and the bureaucratic thread', p. 37.
76. 'La vie de notre Groupe', *Socialisme ou Barbarie*, 1ère Année, no. 4 (October–November 1949) p. 61.
77. In elaborating his conception of a revolutionary theory, Castoriadis stressed that the *sine qua non* objective of a socialist revolution should consist in abolishing this antagonistic division. See 'Socialisme ou Barbarie', *Socialisme ou Barbarie*, p. 42.
78. Singer, 'The early Castoriadis', p. 38.
79. Castoriadis, 'The social regime in Russia', p. 35.
80. Ibid.
81. Lefort, 'What is Bureaucracy?', p. 51.

82. Pierre Chaulieu, 'La voie polonaise de la bureaucratisation', *Socialisme ou Barbarie*, vol. IV, no. 21 (March–May 1957) p. 73.
83. Castoriadis, 'The social regime in Russia', p. 36.
84. Ibid., p. 38.
85. Paul Cardan, 'Le mouvement révolutionnaire sous le capitalisme moderne (suite)', *Socialisme ou Barbarie*, vol. VI, no. 32 (April–June 1961) p. 105.
86. Castoriadis, 'The social regime in Russia', p. 37.
87. Ibid., p. 36.
88. Ibid.
89. Ibid.
90. Zdenek Strmiska, 'Programme socialiste et rapports sociaux en U.R.S.S. et dans les pays socialistes', *Revue d'études comparatives Est–Ouest*, vol. VII, no. 3 (September 1976), p. 167. Writing recently about what he calls 'the fundamental divisions in power relationships' in Soviet-type regimes, Strmiska seems to have introduced nuances in his theoretical position. Thus, paying attention to the phenomenon of the divisions existing within the party, Strmiska has noted that 'certain divisions within the Party have become as important, or more important, than those existing between the Party and society'. See Z. Strmiska, 'Pouvoir politique et inégalités sociales', in P. Kende and Z. Strmiska (eds), *Egalité et inégalités en Europe de l'Est* (Paris: Presses de la Fondation Nationale des Sciences Politiques, 1984) p. 380.
91. Brown, *Soviet politics and political science*, p. 26.
92. Z. Strmiska, 'Pouvoir politique et inégalités sociales', in P. Kende and Z. Strmiska (eds), *Egalité et inégalités en Europe de l'Est*, p. 384.
93. E. Zaleski, *La planification stalinienne – croissance et fluctuations économiques en U.R.S.S. 1933–1952* (Paris: Economica, 1984) p. 615.
94. Pierre Chaulieu, 'La révolution prolétarienne contre la bureaucratie', *Socialisme ou Barbarie*, vol. IV, no. 20 (December 1956–February 1957) pp. 140–1. Almost at the same time when Castoriadis was propounding views of this nature in *Socialisme ou Barbarie*, the then Stalinist scholar Pierre George could write with serene assurance that Soviet central planning was able to ensure the full use of all productive forces and reduce 'to an infinitesimal rate' the wastes of raw materials, time and financial credits! See Pierre George, 'L'U.R.S.S. au seuil du VIe Plan quinquennal', *Cahiers internationaux*, 8ème année, no. 73 (February 1956), p. 64.
95. Castoriadis, 'The social regime in Russia', p. 46.
96. Pierre de Fouquet, 'Marxisme et socialisme étatique', *Revue d'études comparatives Est–Ouest*, vol. XII, no. 1 (March 1981) pp. 114–15.
97. P. Kende, *Logique de l'économie centralisée – Un exemple: La Hongrie* (Paris: Société d'Edition d'Enseignement Supérieur, 1964) p. 497.
98. Gérard Duchêne, 'Le poids du militaire', *Le Débat*, no. 24 (March 1983) p. 189.
99. On this point, see M. Nadeau, *The History of Surrealism* (New York: Macmillan, 1965), esp. Chapter 9 entitled 'The Naville crisis'.
100. P. Naville, *La révolution et les intellectuels* (Paris: Gallimard, 1975) p. 41. The pamphlet was originally published in 1928 by the same publishing house.

101. See the Prologue of L. Trotsky, *The Crisis of the French Section (1935–1936)* (New York: Pathfinder Press, 1977) p. 19.
102. Poster, *Existential Marxism in Postwar France – from Sartre to Althusser*, pp. 180–2.
103. Pierre Naville, 'Le parti nécessaire', *Critique socialiste*, no. 38–9 (1980) pp. 21–9.
104. Pierre Broué, 'Trotsky et les grands débats du Monde communiste', *Annales*, vol. 20, no. 3 (May–June 1965) p. 617.
105. P. Naville, *Le Nouveau Léviathan*, vol. 1. De l'aliénation à la jouissance (Paris: Anthropos, 1967); vol. 2. Le salaire socialiste, premier volume: les rapports de production; vol. 3. Le salaire socialiste, deuxième volume: sur l'histoire moderne des théories de la valeur et de la plus-value (Paris: Anthropos, 1970); vol. 4. Les échanges socialistes (Paris: Anthropos, 1974); vol. 5. La bureaucratie et la révolution (Paris: Anthropos, 1972).
106. Naville, *La révolution et les intellectuels*, p. 97.
107. Naville, *Le Nouveau Léviathan*, vol. 2. *Le salaire socialiste, premier volume: les rapports de production*, p. 63. (my emphasis)
108. Ibid., p. 184.
109. Naville, *Le Nouveau Léviathan*, vol. 5. *La bureaucratie et la révolution*, p. 281.
110. Ibid., p. 257. (my emphasis)
111. Ibid., p. 266.
112. Ibid., p. 11.
113. Ibid., p. 15.
114. Ibid., p. 96.
115. Ibid., p. 222.
116. Ibid., p. 296.
117. Ibid., p. 231.
118. Ibid., p. 296.
119. Ibid., p. 314.
120. Ibid., p. 294.
121. Naville, *Le Nouveau Léviathan*, vol. 2. *Le salaire socialiste, premier volume: les rapports de production*, p. 44.
122. Naville, *Le Nouveau Léviathan*, vol. 5. *La bureaucratie et la révolution*, p. 290.
123. Ibid., p. 348.
124. Pierre Naville, 'Grèves et revendications ouvrières en U.R.S.S.', *Critique socialiste*, no. 40 (1980) p. 96. Twenty-five years before his contribution to *Critique socialiste*, Naville had already shown his awareness about the 'new working class' potential as being determinative in bringing about essential changes in the Soviet society. See Pierre Naville, 'Les Sociétés soviétiques', *La Nef*, vol. 13, no. 12 (March 1956) p. 22.
125. Naville, *Le Nouveau Léviathan*, vol. 5. *La bureaucratie et la révolution*, p. 324.
126. Ibid., p. 314.
127. S. White, *Political Culture and Soviet Politics* (London: Macmillan, 1979) p. 111.

128. Strmiska, 'Programme socialiste et rapports sociaux en U.R.S.S. et dans les pays socialistes', p. 127.
129. Ibid., p. 146.
130. Explicit reference to Naville's theory of mutual exploitation can be found in the writings of Naville's old acquaintance Gilles Martinet. See G. Martinet, *Les cinq communismes* (Paris: Seuil, 1971) esp. pp. 73–7.
131. Thierry Paquot, 'Charles Bettelheim et la "révolution capitaliste" d'Octobre' (interview with C. Bettelheim), *Le Monde Dimanche* (3 October 1982) p. x.
132. C. Bettelheim, *La planification soviétique* (Paris: Librairie Marcel Rivière, 1939).
133. Paquot, interview with C. Bettelheim, p. x.
134. Charles Bettelheim, 'La pensée marxienne à l'épreuve de l'histoire', *Les Temps Modernes*, 41ème Année, no. 472 (November 1985) p. 628.
135. E. Morin, 'L'avenir dans la société française', in J.-D. Reynaud (ed.), *Tendances et volontés de la société française* (Paris: S.é.d.é.i.s., 1966) p. 418.
136. C. Bettelheim, *Cultural Revolution and Industrial Organization in China – Changes in Management and the Division of Labor*, trans. by A. Ehrenfeld (New York and London: Monthly Review Press, 1975) p. 10.
137. Castoriadis, *La société bureaucratique 1 – Les rapports de production en Russie*, p. 283.
138. Cornelius Castoriadis, 'Les divertisseurs', *Le Nouvel Observateur*, no. 658 (20 June 1977) p. 51.
139. C. Bettelheim, *Les luttes de classes en URSS – 1ère période 1917–1923* (Paris: Seuil/Maspéro, 1974), *Les luttes de classes en URSS – 2ème période 1923–1930* (Paris: Seuil/Maspéro, 1977), *Les luttes de classes en URSS – 3ème période 1930–1941 – Les Dominés* (Paris: Seuil/Maspéro, 1982), *Les luttes de classes en URSS – 3ème période 1930–1941 – Les Dominants* (Paris: Seuil/Maspéro, 1983).
140. A number of French writers have employed the theory of state capitalism in their conceptualisation of the Soviet regime. In particular, see the book of an ardent anti-Communist, S. Labin, *Stalin's Russia* (London: Victor Gollancz Ltd, 1949) esp. pp. 420–8; Serge Mallet, 'Bureaucratie et technocratie dans les pays socialistes', *L'Homme et la Société*, 10 (October–November–December 1968) pp. 147–71, in which he distinguishes two phases of state capitalism: 'State capitalism of the bureaucratic phase and the one of the technocratic phase' (p. 160); D. Rousset, *La Société éclatée – De la première à la seconde révolution mondiale* (Paris: Grasset, 1973); Danièle Leborgne and Alain Lipietz, 'Est, Ouest: deux modes de régulation du capitalisme', *Reflets et Perspectives de la vie économique*, vol. XXII, nos 4/5 (1981) pp. 369–76. Finally, Bernard Chavance, 'Sur les rapports de production en URSS (A propos d'un article de Paul Sweezy)', *Les Temps Modernes*, vol. 33, no. 375 (October 1977) pp. 513–26. This writer has developed a new theoretical viewpoint. He now writes of etatist capitalism. See Bernard Chavance, 'La nature du système soviétique, questions et enjeux', *Les Temps Modernes*, vol. 37, no. 419 (June 1981) pp. 2198–213 and

Bernard Chavance, 'Pourquoi le capitalisme étatique? Réponse à:
"Marxisme en crise cherche sociétés socialistes"', *Babylone*, no. 2/3
(Winter 1983–4) pp. 126–42. A. Nove has recently underlined the
distinction now being made by the French economist: 'Among our own
contemporaries it is . . . necessary to mention the interesting ideas of
. . . Chavance, who, in seeing the USSR as a class society, distinguishes
between "state capitalism" (*capitalisme d'Etat*) and "etatist capitalism"
(*capitalisme étatique*). The point of the distinction is that in the former
version the state plays the role of the capitalist, but in the latter (which
he supports), the role is played by specific individuals (officials,
managers) within a system in which ownership is formally vested in the
state and in which these "concrete persons" act as "capitalists" . . .'.
See Alec Nove, 'The Class Nature of the Soviet Union Revisited',
Soviet Studies, vol. xxxv, no. 3 (July 1983) p. 306. Against the new
viewpoint developed by Chavance, see Wladimir Andreff, 'Marxisme
en crise cherche sociétés socialistes. A propos des thèses de P. M.
Sweezy et de B. Chavance', *Babylone*, no. 2/3 (Winter 1983–4) pp. 100–
25.

141. Bettelheim, *Les luttes de classes en URSS – 3ème période 1930–1941 –
Les Dominés*, p. 13.

142. Strmiska, 'Programme socialiste et rapports sociaux en U.R.S.S. et
dans les pays socialistes', p. 179. In the first volume, Bettelheim dwelt
on the party's lack of control and political guidance over the state. He
saw the party's line continually thwarted by a growing number of
important functionaries in the administrative system hostile to the
dictatorship of the proletariat. Bettelheim asserted that the bourgeois
forces present in the state apparatus influenced party leaders and fostered
orientations favourable to their own interests, namely the restoration
of capitalism.

143. Bettelheim rejects any 'juridisme': 'Life has made it its business to
show . . . that changes in legal forms of ownership do not suffice to
cause the conditions for the existence of classes and for class struggle
to disappear. These conditions are rooted . . . not in legal forms of
ownership but in production relations . . .'. C. Bettelheim, *Class
Struggles in the USSR. First period: 1917–1923*, trans. by Brian Pearce
(New York and London: Monthly Review Press, 1976) p. 21.

144. Ibid., p. 139.

145. Ibid., p. 97. In an article published in 1970, Bettelheim was in no doubt
about the 'political domination of the proletariat resulting from the
October Revolution' and about the 'political control possessed by the
working class and its vanguard'. See Charles Bettelheim, 'Remarques
théoriques', *Problèmes de planification*, 14 (1970) pp. 190–1.

146. Bettelheim, *Les luttes de classes en URSS – 3eme période 1930–1941 –
Les Dominés*, p. 9.

147. C. Bettelheim, 'La pertinence des concepts marxiens de classe et de
lutte de classes pour analyser la société soviétique', in B. Chavance
(ed.), *Marx en perspective – Actes du colloque organisé par l'Ecole des
Hautes Etudes en Sciences Sociales, Paris, décembre 1983* (Paris:
Editions de l'Ecole des Hautes Etudes en Sciences Sociales, 1985)
p. 286.

148. Bettelheim, *Les luttes de classes en URSS – 3ème période 1930–1941 – Les Dominés*, p. 10.

149. It is worth comparing this recent viewpoint with what Bettelheim had to say in the first volume about the disappearance of political pluralism. In 1974 Bettelheim had little difficulty in explaining the unsuccessful attempt of the party to give other political formations a place in the political relations emerging under the dictatorship of the proletariat. This failure arose from the illusions of these groups which believed in the possibility of toppling the new proletarian regime by subversive means. Bettelheim, *Class Struggles in the USSR. First Period. 1917– 1923*, p. 269.

150. Bettelheim, *Les luttes de classes en URSS – 3ème période 1930–1941 – Les Dominés*, p. 14.

151. Bettelheim, 'La pertinence des concepts marxiens de classe et de lutte de classes pour analyser la société soviétique', in B. Chavance (ed.), *Marx en perspective – Actes du colloque organisé par l'Ecole des Hautes Etudes en Sciences Sociales, Paris, décembre 1983*, p. 287.

152. Ibid., p. 290. Indeed, such a change in interpretation renders obsolete Bettelheim's previous idea of a 'Stalinist counter-revolution'. On this idea, see Charles Bettelheim, 'La "Crise du marxisme" et l'idéologie stalinienne', *Critique socialiste*, no. 40 (1980) pp. 69–73.

153. Paquot, interview with C. Bettelheim, p. ix.

154. Bettelheim, *Les luttes de classes en URSS – 3ème période 1930–1941 – Les Dominants*, p. 221.

155. C. Bettelheim, 'Le système soviétique: un capitalisme de parti', in *Chronique des petites gens d'URSS* (Paris: Seuil, 1981), p. 160.

156. Bettelheim, *Les luttes de classes en URSS – 3ème période 1930–1941 – Les Dominants*, p. 210 note 3.

157. Ibid., p. 177.

158. Ibid., p. 213. As more recently pointed out by Bettelheim, the 'Party is . . . the matrix of the dominant class; it is through it [the Party] that this class develops'. See Bettelheim, 'La pensée marxienne à l'épreuve de l'histoire', p. 633.

159. Bettelheim, 'La pertinence des concepts marxiens de classe et de lutte de classes pour analyser la société soviétique', in B. Chavance (ed.), *Marx en perspective – Actes du colloque organisé par l'Ecole des Hautes Etudes en Sciences Sociales, Paris, décembre 1983*, p. 290.

160. Ibid.

161. Bettelheim, *Les luttes de classes en URSS – 3ème période 1930–1941 – Les Dominants*, p. 293.

162. Ibid., p. 174–5.

163. Ibid., p. 175.

164. Ibid., p. 221.

165. Ibid.

166. Ibid., p. 304.

167. Ibid., p. 305.

168. Bettelheim, 'Le système soviétique: un capitalisme de parti', in *Chronique des petites gens d'URSS*, p. 161.

169. Ibid., p. 161–2.

170. Charles Bettelheim, 'The specificity of Soviet capitalism', *Monthly Review*, vol. 37 (September 1985) p. 53.
171. Bettelheim, 'Le système soviétique: un capitalisme de parti', in *Chronique des petites gens d'URSS*, p. 162.
172. Bettelheim, 'The specificity of Soviet capitalism', p. 51.
173. Ibid., p. 54.
174. Ibid.
175. M. Lavigne, *Les économies socialistes soviétique et européennes*, 3ème ed. (Paris: Armand Colin, 1979) p. 16.
176. W. Andreff, 'Capitalisme d'Etat ou monopolisme d'Etat en U.R.S.S.? – Propos d'étape' in M. Lavigne, *Economie politique de la planification en système socialiste* (Paris: Economica, 1978) p. 251.
177. Strmiska, 'Programme socialiste et rapports sociaux en U.R.S.S. et dans les pays socialistes', p. 136.
178. Andreff, 'Capitalisme d'Etat ou monopolisme d'Etat en U.R.S.S.?', p. 249.
179. Ibid., pp. 249–50.
180. Nove, 'The Class Nature of the Soviet Union Revisited', p. 309.
181. Strmiska, 'Programme socialiste et rapports sociaux en U.R.S.S. et dans les pays socialistes', p. 225.
182. Nove, 'The Class Nature of the Soviet Union Revisited', p. 303.
183. Jean-Jacques Marie, 'La bureaucratie et l'opposition face à la convergence', *Le Monde diplomatique* (August 1975) p. 10.
184. W. Andreff, 'Vers une théorie de la congruence des systèmes', in M. Lavigne (ed.), *Travail et monnaie en système socialiste* (Paris: Economica, 1981) p. 288.
185. Favouring an analytical approach to the Soviet economy that confronts, in a dialectical fashion, the existing reality with the more abstract Marxist concepts, Andreff lays great stress on the collection and analysis of data as well as on scientific observation. For an example of Andreff's approach, see URGENSE, 'Un taylorisme arythmique dans les économies planifiées du centre', *Critiques de l'économie politique*, no. 19 (April–June 1982) pp. 99–146 and Wladimir Andreff, 'L'organisation du travail dans les entreprises socialistes', *Reflets et Perspectives de la vie économique*, tome xxii, nos 4/5 (1983) pp. 277–87.
186. Lavigne, *Les économies socialistes soviétique et européennes*, p. 16.
187. Ibid., p. 423.
188. M. Lavigne, *Economie internationale des pays socialistes* (Paris: Armand Colin, 1985) p. 96.
189. Lavigne, *Les économies socialistes soviétique et européennes*, p. 277.
190. Ibid., p. 421.
191. Ibid., p. 423.
192. Ibid.
193. Ibid., p. 45.
194. Ibid.
195. Ibid.
196. Ibid., p. 46.
197. B. Kerblay and M. Lavigne, *Les Soviétiques des années 80* (Paris: Armand Colin, 1985) p. 83.

198. Lavigne, *Economie internationale des pays socialistes*, p. 32.
199. Kerblay and Lavigne, *Les Soviétiques des années 80*, p. 57. In recent years, a few young French scholars have devoted some specific attention to the notion of 'crisis' in the context of the Soviet-type economy. See, for instance, M. Drach, *La crise dans les pays de l'Est* (Paris: Editions La Découverte, 1984) and X. Richet, *Crises à l'Est?* (Lyon: Presses Universitaires de Lyon, 1984).
200. As to Soviet agriculture, Lavigne acknowledges that the necessity of reforms in this sector of the Soviet economy is urgent. In her view, the major sources of the difficulties plaguing Soviet agriculture lie outside it, that is, in Soviet industry. One must note that she dismisses as simplistic the idea of a *per se* inefficiency of a planned agriculture such as the Soviet one. For a different viewpoint on this question, see Basile Kerblay, 'Les enseignements de l'expérience soviétique d'agriculture collectiviste (Résultats, problèmes et perspectives)', *Revue d'études comparatives Est–Ouest*, vol. x, no. 3 (September 1979) p. 27.
201. J.-C. Asselain, *Plan et profit en économie socialiste* (Paris: Presses de la Fondation Nationale des Sciences Politiques, 1981), p. 265.
202. Lavigne, *Les économies socialistes soviétique et européennes*, p. 175.

3 Totalitarianism and Ideology

1. A. Brown, 'Political Power and the Soviet State: Western and Soviet Perspectives', in N. Harding (ed.), *The State in Socialist Society* (London: Macmillan, 1984) p. 51.
2. Brown, *Soviet Politics and Political Science*, p. 35.
3. J. Marquès-Rivière, *L'URSS dans le Monde – L'expansion soviétique de 1918 à 1935* (Paris: Payot, 1935) p. 10. (my emphasis)
4. J. Monnerot, *Sociologie du communisme* (Paris: Gallimard, 1949) trans. by J. Degras and R. Rees as *Sociology of Communism* (London: Allen & Unwin, 1953).
5. T. Maulnier, *La face de méduse du communisme* (Paris: Gallimard, 1951).
6. Ibid., p. 109–10.
7. Ibid., p. 113.
8. M. Duverger, *Les orangers du Lac Balaton* (Paris: Seuil, 1980) p. 170. (my emphasis)
9. C. Lefort, 'La logique totalitaire', *Kontinent Skandinavia* (1980), reprinted in Lefort, *L'Invention démocratique – Les limites de la domination totalitaire*, p. 90.
10. Ibid., p. 94.
11. C. Lefort, 'L'image du corps et le totalitarisme', *Confrontation*, 2 (Autumn 1979), reprinted in Lefort, *L'Invention démocratique – Les limites de la domination totalitaire*, p. 159.
12. Lefort, *Eléments d'une critique de la bureaucratie*, p. 22.
13. Pierre Hassner, 'American Foxes and French Hedgehogs? A French Perspective on East European Studies', *Studies in Comparative Communism*, vol. xv, no. 4 (Winter 1982) p. 367.

14. Pierre Hassner, 'Le pacifisme est-il l'aveu d'un pessimisme total?', *Le Nouvel Observateur*, no. 920 (2 June 1982) p. 38.
15. Olivier Mongin, 'Hannah Arendt – Penser ce que nous faisons', *Esprit*, no. 42 (June 1980) pp. 3–4.
16. Raymond Aron, 'L'essence du totalitarisme', *Critique*, vol. 10 (January 1954) p. 68.
17. Raymond Aron, 'Soviet Society in Transition', *Problems of Communism*, vol. vi, no. 6 (November–December 1957) p. 7.
18. Ibid., p. 6.
19. First published in 1946 in a Bulletin de la Société française de philosophie, this lecture has been, in the wake of Aron's death, reprinted in *Commentaire*, vol. 6, no. 24 (Winter 1983–4) pp. 702–10. Interestingly, one observes that Aron does not label the Soviet regime totalitarian. As a matter of fact, such a label is applied only to the German and Italian regimes of the day. At one point, Aron even writes about some kind of opposition existing between these regimes and the Communist one. On the whole, Aron's attitude is somewhat ambiguous, considering that the definition he then gives of a totalitarian regime, that is, a 'particular mixture of demagogy, technique, irrational faith and police' (p. 710) obviously tallies with known 1939 Soviet realities. Such a willingness to be indulgent to the Soviet Union has been explained in the *Mémoires*. As he confesses, not only was his anti-Communist feeling then 'half-repressed' because of his friendships and because of the need for Soviet support against the Third Reich, but also that his definitive rupture with what he calls the '*préjugés de la gauche*' did not take place until 1945. See R. Aron, *Mémoires – 50 ans de réflexion politique* (Paris: Julliard, 1983) p. 158 and p. 153.
20. François Furet, 'Quand Aron raconte notre histoire . . .', *Le Nouvel Observateur*, no. 982 (2 September 1983) p. 48.
21. R. Aron, *Démocratie et totalitarisme* (Paris: Gallimard, 1965) trans. by V. Ionescu as *Democracy and Totalitarianism* (London: Weidenfeld and Nicolson, 1968).
22. Aron, *Democracy and Totalitarianism*, pp. 193–4. Aron was particularly conscious of the uniqueness of totalitarian terror. He was struck by its irrational and absurd character: 'Why, after 1936, did we see the unleashing of the great purge . . . although . . . the regime was no longer in danger? Why was there a purge, when the battle was already won?'. Aron, ibid., p. 199. On a sociological level, Aron maintains that the Party's organisational structure and Leninist modes of action may shed light on the intelligibility of the Great Purge's aberrations, but adds that these features do not imply their necessity. At this point, the sociological explanation gives way to a historical one. As pointed out by C. Polin, 'history arrives in the nick of time to introduce just enough contingency to illuminate the irrational'. See C. Polin, *L'esprit totalitaire* (Paris: Sirey, 1977) p. 34. So, Aron points to a man, Stalin. As he puts it, 'To pass from the potential to the actual, from the comprehensible reasons for the purge to the excesses of the great purge, something quite unique was needed – Stalin himself'. Aron, ibid., p. 202. On Aron's analysis of the totalitarian terror, see Polin's book cited above, esp. pages 30 to 36.

23. R. Aron, *Plaidoyer pour l'Europe décadente* (Paris: Robert Laffont, 1977) p. 472.
24. A. Besançon, *Court traité de soviétologie à l'usage des autorités civiles, militaires et religieuses* (Paris: Hachette, 1976) reprinted in A. Besançon, *Présent soviétique et passé russe* (Paris: Librairie Générale Française, 1980). I am using this recent edition.
25. Ibid., pp. 182–3.
26. Aron, *Democracy and Totalitarianism*, p. 216.
27. Jules Monnerot, 'Le totalitarisme: la droite et la gauche', *La Nef*, 5ème Année, no. 41 (April 1948) pp. 21–37.
28. Monnerot, *Sociology of Communism*, p. 225.
29. Ibid., p. 213.
30. Ibid., p. 216.
31. Ibid., p. 225.
32. Monnerot, 'Le totalitarisme: la droite et la gauche', p. 23.
33. Monnerot, *Sociology of Communism*, p. 223.
34. Ibid., p. 214.
35. Ibid.
36. Monnerot, 'Le totalitarisme: la droite et la gauche', p. 32.
37. Aron, *Democracy and Totalitarianism*, p. 195.
38. Aron, 'L'essence du totalitarisme', p. 63.
39. Aron, *Democracy and Totalitarianism*, p. 195.
40. Ibid., pp. 203–4.
41. Ibid., p. 204.
42. A. Besançon, 'De la difficulté de définir le régime soviétique', *Contrepoint*, no. 20 (February 1976) p. 120. (my emphasis)
43. Aron, *Democracy and Totalitarianism*, p. 185.
44. The word 'ideocracy' is referred to by Aron in *Democracy and Totalitarianism*. But, as indicated, it has come into prominence in recent writings, such as in his book *Plaidoyer pour l'Europe décadente*. In an article contributed to a 1980 issue of *Commentaire*, Aron reiterates his ideas and goes so far as to characterise the Soviet regime as 'militarised ideocracy'. See Raymond Aron, 'L'hégémonisme soviétique: An I', *Commentaire*, vol. III, no. 11 (1980) p. 362.
45. Raymond Aron, 'On Liberalization', *Government and Opposition*, vol. 14, no. 1 (Winter 1979) p. 51.
46. Duverger, *Les orangers du Lac Balaton*, p. 170.
47. Aron, *Democracy and Totalitarianism*, p. 196.
48. Duverger, *Les orangers du Lac Balaton*, p. 171.
49. Ibid., p. 169.
50. Ibid.
51. Ibid.
52. Maurice Duverger, 'La seconde étape', *Le Monde* (28 June 1956) pp. 1 and 6.
53. M. Duverger, *Introduction à la politique* (Paris: Gallimard, 1964) p. 367.
54. M. Duverger, *Janus, les deux faces de l'Occident* (Paris: Fayard, 1972) p. 262.
55. R. Aron, *Dix-huit leçons sur la société industrielle* (Paris: Gallimard, 1962).

56. The theory of convergence, it is worth noting, was also rejected by L. Laurat, who characterised as utopians its advocates. See Lucien Laurat, 'Libéralisme et "libéralisation"', *Le Contrat Social*, vol. xi, no. 1 (1967) p. 18 and Lucien Laurat, 'Convergence Est–Ouest?', *Est et Ouest*, vol. 15, no. 309 (16–30 November 1963) pp. 16–18.

57. Aron, *Mémoires*, pp. 402–3.

58. Raymond Aron, 'Société industrielle, idéologies, philosophie (ii)', *Preuves*, no. 168 (February 1965) p. 19.

59. Aron, *Democracy and Totalitarianism*, p. 251.

60. Ibid., p. 225.

61. Aron, *Plaidoyer pour l'Europe décadente*, p. 301.

62. Aron, 'Société industrielle, idéologies, philosophie (ii)', p. 17.

63. As Aron explains, 'Personally I would say that modern industrial societies . . . are differentiated above all by the way public powers are organized . . . In our century everything happens as if, within the kind of society called industrial, it is politics which determines the different variations'. *Democracy and Totalitarianism*, p. 11.

64. Ibid., p. 6.

65. Ibid., p. 11.

66. Ibid., p. 9.

67. R. Aron, *La lutte de classes – nouvelles leçons sur les sociétés industrielles* (Paris: Gallimard, 1964).

68. Ibid., p. 324.

69. Aron, *Democracy and Totalitarianism*, p. 9.

70. See Aron, *Plaidoyer pour l'Europe décadente*, pp. 101–2.

71. Interview with R. Aron at the Maison des Sciences de l'Homme, Paris, 5 November 1982.

72. Aron, *La lutte de classes – nouvelles leçons sur les sociétés industrielles*, p. 152. Indeed, Aron fully takes account of the presence within Soviet society of diversified and contradictory interests. In the light of such a sociological reality, the regime must assume what Aron calls a necessary 'tâche d'arbitrage' which in the Soviet Union, as pointed out, 'takes place . . . in obscurity, in accordance with procedures that are not "institutionalized" and little-known to observers foreign to the secrets of the system itself'. See Raymond Aron, 'Remarques sur un débat', *Archives européennes de sociologie*, vol. xiii, no. 1 (1972) p. 71.

73. Raymond Aron, 'Classe sociale, classe politique, classe dirigeante', *Archives européennes de sociologie*, vol. i, no. 2 (1960) p. 271.

74. C. Lefort, 'Le Totalitarisme sans Staline', *Socialisme ou Barbarie*, vol. iv, no. 19 (July–September 1956) reprinted in Lefort, *Eléments d'une critique de la bureaucratie*, pp. 155–235.

75. C. Lefort, *Un Homme en trop – Réflexion sur l'Archipel du Goulag* (Paris: Seuil, 1976).

76. Lefort, *L'Invention démocratique – Les limites de la domination totalitaire*.

77. Descamps, 'Claude Lefort le peuple et le pouvoir' (interview with C. Lefort), p. ix.

78. Translated excerpt in Howard, 'Introduction to Castoriadis', p. 120, note 8.

79. Lefort, *Un homme en trop*, p. 72.

80. Lefort, 'L'image du corps et le totalitarisme' (in *L'Invention démocratique*) p. 165.
81. Lefort, 'La logique totalitaire' (in *L'Invention démocratique*), p. 101. In Lefort's mind, Soviet totalitarianism came into existence through sheer and widespread violence exerted by the party on the society. At this point, mention must be made of the 'Egocrat' who is intrinsic, in Lefort's eyes, to the erection or emergence of a totalitarian society. Stalin was an 'Egocrat', a hideous and derisory incarnation of the totalitarian man. Theoretically, as he notes, the totalitarian regime tends at a later stage to get rid of the 'Egocrat', so devastating are his excesses even for the regime itself. See Lefort, 'Staline et le stalinisme' (in *L'Invention démocratique*) pp. 107–27.
82. Lefort, 'La logique totalitaire' (in *L'Invention démocratique*), p. 101.
83. As noted by Monnerot in 1948, 'the totalitarian regime considers itself to be in a state of . . . continual siege'. Monnerot, 'Le totalitarisme: la droite et la gauche', p. 32.
84. M. Heller, *La machine et les rouages – la formation de l'homme soviétique* (Paris: Calmann-Lévy, 1985) p. 285.
85. Descamps, 'Claude Lefort le peuple et le pouvoir', p. x.
86. Lefort, 'L'image du corps et le totalitarisme' (in *L'Invention démocratique'*) pp. 172–3.
87. Lefort, 'Le Totalitarisme sans Staline' (in *Eléments d'une critique de la bureaucratie*) p. 208.
88. Ibid., p. 190.
89. Lefort, 'La logique totalitaire' (in *L'Invention démocratique*) p. 104. Lefort's idea is somewhat reminiscent of Monnerot who, in his 1948 article in *La Nef*, wrote of a single political party that '*occupies* the State, consequently transformed by this very occupation'. Monnerot, 'Le totalitarisme: la droite et la gauche', p. 22.
90. Ibid., p. 105.
91. Marc Ferro, a historian who has written about the genesis of bureaucratic totalitarianism in the Soviet Union, is at variance with Lefort about the question of consensus within the Soviet Union. In Ferro's mind, there exists a simple but essential phenomenon which cannot be overlooked, that is 'the existence, in USSR, of a broad consensus'. In this context, Ferro, unlike Lefort, considers that the social organisations which have recently proliferated help, in the last analysis, to broaden the popular consensus in favour of the Soviet regime. M. Ferro, *Des Soviets au communisme bureaucratique* (Paris: Gallimard/Julliard, 1980) pp. 12 and 226. See also M. Ferro, *L'Occident devant la révolution soviétique* (Bruxelles: Editions Complexe, 1980) pp. 112–13.
92. Claude Lefort, 'La première révolution anti-totalitaire', *Esprit*, no. 1 (January 1977) p. 14.
93. Ibid., p. 15.
94. C. Lefort, 'Reculer les frontières du possible', *Esprit* (January 1981) reprinted in Lefort, *L'Invention démocratique*, p. 329.
95. Lefort, 'La première révolution anti-totalitaire', p. 15.
96. E. Morin, *De la Nature de l'URSS – Complexe totalitaire et nouvel Empire* (Paris: Fayard, 1983).

97. For a presentation of the group and a discussion of its efforts to revitalise Marxist thought, see Poster, *Existential Marxism in Postwar France – From Sartre to Althusser*, pp. 209–63 and Gil Delannoi, 'Arguments, 1956–1962 ou la parenthèse de l'ouverture', *Revue française de science politique*, vol. 34, no. 1 (February 1984) pp. 127–45.

98. Morin, *De la Nature de l'URSS*, p. 271.

99. Eric Vigne, 'Lectures du stalinisme', *Communisme*, 3 (1983) p. 133.

100. Morin, *De la Nature de l'URSS*, p. 165.

101. Morin was receptive to the analysis of the Russian regime propounded in the 1950s by Socialisme ou Barbarie.

102. Pierre Hassner, 'Le miroir totalitaire – Le totalitarisme soviétique vu de l'ouest', *Commentaire*, vol. 7, no. 26 (Summer 1984) p. 202.

103. G. Nivat, *Vers la fin du mythe russe – Essais sur la culture russe de Gogol à nos jours* (Lausanne: L'Age d'Homme, 1982) p. 10.

104. Zaleski, *La planification stalinienne – croissance et fluctuations économiques en U.R.S.S. 1933–1952*, p. 647.

105. Monnerot, 'Le totalitarisme: la droite et la gauche', p. 29.

106. Sophie Lannes and Branko Lazitch, 'La technique du pouvoir en U.R.S.S.', *L'Express*, no. 1430 (2 December 1978) p. 194.

107. Ibid.

108. A. Besançon, *Court traité de soviétologie à l'usage des autorités civiles, militaires et religieuses* (hereafter *Court traité*) (Paris: Hachette, 1976) reprinted in Besançon, *Présent soviétique et passé russe*, p. 280.

109. Alain Besançon, '1984: Orwell et nous', *L'Express*, no. 1685 (28 October 1983) p. 88.

110. Lannes and Lazitch, 'La technique du pouvoir en U.R.S.S.', p. 221. Besançon, as he once made clear, takes it 'to be a general rule that in any one country at any one time there are rarely more than a dozen minds capable of understanding the Soviet phenomenon and of translating what they know into politically usable terms'. See Alain Besançon, 'The End of the Soviet Mirage', *Encounter*, vol. LVII, no. 1 (July 1981) p. 90.

111. Alain Besançon, 'Mort d'un cadavre', *L'Express*, no. 1702 (24 February 1984) p. 29.

112. A. Besançon, *Anatomie d'un spectre – L'économie politique du socialisme réel* (Paris: Calmann-Lévy, 1981) p. 19.

113. Alain Besançon, 'Débat – L'avenir de l'Union soviétique', *Pouvoirs*, 6 (1978) p. 111. One may note that, unlike Besançon, Aron takes the view that the Soviet economy can be well understood through the concepts developed and used in the West. See R. Aron, *Les dernières années du siècle* (Paris: Julliard, 1984) pp. 120–1.

114. Monnerot, *Sociology of Communism*, p. 22.

115. Besançon, *Court traité* (in *Présent soviétique et passé russe*), p. 202.

116. Besançon, 'De la difficulté de définir le régime soviétique', p. 119.

117. The historian and specialist of the PCF Annie Kriegel also views as a dangerous trap the idea of a historical continuity between the Russian Empire and the Soviet Union. In her opinion, the Soviet Union is not just the old Russia that has changed its name. See A. Kriegel, *Le*

système communiste mondial (Paris: Presses Universitaires de France, 1984) p. 14.

118. Alain Besançon, 'Les failles de l'Union Soviétique', *Défense Nationale*, 37ème Année (November 1981) p. 39.

119. A. Besançon, *The Intellectual Origins of Leninism*, trans. by S. Matthews (Oxford: Basil Blackwell, 1981) p. 7, originally *Les Origines intellectuelles du léninisme* (Paris: Calmann-Lévy, 1977).

120. Ibid., p. 52.

121. Marquès-Rivière, '*L'URSS dans le Monde*', p. 361.

122. Monnerot, *Sociology of Communism*, p. 9.

123. B. Kerblay, *La société soviétique contemporaine* (Paris: Armand Colin, 1977) p. 268.

124. Basile Kerblay, 'Où va le régime soviétique?', *Esprit* (1973) p. 658. In this context, see also M. Garder who has unambiguously asserted that the Soviet regime constitutes a 'regime of a religious essence' in which, he adds, the party leadership are the 'priests of a dead religion'. See Michel Garder, 'Un régime condamné', *Contrepoint*, no. 2 (October 1970) pp. 126 and 122. See also 'Où va l'Union soviétique', *Revue politique et parlementaire*, no. 757 (June 1965) pp. 42–50.

125. Kerblay and Lavigne, *Les Soviétiques des années 80*, p. 40.

126. Besançon, 'The Intellectual Origins of Leninism', p. 9.

127. Ibid. In *Sociology of Communism*, Monnerot had written: 'Believers believe they know; they believe only in knowledge and do not know that they believe'. See Monnerot, *Sociology of Communism*, p. 155.

128. Ibid.

129. Alain Besançon, 'La conviction idéologique: avant et après la prise du pouvoir', *Cadmos*, 3ème Année, no. 11 (Fall 1980) p. 41.

130. Besançon, *Court traité* (in *Présent soviétique et passé russe*) pp. 276–7.

131. Besançon, 'Les failles de l'Union Soviétique', p. 35.

132. For him, this chimera for Eastern Europe has been 'the school of under-development'. See Alain Besançon, 'L'autre Europe', *L'Express*, no. 1747 (4 January 1985) p. 69.

133. D. Colas, *Le léninisme – Philosophie et sociologie politiques du léninisme* (Paris: Presses Universitaires de France, 1982) p. 262.

134. Alain Besançon, 'Présent soviétique et passé russe', *Contrepoint*, no. 14 (May 1974) p. 31.

135. Besançon, *The Intellectual Origins of Leninism*, p. 282.

136. Besançon, *Court traité* (in *Présent soviétique et passé russe*) p. 196. For Aron's viewpoint as to Besançon's idea of alternation, see Aron, *Plaidoyer pour l'Europe décadente*, pp. 162–3.

137. Besançon, 'La conviction idéologique: avant et après la prise du pouvoir', p. 45.

138. Ibid.

139. The term 'surreality' also appears in Aron's *Democracy and Totalitarianism*, p. 193. In his *Plaidoyer pour l'Europe décadente*, Aron praises Besançon for having 'rediscovered' and brilliantly used the notion of 'surreality' in his *Court traité de soviétologie*.

140. Bruno Frappat and Dominique Wolton, 'L'optimisme glacé de

Raymond Aron' (interview with R. Aron), *Le Monde Dimanche* (21 September 1980) p. XVII. It may be worth observing that Aron argues, as far back as 1954, that the source of such a phenomenon, or what he calls 'the principle of all lies', was already well established during Lenin's lifetime. In Aron's view, Lenin must be held responsible for the permanent substitution of ideology to reality in the Soviet Union. See Aron, 'L'essence du totalitarisme', p. 63. Such an early viewpoint was recently reiterated by Aron in his *Plaidoyer pour l'Europe décadente*, p. 81. Finally, mention ought to be made of the fact that the characterisation of the Soviet Union as a land where the 'mensonge' triumphantly reigns was advocated as far back as the 1930s by B. Souvarine: 'The U.S.S.R. is the land of the lie, of the absolute lie . . . The Constitution contains many lies per clause. The lie is the natural element of the pseudo-Soviet society . . . The Party, Élite of the population: lie. The rights of the people, democracy . . . lies. The five-year plans, statistics, results . . . lies. The meetings and congresses: theatre, stage-settings. The dictatorship of the proletariat: immense imposture. The masses' spontaneity: meticulous organisation'. See Boris Souvarine, 'Aveux à Moscou', *La vie intellectuelle* (10 April 1938) pp. 59–60. See also S. Labin, *Stalin's Russia*, p. 161; C. Wilczkowski, 'L'aspect czariste du régime stalinien', *Travaux de l'Action populaire*, Nlle série, no. 16 (January 1948) p. 58; E. Delimars, 'Mentalité des cadres en U.R.S.S.', *Le Contrat Social*, vol. V, no. 3 (May–June) p. 164 and, more recently, Jacques Laurent, 'Connaissons-nous l'armée soviétique?', *L'autre Europe*, no. 3 (1984) p. 10.

141. Lannes and Lazitch, 'La technique du pouvoir en U.R.S.S', p. 207.
142. Besançon, *The Intellectual Origins of Leninism*, p. 284.
143. Ibid., p. 287.
144. Ibid., p. 288.
145. A. Besançon, 'Eloge de la corruption en Union soviétique', Foreword to Ilja Zemtsov, *La corruption en Union soviétique* (Paris: Hachette, 1976). This foreword is reprinted in Besançon, *Présent soviétique et passé russe*, p. 308.
146. Besançon, *Court traité* (in *Présent soviétique et passé russe*) p. 210.
147. Basile Kerblay, 'Les problèmes de la socialisation dans le milieu rural soviétique', *Cahiers du Monde Russe et Soviétique*, vol. XXI, no. 3–4 (July–December 1980) p. 272. As P. Lorrain has observed, 'At home, the individual can really . . . rediscover his true nature, be natural and indulge in 'exteriorizing'' his personality'. See P. Lorrain, *L'Évangile selon Saint-Marx – La pression idéologique dans la vie quotidienne en URSS* (Paris: Belfond, 1982) p. 199.
148. Ibid., p. 268.
149. Besançon, *Anatomie d'un spectre – L'économie politique du socialisme réel*, p. 147.
150. As far as this specific aspect of Besançon's analysis is concerned, there is little doubt that an evolution has taken place. This change, as mentioned, may be linked to some of the ideas put forward in the late 1970s by Zinoviev. One may gauge this change when reading, for instance, a 1973 assertion by Besançon as to who benefits from the

Soviet regime. As he then explained: 'Who, in the Soviet Union, is objectively interested in maintaining the present regime? Neither the peasants, . . . Nor the workers . . . Nor the employees . . . The regime can only count upon the direct beneficiaries, the members of the Party, the privileged cadres'. See Alain Besançon *et al.*, 'Où va le régime soviétique?', *Esprit* (November 1973) p. 625.

151. Besançon, *Anatomie d'un spectre – L'économie politique du socialisme réel*, pp. 149–50.

152. Emmanuel LeRoy Ladurie, 'L'Union soviétique analysée par Alain Besançon', *Le Monde* (11 April 1980) p. 18.

153. Edgar Morin, 'From the Stalinist era to the Stalinistic era (Fragments)', *The Review*, vol. 5, no. 3 (1963) p. 6.

154. Georges Nivat, '"Langue de bois" et "Langue de vie" dans la Russie d'aujourd'hui', *Cadmos*, no. 26/7 (Summer/Fall 1984) p. 109. A few writers have dismissed the expression as being too polemical and journalistic and have chosen to refer to the 'Soviet political discourse'. See, for instance, P. Seriot, *Analyse du discours politique soviétique* (Paris: Institut d'Etudes Slaves, 1985). The book, concerned with syntactical phenomena, is an example of semiological erudition. In this context, see also the periodical *Essais sur le discours soviétique* published by the University of Grenoble since the early 1980s.

155. Louis Martinez, 'La "langue de bois" soviétique', *Commentaire*, vol. 4, no. 16 (Winter 1981–2) p. 508.

156. Ibid., p. 511.

157. Ibid., p. 515.

158. In Besançon's opinion, 'heteroglossy is the first sign of rebellion'. See Besançon, *The Intellectual Origins of Leninism*, p. 308.

159. Other writers disagree with the use of the notion of 'ideocracy'. L. Sochor, for one, argues that the notion is somewhat obsolete, since the Soviet élite clearly does not exercise its domination in the name of ideas, as it used to do in the early period of the Soviet regime. See Lubomir Sochor, 'Le "socialisme réel", une idéologie tournée vers le passé', *Les Temps Modernes*, 41ème Année, no. 468/9 (July–August 1985) p. 232.

160. Bettelheim, *Les luttes de classes en URSS – 3ème période 1930–1941 – Les Dominants*, p. 66.

161. Ibid.

162. C. Orsini, 'Le régime idéologique soviétique et la dissidence', in *Chronique des petites gens d'URSS*, p. 167. See also Lorrain, *L'Évangile selon Saint-Marx – La pression idéologique dans la vie quotidienne en URSS*, p. 99.

163. Besançon, 'Eloge de la corruption en Union soviétique' (in *Présent soviétique et passé russe*), p. 308.

164. Besançon, *The Intellectual Origins of Leninism*, p. 288.
     The same idea is also spelled out in Besançon, 'La conviction idéologique: avant et après la prise du pouvoir', p. 51.

165. Heller, *La machine et les rouages – la formation de l'homme soviétique*, p. 243.

166. Sochor, 'Le "socialisme réel"', une idéologie tournée vers le passé', p. 231.
167. Besançon, *Court traité* (in *Présent soviétique et passé russe*), p. 236.
168. Ibid., p. 287.
169. Monnerot, *Sociology of Communism*, p. 115.
170. Besançon, 'La conviction idéologique: avant et après la prise du pouvoir', p. 52.
171. Besançon, *The Intellectual Origins of Leninism*, p. 289.
172. Alain Besançon, 'Pourquoi aller à Moscou?', *L'Express*, no. 1709 (13 April 1984) p. 49.
173. Besançon, 'La conviction idéologique: avant et après la prise du pouvoir', p. 47. In this context, it is interesting to note that Besançon has wondered about the reasons which caused Lenin to become an ideologue. As he points out, 'What internal catastrophe forced Lenin to secrete this huge and complicated prosthesis of self, this elementary but coherent "Marxism", which he could not question without endangering his own identity, without feeling a threat which he exorcized . . . by annihilating the instigators of doubt? . . . It is hopeless to speculate, we will never know'. See Besançon, *The Intellectual Origins of Leninism*, p. 197.
174. Todd, *La Chute finale – essai sur la décomposition de la sphère soviétique*, p. 58.
175. Besançon, 'La conviction idéologique: avant et après la prise du pouvoir', p. 52.
176. On this phenomenon of rampant corruption in the Soviet Union see P. Meney, *La Kleptocratie – La délinquance en URSS* (Paris: La Table Ronde, 1982) esp. Chapter 5. See also Christian Jelen and Leopold Unger, 'L'Etat kleptocratique ou comment gagner de l'argent à l'Est', *L'Express*, no. 1465 (11 August 1979) pp. 58–64 and Alexandre Adler, 'Le problème de la corruption en U.R.S.S.', *Pouvoirs*, 31 (1984) pp. 105–13.
177. Besançon, *Anatomie d'un spectre – L'économie politique du socialisme réel*, p. 66.
178. Besançon, 'Eloge de la corruption en Union soviétique' (in *Présent soviétique et passé russe*), p. 302.
179. Ibid., p. 305. (my emphasis)
180. Besançon, 'Les failles de l'Union Soviétique', p. 40.
181. Besançon, 'Eloge de la corruption en Union soviétique' (in *Présent soviétique et passé russe*), p. 310.
182. Ibid., p. 311.
183. Besançon, 'Les failles de l'Union Soviétique', p. 41.
    See also A. Besançon, 'L'Empire russe et la domination soviétique', in M. Duverger (ed.) *Le concept d'empire* (Paris: Presses Universitaires de France, 1980) p. 373.
184. Besançon, 'Eloge de la corruption en Union soviétique' (in *Présent soviétique et passé russe*), p. 312.
185. Aron, *Plaidoyer pour l'Europe décadente*, p. 472. We believe that Aron, in this affirmation, shows a degree of theoretical laxity in the

choice of well-defined notions which are steadily present throughout his analysis of the social structure of the Soviet Union. It is our opinion that the notion of 'political class' which Aron regards as *the* essential component of the Soviet élite should have been used. It would have reflected with more accuracy what Aron really meant in 1977. See Aron, 'Remarques sur un débat', p. 78. For a viewpoint close to Aron's see Jean Vineuil, 'Les hommes de Moscou', *Preuves*, no. 167 (January 1965) p. 65.

186. G. Nivat, *Vers la fin du mythe russe – Essais sur la culture russe de Gogol à nos jours*, p. 189.

187. Strmiska, 'Programme socialiste et rapports sociaux en U.R.S.S. et dans les pays socialistes', p. 196.
On this general question, the analysis developed by Henri Chambre is worthy of mention. In a number of writings Chambre sets out to study the Soviet superstructure, seeking more particularly to establish the extent to which some of its major components – such as law, ethics and economic science – may have strayed, with the passing of time, from original Marxist tenets. He shows how ideology has historically undergone serious transformations in contact with the Soviet Union's realities. See Chambre's classic *Le Marxisme en Union soviétique – Idéologie et institutions Leur évolution de 1917 à nos jours* (Paris: Seuil, 1955). Finally, see also *L'évolution du marxisme soviétique – Théorie économique et droit* (Paris: Seuil, 1974). This book corresponds to Chambre's need to examine some aspects of the Soviet Union's ideological evolution in the post-Stalin era. Concentrating, as the title reveals, on Soviet law and economic theory, Chambre formulates the idea that these superstructural components have evolved in response to a real Soviet concern for greater rationality. Needless to say Chambre had very little impact, if any at all, on Besançon, who has been very ready, with a stroke of the pen, to discard his colleague's erudite work.

188. See M.-C. Maurel, *La campagne collectivisée – société et espace rural en Russie* (Paris: Editions Anthropos, 1980) pp. 231, 275–6 and 279.

189. Aron, *Les dernières années du siècle*, p. 117. In this connection, Aron once wrote that detente, in Soviet minds, can only be 'a mere modality of the ruthless struggle between the two camps'. See Raymond Aron, 'Ils ont choisi le plus intelligent', *L'Express*, no. 1637 (26 November 1982) p. 55. The point made by Aron in his posthumously published book has often been made in French writings on the Soviet Union. See, for instance, Michel Mouskhély, 'La révolution communiste en marche – A propos du nouveau programme', *Res Publica*, vol. iv, 4 (1962) p. 330 and, more recently M. Tatu, *Eux et nous – Les relations Est–Ouest entre deux détentes* (Paris: Fayard, 1985) pp. 35 and 39–40.

190. The question of ideological 'overestimating' has been touched on by Georges Lavau in a short article investigating the link between Communist states' foreign policy and ideology. According to the published summary, Lavau claims that any understanding of the role of ideology in foreign policy 'requires to distinguish *a*) between various ideology's levels, *b*) between its various uses (motivation, tool for analysis, rationalizing, resource of power, resource for the system's

cohesion)'. See Georges Lavau, 'Le rapport entre l'idéologie et la politique extérieure', *Pouvoirs*, 21 (1982) p. 138.

191. J. M. Vincent, 'Le marxisme et les contradictions du "socialisme réellement existant"', in E. Pisier-Kouchner (ed.), *Les interprétations du Stalinisme*, p. 293.

192. Aron, *Democracy and Totalitarianism*, pp. 215–16.

4 Institutional Analyses

1. Carrère d'Encausse, Introduction to L. Marcou, *L'Union soviétique*, p. 23.

2. P. Gélard, *L'administration locale en U.R.S.S.* (Paris: Presses Universitaires de France, 1972).

3. P. Gélard, *Les systèmes politiques des Etats socialistes*, Tome premier – Le modèle soviétique, Tome deux – Transpositions et transformations du modèle soviétique (Paris: Cujas, 1975).

4. Gélard, *Les systèmes politiques des Etats socialistes*, Tome premier, p. 297.

5. Patrice Gélard, 'Le consensus en Union soviétique', *Pouvoirs*, 5 (1978) p. 135.

6. Ibid., pp. 135–6.

7. Gélard, *Les systèmes politiques des Etats socialistes*, Tome premier, p. 367.

8. P. Gélard, 'Le phénomène du parti unique dans les Etats socialistes', in G. Conac, H. Maisl and J. Vaudiaux (eds), *Itinéraires – Etudes en l'honneur de Léo Hamon* (Paris: Economica, 1982) p. 290.

9. Gélard, *Les systèmes politiques des Etats socialistes*, Tome premier, p. 312.

10. Ibid.

11. Gélard, 'Le consensus en Union soviétique', p. 137.

12. Patrice Gélard, 'Des enjeux nouveaux', *La Nouvelle Critique*, no. 108 (November 1977) p. 60.

13. Patrice Gélard, 'La Constitution d'octobre 1977', *Problèmes politiques et sociaux*, no. 326 (23 December 1977) p. 37.

14. Gélard, *Les systèmes politiques des Etats socialistes*, Tome premier, p. 178.

15. Gélard, 'Le consensus en Union soviétique', p. 137.

16. M. Lesage, *Les régimes politiques de l'U.R.S.S. et de l'Europe de l'Est* (Paris: Presses Universitaires de France, 1971).

17. Gélard, *Les systèmes politiques des Etats socialistes*, Tome deux, p. 652.

18. Strmiska, 'Programme socialiste et rapports sociaux en U.R.S.S. et dans les pays socialistes', p. 161. On the real meaning given by the party leadership to the popular discussion on the draft of the Constitution of 1977, see Francis Conte and Dimitri G. Lavroff, 'La Constitution de l'Union des républiques socialistes soviétiques du 7 Octobre 1977', *Revue du droit public et de la science politique en France et à l'étranger*, vol. 94. no. 3 (May–June 1978) pp. 694 and 696.

19. C. Revuz, *Ivan Ivanovitch écrit à 'la Pravda'* (Paris: Editions Sociales, 1980) p. 292.
20. Z. Strmiska, 'Pouvoir politique et inégalités sociales', in P. Kende and Z. Strmiska (eds), *Egalité et inégalités en Europe de l'Est*, p. 376.
21. Maurice Duverger, 'Les régimes de type russe', *La Vie intellectuelle*, 16ème Année (February 1948) p. 55.
22. Thomas Lowit, 'Le parti polymorphe en Europe de l'Est', *Revue française de science politique*, vol. 29, no. 4–5 (August–October 1979) p. 827.
23. Ibid., p. 813.
24. Thomas Lowit, 'Y-a-t-il des Etats en Europe de l'Est?', *Revue française de sociologie*, vol. xx, no. 2 (April–June 1979) p. 447. In the context of Lowit's argument, ideas expressed decades earlier by G. Langrod in an article canvassing the role of the party in the Soviet state deserve attention. See Georges Langrod, 'Le rôle du parti unique dans l'Etat soviétique', *Revue politique et parlementaire*, vol. cciv (April–June 1951) p. 51.
25. Ibid., p. 448.
26. Lowit, 'Le parti polymorphe en Europe de l'Est', p. 836.
27. In this general context, M. Lesage has recently advanced the idea that conflicts arising between the vanguard party and the Soviet administration under its tutelage play a positive role for the system. As he explains: 'the conflicts play a positive role as they constitute, for the higher authorities, a means of information about tensions existing in the system. The advent of a conflict between two authorities of a similar level may enable the higher authority to intervene in an attempt to solve the underlying problem'. See M. Lesage, *L'administration soviétique* (Paris: Economica, 1981) p. 116.
28. Lowit, 'Y-a-t-il des Etats en Europe de l'Est?', p. 448. Lowit takes the view that the notion of state bureaucracy should now be dropped as there is just one single bureaucracy in the Soviet Union – that is the party's bureaucracy.
29. Lowit, 'Le parti polymorphe en Europe de l'Est', p. 834.
30. Hassner, 'American Foxes and French Hedgehogs? A French Perspective on East European Studies', p. 370. One notes that the concept developed by Lowit has been borrowed and used by W. Pańków, a researcher at the Polish Academy of Sciences. See Wlodzimierz Pańków, 'L'été polonais – un système de pouvoir en crise', *Revue française de sociologie*, vol. xxiv, no. 2 (April–June 1983) pp. 271–83 (article written before the imposition of martial law).
31. Kerblay and Lavigne, *Les Soviétiques des années 80*, pp. 26–7.
32. Bettelheim, *Les luttes de classes en URSS – 3ème période 1930–1941 – Les Dominants*, p. 220.
33. Z. Strmiska, 'Pouvoir politique et inégalités sociales', p. 382.
34. Fred Kupferman, 'L'oeil sur Moscou', *L'Express*, no. 1766 (17 May 1985) p. 40.
35. Ibid.
36. H. Carrère d'Encausse, *L'empire éclaté – la révolte des nations en U.R.S.S.* (Paris: Flammarion, 1978).
37. H. Carrère d'Encausse, *Le pouvoir confisqué – gouvernants et gouvernés*

en U.R.S.S. (Paris: Flammarion, 1980) trans. by G. H. Hålôch as *Confiscated Power – How Soviet Russia Really Works* (New York: Harper and Row, 1982).

38. H. Carrère d'Encausse, *Le grand frère – l'Union soviétique et l'Europe soviétisée* (Paris: Flammarion, 1983) p. 246.
39. H. Carrère d'Encausse, *Confiscated Power*, p. 25.
40. Nove, 'The Class Nature of the Soviet Union Revisited', p. 310.
41. Annie Kriegel, 'Qui détient le pouvoir en U.R.S.S.?', *Le Figaro* (13 November 1980) p. 2.
42. H. Carrère d'Encausse, *Confiscated Power*, p. 150.
43. Ibid., p. 17.
44. Ibid., p. 329.
45. Hélène Carrère d'Encausse, 'La puissance soviétique aujourd'hui', *Relations internationales (Genève)*, no. 17 (Spring 1979) p. 48. One notes that, for Carrère d'Encausse, international power constitutes a remarkable means to protect the Soviet system from its internal difficulties. See *Confiscated Power*, p. 331.
46. Carrère d'Encausse has defined Khrushchevism as follows: 'Khruschevism meant becoming aware of all the new factual elements of the Soviet society and of the world, in addition to attempting to salvage the structures and ideology inherited from the revolution by bringing to them a new dynamism'. See Hélène Carrère d'Encausse, 'Khrouchtchev était-il vraiment nécessaire?', *Revue française de science politique*, vol. xv, no. 6 (December 1965) p. 1077.
47. Carrère d'Encausse, *Confiscated Power*, p. 207.
48. Kerblay and Lavigne, *Les Soviétiques des années 80*, p. 25; Marc Ferro, 'Y-a-t-il "trop de démocratie" en URSS?', *Annales*, 40ᵉᵐᵉ Année, no. 4 (July–August 1985) p. 822 and A. Smolar, 'Le monde soviétique: transformation ou décadence?', in G. Hermet (ed.), *Totalitarismes* (Paris: Economica, 1984) p. 165.
49. Carrère d'Encausse, *Confiscated Power*, p. 319.
50. Hélène Carrère d'Encausse, 'Lire la nouvelle Constitution', *Le Monde diplomatique* (July 1977) p. 10.
51. Hélène Carrère d'Encausse, 'Party and Federation in the USSR: The Problem of the Nationalities and Power in the USSR', *Government and Opposition*, vol. 13, no. 2 (Spring 1978) p. 148.
52. Ibid. On this point, see also Hélène Carrère d'Encausse, 'URSS: le changement sans alternance?', *Pouvoirs*, i (1977) p. 101 *in fine*.
53. Carrère d'Encausse, *Confiscated Power*, p. 145.
54. Ibid., p. 208.
55. Ibid., p. 327.
56. On this particular question of participation, see the interesting article of Georges Langrod, 'Les formes de la participation des masses dans le gouvernement et l'administration de l'U.R.S.S.', *Annuaire de l'U.R.S.S. Droit-Economie-Sociologie-Politique-Culture*, vol. i (1962) pp. 101–39.
57. Ibid., p. 323. (my emphasis)
58. Ibid., p. 278.
59. Hélène Carrère d'Encausse, 'Les failles de l'Union soviétique', *Défense nationale,* 37ᵉ Année (November 1981) p. 66.

60. Carrère d'Encausse, *Le pouvoir confisqué*, p. 294.
61. Carrère d'Encausse, 'Les failles de l'Union soviétique', p. 59. (my emphasis)
62. Ibid., p. 70.
63. As she explains, three elements of the 1977 Constitution appreciably weaken the significance of Soviet federalism: 'First, the Constitution repeatedly asserts that the development of Soviet society leads to an ultimate rapprochement of nations and ethnic groups, and stresses the existence of the Soviet people. In addition, the Constitution of 1977 is much less precise than the 1936 Constitution with regard to federal and republican powers. . . . Finally, and this is the key point, by turning the Party – this unitary organisation, the vocation of which is to transcend national differences – into the central axis of the Soviet society of tomorrow, and by stressing democratic centralism, those in charge of the Constitution (*constituants*) have stressed the will for unity, and reopened the contents of Soviet federalism'. See also Carrère d'Encausse, 'Lire la nouvelle Constitution', p. 10. See also Hélène Carrère d'Encausse, 'La Constitution de 1977: continuité et changement', *Problèmes politiques et sociaux*, no. 326 (23 December 1977) p. 26.
64. Carrère d'Encausse, *L'empire éclaté*, p. 128.
65. Ibid., p. 275.
66. Ibid., p. 252.
67. In addition to its impact on the operations of some specific institutions such as universities, the clan/tribe structure influences the selection of cadres in local party or government organs. Also, as Bennigsen points out, 'in some cases, these survivals of the clan/tribe system provide the basis for illegal religious organizations'. The writer refers here to the Sufi orders which he depicts as being violently hostile to the Soviet regime (these mystical brotherhoods represent the *jihad* or 'holy war' aspects of Islam). See Alexandre Bennigsen, 'Several Nations or One People? Ethnic Consciousness among Soviet Central Asian Muslims', *Survey*, vol. 24, no. 3 (Summer 1979) p. 52.
68. A. Bennigsen and C. Lemercier-Quelquejay, *Les musulmans oubliés – L'Islam en Union soviétique* (Paris: Maspéro, 1981) pp. 279–80.
69. This particular viewpoint relating to the vitality and importance of both the subnational and supranational levels of consciousness is somewhat at variance with conclusions reached by Bennigsen in earlier writings. For instance, we read in a book published in 1967 that 'ill-defined tribal on ethnic "subnational" consciousness has disappeared; supranational pan-Islamic or pan-Turkic consciousness . . . may have survived in the minds of a few but it is barely discernible on the surface'. See A. Bennigsen and C. Lemercier-Quelquejay, Islam in the Soviet Union (New York and Washington: Praeger, 1967) p. 224.
70. Bennigsen, 'Several Nations or One People? Ethnic Consciousness among Soviet Central Asian Muslims', p. 51. See also A. Bennigsen and M. Broxup, *The Islamic Threat to the Soviet State* (London and Canberra: Croom Helm, 1983) pp. 135–6.
71. As remarked by J.-P. Brûlé, the Soviet Muslims 'today play more the Communist than the Islamic game'. See Jean-Pierre Brûlé, 'L'U.R.S.S. et ses musulmans', *Est et Ouest*, no. 666 (September 1982) p. 30.

72. Alexandre Bennigsen, 'Les Musulmans de l'URSS et la crise afghane', *Politique étrangère*, vol. 45, no. 1 (1980) pp. 19–20. In this regard, Bennigsen mentions the curious symbiosis existing between party apparatus and clan/tribe system.
73. Carrère d'Encausse, *L'empire éclaté*, p. 245.
74. Ibid., p. 270.
75. In an article written in the early 1950s, Bennigsen had already underscored the emergence of Muslim 'separatism'. See Alexandre Bennigsen, 'Les peuples musulmans de l'U.R.S.S. et les Soviets: IV. Les problèmes politiques', *L'Afrique et l'Asie*, no. 23 (3rd Trim. 1953) p. 33.
76. Bennigsen and Lemercier-Quelquejay, *Les musulmans oubliés – L'Islam en Union soviétique*, p. 299.
77. Alexandre Bennigsen, 'Mullahs, Mujahidin and Soviet Muslims', *Problems of Communism*, vol. XXXIII, (November–December 1984) p. 32.
78. Bennigsen, 'Les Musulmans de l'URSS et la crise afghane', p. 19. See also Alexandre Bennigsen and Chantal Lemercier-Quelquejay, 'L'impact des évènements d'Iran et d'Afghanistan sur l'Islam soviétique', *L'Alternative*, no. 31 (January–February 1985) p. 17.
79. Ibid.
80. While writing about this idea of 'Russian masters', Bennigsen is indeed far too well-informed a specialist not to bear in mind the evolution towards greater participation and authority of native cadres in their republics' national affairs. See Bennigsen and Broxup, *The Islamic Threat to the Soviet State*, p. 134.
81. XXX, 'Des musulmans tranquilles – L'Islam en Chine et en URSS', *Etudes*, Tome 363, no. 5 (November 1985) p. 446.
82. Bennigsen and Broxup, *The Islamic Threat to the Soviet State*, p. 152. Bennigsen is in no doubt of the fact that 'Muslim territories of the Soviet Union, forgotten by world public opinion and even by specialists, may well become, in a fairly near future, one of the hottest items in the news'. See Alexandre Bennigsen, 'L'islam en U.R.S.S.', *L'Afrique et l'Asie modernes*, no. 120 (1st trim. 1979) pp. 21–2.
83. Carrère d'Encausse, 'Les failles de l'Union soviétique', p. 61.
84. Carrère d'Encausse, *Confiscated Power*, p. 335. For an early depiction of the Soviet Union's contradictions, see Hélène Carrère d'Encausse, 'La crise de juin 1957 en U.R.S.S.', *Revue de défense nationale*, vol. 13 (November 1957) pp. 1669–72. It is worth noting the relationship existing between the most fundamental contradiction that Carrère d'Encausse underlines in this early writing – that is the opposition between '*la classe des gouvernants-quels qu'ils soient . . . à celle des gouvernés . . .*' (pp. 1669–70) – and the title of her book published in 1980.
85. Ibid., p. 336.
86. Michel Tatu, 'Les institutions communistes face aux crises: les militaires seront-ils le recours?', *Défense nationale*, 37ᵉ Année (November 1981) pp. 52 and 54. Tatu's hypothesis has been echoed by E. Morin, for whom the totalitarian era in the Soviet Union might on the occasion of a succession crisis come to an end through action undertaken and led by the Soviet military. See Morin, *De la Nature de l'URSS – Complexe*

totalitaire et nouvel Empire, p. 249. Both writers seem to believe that a military rule would probably mean less bellicosity on the part of the Soviet Union in the sphere of international relations. Tatu points here to the fact that the military, unlike the party, would not have to seek its legitimacy in foreign adventurism. For Morin, the military would display greater political realism than the party and would, importantly, abandon universal Communist messianism. Another reason leading Morin to think that seizure of power by the Soviet military would constitute the most favourable evolution relates to the disappearance of an acute danger inherent in the nature of the totalitarian CPSU. As he explains, the party can only be 'all or nothing' in the Soviet Union. According to Morin, the party knows that, if confronted by a serious democratic threat to its domination, it will then have to stake its all. Were the party's disappearance to become imminent, the party would likely choose to provoke the nuclear destruction of the planet, so bringing down the whole world in its fall. Ibid., p. 252.

87. On this general point, see Jean-Christophe Romer, 'Le facteur militaire dans la politique soviétique', *Projet*, no. 167 (July–August 1982) p. 845; M. Garder, *Histoire de l'armée soviétique* (Paris: Plon, 1959) pp. 199–200 and Michel Garder, 'De l'armée impériale russe aux forces armées soviétiques (1917–1977)', *Esope*, no. 387 (16 October 1977) p. 17.

88. Carrère d'Encausse, *Confiscated Power*, p. 188. On this point, see also R. Fritsch-Bournazel: 'Thus, a fundamental consensus unites the party apparatus with the military for the pursuit of common goals'. Renata Fritsch-Bournazel, 'Les Forces armées et la "société socialiste avancée"', *Pouvoirs* 6 (1978) p. 64.

89. H. Carrère d'Encausse, *Staline – l'ordre par la terreur* (Paris: Flammarion, 1979) trans. by V. Ionescu as *Stalin – Order Through Terror* (London and New York: Longman, 1981) p. 165.

90. H. Carrère d'Encausse, 'L'URSS ou le totalitarisme exemplaire', in M. Grawitz and J. Leca (eds), *Traité de science politique. Vol. 2 – Les régimes politiques contemporains* (Paris: Presses Universitaires de France, 1985) pp. 233–4.

91. Ibid.

92. Hélène Carrère d'Encausse, 'Les nouveaux Russes', *Le Nouvel Observateur*, no. 1136 (15 August 1986) p. 37. (my emphasis)

93. Ibid.

94. Michel Heller, 'Teeth 'n' Smiles – Gorbachov for Beginners', *Survey*, vol. 29, no. 1 (Spring 1985) p. 18.

95. Ibid.

96. See Archie Brown, 'Soviet Political Developments and Prospects', *World Policy Journal*, vol. IV, no. 1 (Winter 1986/87) pp. 81–3.

97. Dominique Dhombres, 'M. Gorbatchev engage une profonde réforme du mode de sélection des responsables', *Le Monde* (29 January 1987) pp. 1 and 4.

98. Wlodzimierz Brus, 'Prospects of Reconstruction of Socialism by Political Democratisation and Economic Reform', paper delivered at St Antony's College, Oxford (October 1983) p. 9.

99. Kende, *Logique de l'économie centralisée*, p. 281. In our view, the law

adopted in 1986 by the Supreme Soviet of the USSR legalising different types of private activities such as car repair, furniture making and tailoring does not constitute a significant departure from Soviet ideological orthodoxy. Such a measure, the scope of which seems much restricted, is still rooted within the Leninist heritage. See Patrick Cockburn, 'Moscow legalises private enterprise in service sector', *The Financial Times* (29 November 1986) p. 1.

100. Brus, 'Prospects of Reconstruction of Socialism by Political Democratisation and Economic Reform', p. 12. See also E. Egnell and M. Peissik, *URSS – L'entreprise face à l'Etat* (Paris: Seuil, 1974) p. 172.
101. Lorrain, *L'Évangile selon Saint-Marx*, p. 37.
102. Sochor, 'Le "socialisme réel", une idéologie tournée vers le passé', pp. 173–4.
103. Georges Sokoloff, 'La dynamique Gorbatchev', *Politique étrangère*, no. 3 (Fall 1985) p. 623.
104. Olivier Duhamel and Jean-Luc Parodi, '*Images du communisme*: *1*. La dégradation de l'image de l'Union soviétique', *Pouvoirs*, 21 (1982) pp. 169–80.
105. Cornelius Castoriadis, 'Facing the war', *Telos*, no. 46 (Winter 1980–1) p. 52, note 7. Originally published in *Libre*, 8 (1980) pp. 217–50 and translated by J. Light.
106. Ibid., p. 48.
107. When Castoriadis refers to the power of the stratocracy he does not mean the presence in the Politburo of a majority of military officers, nor that the latter's signed intervention is necessary for the taking of any particular decision.
108. Ibid., p. 48.
109. Ibid., p. 47.
110. Dominique Frager, 'I. URSS: quelle stratégie? – Interview de Cornelius Castoriadis', *Critique socialiste*, no. 43 (April 1982) p. 12.
111. Castoriadis, *Devant la guerre*, pp. 109–10.
112. Castoriadis considers that his hypothesis of a separate military society is plainly confirmed by the very existence of the 'closed enterprises'. Ibid., p. 122.
113. Castoriadis, 'Facing the war', p. 52.
114. Castoriadis, *Devant la guerre*, p. 256.
115. Louis-Bernard Robitaille, 'Le pouvoir au bout du char' (interview with C. Castoriadis), *Le Nouvel Observateur*, no. 895 (2 January 1982) p. 15.
116. Ibid.
117. Castoriadis, *Devant la guerre*, p. 263.
118. Ibid., p. 264.
119. Ibid., p. 161.
120. See Paul Thibaud, 'Le plus dur et le plus fragile des régimes – Entretien avec Cornelius Castoriadis', *Esprit*, no. 63 (March 1982) pp. 140–6.
121. Ibid., p. 143.
122. Robitaille, 'Le pouvoir au bout du char', p. 19.
123. Morin, *De la Nature de l'URSS – Complexe totalitaire et nouvel Empire*, p. 213.

124. Ibid., p. 214.
125. Caroline Ost and Gilles Lourmel, 'La stratocratie: une interprétation hâtive', *Critique*, vol. 37, no. 411–12 (August–September 1981) p. 745.
126. Paul Thibaud, 'Le socialisme mûr – Entretien avec Michel Heller', *Esprit*, no. 74 (February 1983) p. 42.
127. Thierry Maulnier, 'Le bien-être et la puissance', *Preuves*, no. 74 (April 1957) p. 67.
128. Jacques Sapir, 'L'armée dans la société soviétique', *République Moderne*, no. 2 (Fall 1985) p. 33.
129. Ibid.

5 Conclusions

1. J. Bonamour, 'Soviet and East European Studies in France' in A. Buchholz (ed.), *Soviet and East European Studies in the International Framework*, p. 54.
2. Interview with Marc Ferro in Paris, 16 May 1986.
3. Lannes and Lazitch, 'La technique du pouvoir en U.R.S.S.', p. 221.
4. Interview with H. Carrère d'Encausse in Paris, 5 November 1982.
5. Jean-Pierre Chevènement, 'Comprendre', *République Moderne*, no. 2 (Fall 1985) p. 5.
6. Interview with Lilly Marcou in Paris, 29 June 1984.
7. Hassner, 'American Foxes and French Hedgehogs? A French Perspective on East European Studies', p. 368.
8. J. Rupnik, 'Le totalitarisme vu de l'Est', in G. Hermet (ed.), *Totalitarismes*, pp. 52–3.
9. Hassner, 'Le miroir totalitaire – Le totalitarisme soviétique vu de l'ouest', p. 204.
10. Brown, 'Political Power and the Soviet State: Western and Soviet Perspectives', in N. Harding (ed.), *The State in Socialist Society*, p. 87.
11. Aron, *Democracy and Totalitarianism*, pp. 215–16.

Bibliography

1 Books

ADLER, ALEXANDRE, COHEN, FRANCIS, DECAILLOT, MAURICE, FRIOUX, CLAUDE and ROBEL, LEON, *L'URSS et Nous* (Paris: Editions Sociales, 1978).

ANDREFF, WLADIMIR, 'Capitalisme d'Etat ou Monopolisme d'Etat en U.R.S.S.? – Propos d'étape', in *Economie politique de la planification en système socialiste*, Marie Lavigne (ed.) (Paris: Economica, 1978) pp. 243–86.

——, 'Vers une théorie de la congruence des systèmes', in *Travail et monnaie en système socialiste*, Marie Lavigne (ed.) (Paris: Economica, 1981) pp. 288–310.

——, 'Pour un marxisme éclectique: au-delà des approches dogmatiques des économies soviétiques et est-européennes', in *Les aventures du Marxisme*, René Gallissot (ed.) (Paris: Syros, 1984) pp. 171–200.

ARON, RAYMOND, *Dix-huit leçons sur la société industrielle* (Paris: Gallimard, 1962).

——, *La lutte de classes – nouvelles leçons sur les sociétés industrielles* (Paris: Gallimard, 1964).

——, *Democracy and Totalitarianism*, trans. V. Ionescu (London: Weidenfeld and Nicolson, 1968).

——, *Plaidoyer pour l'Europe décadente* (Paris: Robert Laffont, 1977).

——, *Mémoires – 50 ans de réflexion politique* (Paris: Julliard, 1983).

——, *Les dernières années du siècle* (Paris: Julliard, 1984).

ASSELAIN, JEAN-CHARLES, *Plan et profit en économie socialiste* (Paris: Presses de la Fondation Nationale des Sciences Politiques, 1981).

BENNIGSEN, ALEXANDRE and LEMERCIER-QUELQUEJAY, CHANTAL, *Islam in the Soviet Union* (New York and Washington: Praeger, 1967).

——, *Les musulmans oubliés – L'Islam en Union soviétique* (Paris: Maspéro, 1981).

—— and BROXUP, MARIE, *The Islamic Threat to the Soviet State* (London and Canberra: Croom Helm, 1983).

BESANÇON, ALAIN, *Court traité de soviétologie à l'usage des autorités civiles, militaires et religieuses* (Paris: Hachette, 1976).

——, *The Intellectual Origins of Leninism*, trans. S. Matthews (Oxford: Basil Blackwell, 1981).

——, *Présent soviétique et passé russe* (Paris: Librairie Générale Française, 1980).

——, 'L'Empire russe et la domination soviétique', in *Le concept d'empire*, Maurice Duverger (ed.) (Paris: Presses Universitaires de France, 1980) pp. 365–77.

——, *Anatomie d'un spectre – L'économie politique du socialisme réel* (Paris: Calmann-Lévy, 1981).

BETTELHEIM, CHARLES, *La planification soviétique* (Paris: Librairie Marcel Rivière, 1939).

——, *Class Struggles in the USSR. First Period: 1917–1923*, trans. B. Pearce (New York and London: Monthly Review Press, 1976).

——, *Les luttes de classes en URSS – 2ème période 1923–1930* (Paris: Seuil/Maspéro, 1977).

——, *Les luttes de classes en URSS – 3ème période 1930–1941 – Les Dominés* (Paris: Seuil/Maspéro, 1982).

——, *Les luttes de classes en URSS – 3ème période 1930–1941 – Les Dominants* (Paris: Seuil/Maspéro, 1983).

——, 'La pertinence des concepts marxiens de classe et de lutte de classes pour analyser la société soviétique', in *Marx en perspective – Actes du colloque organisé par l'Ecole des Hautes Etudes en Sciences Sociales, Paris, décembre 1983*, Bernard Chavance (ed.) (Paris: Editions de l'Ecole des Hautes Etudes en Sciences Sociales, 1985) pp. 277–300.

BONAMOUR, JEAN, 'Soviet and East European Studies in France', in *Soviet and East European Studies in the International Framework – Organization, Financing and Political Relevance*, Arnold Buchholz (ed.) (New York: Transnational Publishers, 1982) pp. 50–9.

BORDAZ, ROBERT, *La nouvelle économie soviétique 1953–1960* (Paris: Grasset, 1960).

BOUDON, RAYMOND, 'L'intellectuel et ses publics: les singularités françaises', in *Français, qui êtes-vous? – des essais et des chiffres*, Jean-Daniel Reynaud and Yves Grafmeyer (eds) (Paris: La Documentation française, 1981) pp. 465–80.

BOURRICAUD, FRANÇOIS, *Le bricolage idéologique – Essai sur les intellectuels et les passions démocratiques* (Paris: Presses Universitaires de France, 1980).

BROUE, PIERRE, *Le parti bolchevique – Histoire du P.C. de l'U.R.S.S.* 2nd edn (Paris: Editions de Minuit, 1972).

BROWN, ARCHIE H., *Soviet Politics and Political Science* (London: Macmillan, 1974).

——, 'Political Power and the Soviet State: Western and Soviet Perspectives', in *The State in Socialist Society*, Neil Harding (ed.) (London: Macmillan, 1984) pp. 51–103.

BURDEAU, GEORGES, *Méthode de la science politique* (Paris: Dalloz, 1959).

CARRERE D'ENCAUSSE, HELENE, *L'empire éclaté – la révolte des nations en U.R.S.S.* (Paris: Flammarion, 1978).

——, *Lénine – la révolution et le pouvoir* (Paris: Flammarion, 1979).

——, *Staline – l'ordre par la terreur* (Paris: Flammarion, 1979).

——, *Confiscated Power – How Soviet Russia Really Works*, trans. G. Hålôch (New York: Harper and Row, 1982).

——, *Le grand frère – l'Union soviétique et l'Europe soviétisée* (Paris: Flammarion, 1983).

——, *La déstalinisation commence* (Brussels: Editions Complexe, 1984).

——, 'L'URSS ou le totalitarisme exemplaire', in *Traité de science politique Volume 2 – Les régimes politiques contemporains*, Madeleine Grawitz and

Jean Leca (eds) (Paris: Presses Universitaires de France, 1985) pp. 210–37.

CASTORIADIS, CORNELIUS, *La société bureaucratique 1: Les rapports de production en Russie* (Paris: Union Générale d'Editions, 1973).

——, *La société bureaucratique 2: La révolution contre la bureaucratie* (Paris: Union Générale d'Editions, 1973).

——, *Devant la guerre – Les réalités* (Paris: Fayard, 1981).

CHAMBRE, HENRI, *Le Marxisme en Union soviétique – Idéologie et institutions Leur évolution de 1917 à nos jours* (Paris: Seuil, 1955).

——, *L'Union Soviétique – Introduction à l'étude de ses institutions*, 2nd edn (Paris: LGDJ, 1966).

——, *L'évolution du marxisme soviétique – Théorie économique et droit* (Paris: Seuil, 1974).

CHARLIER, FERNAND, *L'union soviétique et les pays de l'est: capitalisme ou socialisme?* (Paris: Maspéro Cahier Rouge, 1970).

CHARVIN, ROBERT, *Les Etats socialistes européens – Institutions et vie politique* (Toulouse: Dalloz, 1975).

CHAVANCE, BERNARD, *Le système économique soviétique* (Paris: Editions le Sycomore, 1983).

CHIAMA, JEAN and SOULET, JEAN-FRANÇOIS, *Histoire de la dissidence* (Paris: Seuil, 1982).

Chronique des petites gens d'URSS (Paris: Seuil, 1981).

CLARION, NICOLAS, *Le Glacis soviétique – Théorie et pratique de la démocratie nouvelle* (Paris: Somogy, 1948).

COHEN, FRANCIS, *L'U.R.S.S. en mouvement* (Paris: Editions Sociales, 1963).

——, *Les Soviétiques – Classes et société en U.R.S.S.* (Paris: Editions Sociales, 1974).

COHN-BENDIT, DANIEL and COHN-BENDIT, G., *Obsolete Communism. The Left-Wing Alternative* (London: André Deutsch, 1968).

COLAS, DOMINIQUE, *Le léninisme – Philosophie et sociologie politiques du léninisme* (Paris: Presses Universitaires de France, 1982).

COLLIGNON, JEAN-GUY, 'L'idéologie soviétique devant la soviétologie scientifique française', in Centre d'étude de la pensée politique, *Analyse de l'idéologie – Tome 1: problématiques* (Paris: Editions Galilée, 1980) pp. 309–27.

CONTE, FRANCIS and MARTRES, JEAN-LOUIS (eds), *L'Union Soviétique dans les relations internationales* (Paris: Economica, 1982).

CRAIPEAU, YVAN, *Ces pays que l'on dit socialistes – La face cachée du capitalisme* (Paris: E.D.I., 1982).

DAIX, PIERRE, *L'avènement de la Nomenklatura – la chute de Khrouchtchev* (Brussels: Editions Complexe, 1982).

DEVILLERS, PHILIPPE, *Guerre ou paix?* (Paris: Balland, 1979).

DRACH, MARCEL, *La crise dans les pays de l'Est* (Paris: Editions La Découverte, 1984).

——, 'Les trois crises', in *La Réalité Socialiste – Crise, Adaptation, Progrès*, Marie Lavigne and Wladimir Andreff (eds) (Paris: Economica, 1985) pp. 55–62.

DUHAMEL, OLIVIER and RACINE, NICOLE, 'Léon Blum, les socialistes français et l'Union soviétique', in *L'U.R.S.S. vue de gauche*, Lilly Marcou (ed.) (Paris: Presses Universitaires de France, 1982) pp. 124–53.

DUPEUX, LOUIS, 'Le débat sur le totalitarisme en Allemagne', in Centre d'étude de la pensée politique, *Analyse de l'idéologie Tome 2: thématiques* (Paris: Editions Galilée, 1983) pp. 434–8.

DUPUIS, GEORGES, GEORGEL, JACQUES, MONCONDUIT, FRANCOIS and MOREAU, JACQUES, *La Direction collégiale en Union soviétique* (Paris: Armand Colin, 1972).

DUVERGER, MAURICE, *Introduction à la politique* (Paris: Gallimard, 1964).

——, *Janus, les deux faces de l'Occident* (Paris: Fayard, 1972).

——, *Les orangers du Lac Balaton* (Paris: Seuil, 1980).

EGNELL, ERIK and PEISSIK, MICHEL, *URSS – L'entreprise face à l'Etat* (Paris: Seuil, 1974).

ELLEINSTEIN, JEAN, *L'U.R.S.S. contemporaine – histoire de l'U.R.S.S.* (Tome 4) (Paris: Editions Sociales, 1975).

——, *The Stalin Phenomenon* (London: Lawrence and Wishart, 1976).

FAVRE, PIERRE, 'Histoire de la science politique', in *Traité de science politique – Volume I – La science politique, science sociale*, Madeleine Grawitz and Jean Leca (eds) (Paris: Presses Universitaires de France, 1985) pp. 3–45.

FERRO, MARC, *Des Soviets au communisme bureaucratique* (Paris: Gallimard/Julliard, 1980).

——, *L'Occident devant la révolution soviétique* (Brussels: Editions Complexe, 1980).

FRANK, PIERRE, *Le stalinisme* (Paris, Maspéro, 1977).

FREMEAUX, PHILIPPE and DURAND, CHRISTINE, *Comprendre l'économie soviétique* (Paris: Syros, 1985).

FRIEDMANN, GEORGES, *De la Sainte Russie à l'U.R.S.S.* (Paris: Gallimard, 1938).

GARDER, MICHEL, *Histoire de l'armée soviétique* (Paris: Plon, 1959).

GELARD, PATRICE, *L'administration locale en U.R.S.S.* (Paris: Presses Universitaires de France, 1972).

——, *Les systèmes politiques des Etats socialistes, Tome premier – Le modèle soviétique* (Paris: Cujas, 1975).

——, *Les systèmes politiques des Etats socialistes, Tome deux – Transpositions et transformations du modèle soviétique* (Paris: Cujas, 1975).

——, 'Le phénomène du parti unique dans les Etats socialistes', in *Itinéraires – Etudes en l'honneur de Léo Hamon*, Gérard Conac, Herbert Maisl and Jacques Vaudiaux (eds) (Paris: Economica, 1982) pp. 279–95.

GLUCKSMANN, ANDRE, *La cuisinière et le mangeur d'hommes – Essai sur l'Etat, le marxisme, les camps de concentration* (Paris: Seuil, 1975).

HELLER, MICHEL and NEKRICH, ALEKSANDR, *L'utopie au pouvoir – Histoire de l'U.R.S.S. de 1917 à nos jours* (Paris: Calmann-Lévy, 1982).

——, *La machine et les rouages – la formation de l'homme soviétique* (Paris: Calmann-Lévy, 1985).

HOFFMAN, STANLEY, LEONTIEFF, WASSILY and TAJFEL, HENRY, *Social Sciences Policy – France – Examiners' Report* (Paris: OECD, 1975).

HOUGH, JERRY F. and FAINSOD, MERLE, *How the Soviet Union is Governed* (Cambridge and London: Harvard University Press, 1979).

ISTRATI, PANAIT, *Vers l'autre flamme. La Russie nue* (Paris: Ed. Rieder, 1929).

KEHAYAN, JEAN and KEHAYAN, NINA, *Rue du prolétaire rouge* (Paris: Seuil, 1978).

——, *Le tabouret de Piotr* (Paris: Seuil, 1980).

KENDE, PIERRE, *Logique de l'économie centralisée. Un exemple: La Hongrie* (Paris: Société d'Edition d'Enseignement Supérieur, 1964).

—— and POMIAN, KRZYSZTOF (eds), *1956 Varsovie – Budapest – La deuxième révolution d'Octobre* (Paris: Seuil, 1978).

KERBLAY, BASILE, *La société soviétique contemporaine* (Paris: Armand Colin, 1977).

—— and LAVIGNE, MARIE, *Les Soviétiques des années 80* (Paris: Armand Colin, 1985).

KRIEGEL, ANNIE, *Le système communiste mondial* (Paris: Presses Universitaires de France, 1984).

LABIN, SUZANNE, *Stalin's Russia* (London: Victor Gollancz Ltd., 1949).

LAURAT, LUCIEN, *L'économie soviétique. Sa dynamique. Son mécanisme* (Paris: Libraire Valois, 1931).

——, *Problèmes actuels du Socialisme* (Paris: Les Iles d'Or, 1955).

LAVAU, GEORGES, *A quoi sert le parti communiste français?* (Paris: Fayard, 1981).

LAVIGNE, MARIE, *Les économies socialistes soviétique et européennes*, 3rd edn (Paris: Armand Colin, 1979).

—— and TIRASPOLSKY, ANITA, *L'U.R.S.S. – Pouvoir et Société* (Paris: Hatier, 1981).

—— and ANDREFF, WLADIMIR (eds), *La Réalité Socialiste – Crise, Adaptation, Progrès* (Paris: Economica, 1985).

——, *Economie internationale des pays socialistes* (Paris: Armand Colin, 1985).

LEFORT, CLAUDE, *Un homme en trop – Réflexion sur l'Archipel du Goulag* (Paris: Seuil, 1976).

——, *Eléments d'une critique de la bureaucratie* (Paris: Gallimard, 1979).

——, *L'Invention démocratique – Les limites de la domination totalitaire* (Paris: Fayard, 1981).

LESAGE, MICHEL, *Les régimes politiques de l'U.R.S.S. et de l'Europe de l'Est* (Paris: Presses Universitaires de France, 1971).

——, *Les institutions soviétiques* (Paris: Presses Universitaires de France, 1975).

——, *L'administration soviétique* (Paris: Economica, 1981).

LORRAIN, PIERRE, *L'Évangile selon Saint Marx – La pression idéologique dans la vie quotidienne en URSS* (Paris: Belfond, 1982).

LYON, JACQUES, *La Russie Soviétique* (Paris: Librairie Félix Alcan, 1927).

MARCOU, LILLY, *L'Union Soviétique* (Paris: Armand Colin, 1971).

—— (ed.) *L'U.R.S.S. vue de gauche* (Paris: Presses Universitaires de France, 1982).

MARCZEWSKI, JEAN, *Crise de la planification socialiste?* (Paris: Presses Universitaires de France, 1973).

MARQUES-RIVIERE, JEAN, *L'URSS dans le Monde – L'expansion soviétique de 1918 à 1935* (Paris: Payot, 1935).

MARTINET, GILLES, *Les cinq communismes* (Paris: Seuil, 1971).

MAULNIER, THIERRY, *La face de méduse du communisme* (Paris: Gallimard, 1951).

MAUREL, MARIE-CLAUDE, *La campagne collectivisée – société et espace rural en Russie* (Paris: Anthropos, 1980).

MENEY, PATRICK, *La Kleptocratie – La délinquance en URSS* (Paris: La Table Ronde, 1982).

MONNEROT, JULES, *Sociology of Communism*, trans. J. Degras and R. Rees (London: Allen and Unwin, 1953).

MONTEIL, VINCENT, *Les Musulmans soviétiques* (Paris: Seuil, 1982).

MORIN, EDGAR, 'L'avenir dans la société française', in *Tendances et volontés de la société française*, Jean-Daniel Reynaud (ed.) (Paris: S.é.d.é.i.s., 1966) pp. 402–22.

——, *De la Nature de l'URSS – Complexe totalitaire et nouvel Empire* (Paris: Fayard, 1983).

MOSSE, ROBERT, *L'Union soviétique au carrefour – Socialisme ou Capitalisme?* (Paris: Editions du Sagittaire, 1936).

MOULIN, GERARD, *UBURSS* (Paris: Gallimard, 1980).

MOUSKHELY, MICHEL and JEDRYKA, ZYGMUNT, *Le gouvernement de l'U.R.S.S.* (Paris: Presses Universitaires de France, 1961).

——, *L'URSS au seuil du Communisme?* (Paris: Dalloz, 1962).

NAVILLE, PIERRE, *Le Nouveau Léviathan, Vol. 1. De l'aliénation à la jouissance* (Paris: Anthropos, 1967).

——, *Le Nouveau Léviathan, Vol. 2. Le salaire socialiste, premier volume: les rapports de production* (Paris: Anthropos, 1970).

——, *Le Nouveau Léviathan, Vol. 3. Le salaire socialiste, deuxième volume: sur l'histoire moderne des théories de la valeur et de la plus-value* (Paris: Anthropos, 1970).

——, *Le Nouveau Léviathan, Vol. 5. La bureaucratie et la révolution* (Paris: Anthropos, 1972).

——, *Le Nouveau Léviathan, Vol. 4. Les échanges socialistes* (Paris: Anthropos, 1974).

——, *La Révolution et les intellectuels* (Paris: Gallimard, 1975).

NIVAT, GEORGES, *Vers la fin du mythe russe – Essais sur la culture russe de Gogol à nos jours* (Lausanne: L'Age d'Homme, 1982).

PIERRE, ANDRE, *Qui succédera à Staline?* (Paris: Flammarion, 1952).

PISIER-KOUCHNER, EVELYNE, *Les interprétations du stalinisme* (Paris: Presses Universitaires de France, 1983).

POLIN, CLAUDE, *L'esprit totalitaire* (Paris: Sirey, 1977).

—— and ROUSSEAU, CLAUDE, *Les illusions de l'Occident* (Paris: Albin Michel, 1981).

——, *Le totalitarisme* (Paris: Presses Universitaires de France, 1982).

POLLAK, MICHAEL, *Social Sciences Policy – France – Background Report* (Paris: OECD, 1975).

POSTER, MARK, *Existential Marxism in Postwar France – From Sartre to Althusser* (Princeton: Princeton University Press, 1977).

RAIN, PAUL, *L'Ecole libre des Sciences politiques, 1871–1945* (Paris: Fondation Nationale des Sciences Politiques, 1963).

RAYNAUD, PHILIPPE, 'L'évolution du régime soviétique: stratocratie ou idéocratie? Remarques sur l'analyse du régime soviétique chez Cornelius Castoriadis et Alain Besançon', in *Les interprétations du stalinisme*, Evelyne Pisier-Kouchner (ed.) (Paris: Presses Universitaires de France, 1983) pp. 257–89.

REVUZ, CHRISTINE, *Ivan Ivanovitch écrit à 'la Pravda'* (Paris: Editions Sociales, 1980).

RICHET, XAVIER (ed.), *Crises à l'Est?* (Lyon: Presses Universitaires de Lyon, 1984).

ROUSSET, DAVID, *La Société éclatée – De la première à la seconde révolution mondiale* (Paris: Grasset, 1973).

RUPNIK, JACQUES, 'Le totalitarisme vu de l'Est', in *Totalitarismes*, Guy Hermet (ed.) (Paris: Economica, 1984) pp. 43–71.

SAPIR, JACQUES, *Pays de l'Est vers la crise généralisée?* (Lyon: Fédérop, 1980).

SERIOT, PATRICK, *Analyse du discours politique soviétique* (Paris: Institut d'études slaves, 1985).

SMOLAR, ALEKSANDER, 'Le monde soviétique: transformation ou décadence?', in *Totalitarismes*, Guy Hermet (ed.) (Paris: Economica, 1984) pp. 159–77.

SOKOLOFF, GEORGES, *L'économie obéissante – Décisions politiques et vie économique en U.R.S.S.* (Paris: Calmann-Lévy, 1976).

——, *L'économie de la détente – L'U.R.S.S. et le capital occidental* (Paris: Presses de la Fondation Nationale des Sciences Politiques, 1983).

SORLIN, PIERRE, *La société soviétique 1917–1964* (Paris: Armand Colin, 1964).

SOUVARINE, BORIS, *Staline – Aperçu historique du bolchevisme* (Paris: Plon, 1935).

——, *L'Observateur Des Deux Mondes et autres textes* (Paris: Editions de la différence, 1982).

STRMISKA, ZDENEK, 'Pouvoir politique et inégalités sociales', in *Egalité et inégalités en Europe de l'Est*, Pierre Kende and Zdenek Strmiska (eds) (Paris: Presses de la Fondation Nationale des Sciences Politiques, 1984) pp. 369–409.

TATU, MICHEL, *Le pouvoir en U.R.S.S. – Du déclin de Khrouchtchev à la direction collective* (Paris: Grasset, 1967).

——, *La bataille des euromissiles* (Paris: Fondation pour les études de défense nationale, 1983).

——, *Eux et nous – Les relations Est-Ouest entre deux détentes* (Paris: Fayard, 1985).

TERUEL-MANIA, PIERRE, *De Lénine au panzer-communisme* (Paris: Maspéro, 1971).

TODD, EMMANUEL, *Le chute finale – Essai sur la décomposition de la sphère soviétique* (Paris: Robert Laffont, 1976).

TOURAINE, ALAIN, *Un désir d'Histoire* (Paris: Stock, 1977).

VERDES-LEROUX, JEANNINE, *Au service du Parti – Le parti*

communiste, les intellectuels et la culture (1944–1956) (Paris: Fayard/Editions de Minuit, 1983).

VIET, J., *Les sciences de l'homme en France – tendances et organisation de la recherche* (Paris: Mouton, 1966).

VOSLENSKY, MICHAEL, *La Nomenklatura – Les privilégiés en URSS* (Paris: Belfond, 1980).

WHITE, STEPHEN, *Political Culture and Soviet Politics* (London: Macmillan, 1979).

WRIGHT, VINCENT, 'The French Communist Party during the Fifth Republic: the troubled path', in *National Communism in Western Europe: a third way to socialism?*, Howard Machin (ed.) (London and New York: Methuen, 1983) pp. 90–123.

YVON, MARCEL, *L'U.R.S.S. telle qu'elle est* (Paris: Gallimard, 1938).

ZALESKI, EUGENE, *Planification de la croissance et fluctuations économiques en U.R.S.S. – Tome I 1918–1932* (Paris: Société d'Edition d'Enseignement Supérieur, 1962).

——, *La planification stalinienne – croissance et fluctuations économiques en U.R.S.S. 1933–1952* (Paris: Economica, 1984).

2 Journals, newspapers and documents

ADLER, ALEXANDRE, 'Le problème de la corruption en U.R.S.S.', *Pouvoirs*, 31 (1984) pp. 105–13.

AMBARTSUMOV, E., BURLATSKY, F., KRASIN, Y. and PLETNYOV, E., 'Against distortion of the experience of real, existing socialism', *New Times*, 52 (December 1978) pp. 18–28.

ANDREFF, WLADIMIR, 'L'organisation du travail dans les entreprises socialistes', *Reflets et Perspectives de la vie économique*, tome XXII, nos 4/5 (1983) pp. 277–87.

——, 'Marxisme en crise cherche sociétés socialistes. A propos des thèses de P. M. Sweezy et de B. Chavance', *Babylone*, no. 2/3 (Winter 1983/4) pp. 100–25.

ANTI-MYTHES, 'An interview with Claude Lefort', *Telos*, no. 30 (Winter 1976–77) pp. 173–92.

ARON, RAYMOND, 'L'essence du totalitarisme', *Critique*, vol. 10 (January 1954) pp. 51–70.

——, 'Fascinés par l'Union Soviétique', *La Nef*, vol. 13, no. 12 (March 1956) pp. 213–23.

——, 'Soviet Society in Transition', *Problems of Communism*, vol. VI, no. 6 (November–December 1957) pp. 5–10.

——, 'Classe sociale, classe politique, classe dirigeante', *Archives européennes de sociologie*, vol. I, no. 2 (1960) pp. 260–81.

——, 'Société industrielle, idéologies, philosophie', *Preuves*, no. 167 (January 1965) pp. 3–13.

——, 'Société industrielle, idéologies, philosophie (II)', *Preuves*, no. 168 (February 1965) pp. 12–24.

——, 'Société industrielle, idéologies, philosophie (III)', *Preuves*, no. 169 (March 1965) pp. 23–41.

——, 'Remarques sur un débat', *Archives européennes de sociologie*, vol. xiii, no. 1 (1972) pp. 63–79.

——, 'On Liberalization', *Government and Opposition*, vol. 14, no. 1 (Winter 1979) pp. 37–57.

——, 'L'hégémonisme soviétique: An I', *Commentaire*, vol. iii, no. 11 (1980) pp. 349–62.

——, 'La puissance et la faillite', *L'Express*, no. 1583 (13 November 1981) pp. 47–8.

——, 'Ils ont choisi le plus intelligent', *L'Express*, no. 1637 (26 November 1982) pp. 54–5.

——, 'Etats démocratiques et Etats totalitaires (Juin 1939)', *Commentaire*, vol. 6, no. 24 (Winter 1983–1984) pp. 701–10.

BARRY, FRANÇOISE, 'La prise de décision en U.R.S.S.', *Economies et Sociétés*, Cahiers de l'ISMEA, Série G, no. 33 (February–March 1976) pp. 365–87.

BARTON, PAUL, 'Despotisme et totalitarisme', *Le Contrat Social*, vol. iii, no. 4 (July 1959) pp. 213–17.

——, 'Le système concentrationnaire soviétique', *Le Contrat Social*, vol. V, no. 4 (July–August 1961) pp. 223–30.

BAUDOUIN, JEAN, 'Le P.C.F.: retour à l'archaïsme?', *Revue politique et parlementaire*, vol. 82, no. 889 (November–December 1980) pp. 30–40.

BAUTIER, R. and ROGULSKA, BARBARA, 'La communication sociale, langue de bois ou de caoutchouc', *Economie et Humanisme*, no. 278 (1984) pp. 21–31.

BENNIGSEN, ALEXANDRE, 'Les peuples musulmans de l'U.R.S.S. et les Soviets: IV. Les problèmes politiques', *L'Afrique et l'Asie*, no. 23 (3rd Trimester 1953) pp. 15–34.

——, 'L'agitation et le durcissement idéologique en U.R.S.S.', *Etudes*, vol. 294 (July–August–September 1957) pp. 243–51.

——, 'L'U.R.S.S. aux deux visages: Socialisme et tradition russe', *Revue militaire d'information*, 291 (February 1958) pp. 7–30.

——, 'L'islam en U.R.S.S.', *L'Afrique et l'Asie modernes*, no. 120 (1st Trimester 1979) pp. 3–24.

——, 'Several Nations or One People? Ethnic Consciousness among Soviet Central Asian Muslims', *Survey*, vol. 24, no. 3 (Summer 1979) pp. 51–64.

——, 'Les Musulmans de l'URSS et la crise afghane', *Politique étrangère*, vol. 45, no. 1 (1980) pp. 13–25.

——, 'L'U.R.S.S. et l'islam', *Géopolitique*, 7 (Fall 1984) pp. 53–60.

——, 'Mullahs, Mujahidin and Soviet Muslims', *Problems of Communism*, vol. xxxiii, no. 6 (November–December 1984) pp. 28–44.

—— and LEMERCIER-QUELQUEJAY, CHANTAL, 'L'impact des évènements d'Iran et d'Afghanistan sur l'Islam soviétique', *L'Alternative*, no. 31 (January–February 1985) pp. 15–17.

BESANÇON, ALAIN, *et al.*, 'Où va le régime soviétique?', *Esprit* (November 1973) pp. 611–59.

——, 'Présent soviétique et passé russe', *Contrepoint*, no. 14 (May 1974) pp. 21–36.

——, 'De la difficulté de définir le régime soviétique', *Contrepoint*, no. 20 (February 1976) pp. 115–28.

——, 'Débat – L'avenir de l'Union soviétique', *Pouvoirs*, 6 (1978) pp. 111–15.

——, 'La conviction idéologique: avant et après la prise du pouvoir', *Cadmos*, 3ème Année, no. 11 (Fall 1980) pp. 37–54.

——, 'The End of the Soviet Mirage', *Encounter*, vol. LVII, no. 1 (July 1981) pp. 90–92.

——, 'Les failles de l'Union Soviétique', *Défense Nationale*, 37e Année (November 1981) pp. 33–44.

——, 'Economie: une pénurie planifiée', *L'Express*, no. 1583 (13 November 1981) pp. 58–9.

——, '1984: Orwell et nous', *L'Express*, no. 1685 (28 October 1983) pp. 84–90.

——, 'Mort d'un cadavre', *L'Express*, no. 1702 (24 February 1984) p. 29.

——, 'Pourquoi aller à Moscou?', *L'Express*, no. 1709 (13 April 1984) p. 49.

——, 'Aider le régime soviétique?', *L'Express*, no. 1735 (12 October 1984) p. 41.

——, 'L'autre Europe', *L'Express*, no. 1747 (4 January 1985) p. 69.

——, 'Ne pas se tromper d'ennemi', *L'Express*, no. 1767 (24 May 1985) p. 9.

——, 'Lire Michel Heller', *Commentaire*, vol. 8, no. 3 (Fall 1985) pp. 938–40.

BESSE, GUY, '"L'URSS et Nous"', *Cahiers du Communisme*, 54ème Année, no. 10 (October 1978) pp. 96–101.

BEST, ROBERT, 'Idéologie et information: le cas de la presse soviétique', *Essais sur le discours soviétique*, 1 (1981) pp. 161–4.

BETTELHEIM, CHARLES, 'Remarques théoriques', *Problèmes de planification*, 14 (1970) pp. 174–201.

—— and CHAVANCE, BERNARD, 'Le stalinisme en tant qu'idéologie du capitalisme d'état', *Les Temps Modernes*, vol. 34, no. 394 (May 1979) pp. 1731–67.

——, 'La "Crise du marxisme" et l'idéologie stalinienne', *Critique socialiste*, no. 40 (1980) pp. 69–73.

——, 'The specificity of Soviet capitalism', *Monthly Review*, vol. 37, no. 4 (September 1985) pp. 43–61.

——, 'La pensée marxienne à l'épreuve de l'histoire (Un entretien avec G. Boismenu), *Les Temps Modernes*, 41ème Année, no. 472 (November 1985) pp. 620–51.

BOD, LADISLAS, 'Langage et pouvoir politique – Réflexions sur le stalinisme', *Etudes*, vol. 342 (February 1975) pp. 177–213.

BOURDIEU, PIERRE, 'Le champ scientifique', *Actes de la recherche en sciences sociales*, no. 2–3 (June 1976) pp. 89–104.

——, 'La représentation politique – Eléments pour une théorie du champ politique', *Actes de la recherche en sciences sociales*, no. 36–7 (February–March 1981) pp. 3–24.

BOURMEYSTER, ALEXANDRE, 'Le discours politique soviétique, le programme narratif et la théorie du skaz', *Essais sur le discours soviétique*, 5 (1985) pp. 2–15.

BROUE, PIERRE, 'Trotsky et les grands débats du Monde communiste', *Annales*, vol. 20, no. 3 (May–June 1965) pp. 617–23.

BROWN, ARCHIE, 'Soviet political developments and prospects', *World Policy Journal*, vol. IV, no. 1 (Winter 1986–7) pp. 55–87.

BRULE, JEAN-PIERRE, 'L'U.R.S.S. et ses musulmans', *Est et Ouest*, no. 666 (September 1982) pp. 21–30.

BRUS, WLODZIMIERZ, 'Prospects of Reconstruction of Socialism by Political Democratisation and Economic Reform', Paper delivered at St. Antony's College, Oxford, October 1983, 15 pages.

BURNETT, PETER, 'Pierre Frank', *The Journal of Communist Studies*, vol. 1, no. 1 (March 1985) p. 90.

CALVEZ, JEAN-YVES, 'La Place de l'Idéologie', *Revue française de science politique*, vol. XVII, no. 6 (December 1967) pp. 1050–61.

CARDAN, PAUL, 'Socialisme ou Barbarie', *The Review*, vol. 2, no. 6 (October 1960) pp. 96–101.

——, 'Le mouvement révolutionnaire sous le capitalisme moderne (suite)', *Socialisme ou Barbarie*, vol. VI, no. 32 (April–June 1961) pp. 84–111.

CARRERE D'ENCAUSSE, HELENE, 'La crise de juin 1957 en U.R.S.S.', *Revue de défense nationale*, vol. 13 (November 1957) pp. 1668–83.

—— and BENNIGSEN, ALEXANDRE, 'Pouvoir apparent et pouvoir réel dans les républiques musulmanes de l'U.R.S.S.', *Problèmes soviétiques*, no. 1 (April 1958) pp. 57–73.

——, 'Le parti communiste de l'Union Soviétique', *Revue militaire d'information*, no. 300 (December 1958) pp. 29–44.

——, 'Khrouchtchev était-il vraiment nécessaire?', *Revue française de science politique*, vol. XV, no. 6 (December 1965) pp. 1050–78.

——, 'URSS: le changement sans alternance?', *Pouvoirs*, 1 (1977) pp. 97–103.

——, 'Lire la nouvelle Constitution', *Le Monde diplomatique* (July 1977) pp. 9–10.

——, 'Forces et vulnérabilité de l'URSS', *Projet*, 117 (July–August) pp. 815–26.

——, 'La Constitution de 1977: continuité et changement', *Problèmes politiques et sociaux*, no. 326 (23 December 1977) pp. 25–7.

——, 'Party and Federation in the USSR: The Problem of the Nationalities and Power in the USSR', *Government and Opposition*, vol. 13, no. 2 (Spring 1978) pp. 133–50.

——, 'La puissance soviétique aujourd'hui', *Relations internationales* (Genève), no. 17 (Spring 1979) pp. 29–48.

——, 'Les failles de l'Union soviétique', *Défense Nationale*, 37e Année (November 1981) pp. 57–70.

——, 'Les guerres de succession du Kremlin (1924–1984)', *Vingtième siècle – revue d'histoire*, no. 4 (October 1984) pp. 3–17.

——, 'Paris–Moscou L'U.R.S.S. au purgatoire?', *Le Débat*, no. 36 (September 1985) pp. 164–74.

——, 'Les nouveaux Russes', *Le Nouvel Observateur*, no. 1136 (15 August 1986) pp. 34–7.

CASTORIADIS, CORNELIUS, 'Les divertisseurs', *Le Nouvel Observateur*, no. 658 (20 June 1977) pp. 50–1.

——, 'The social regime in Russia', *Telos*, no. 38 (Winter 1978–9) pp. 32–47.

——, 'Facing the war', *Telos*, no. 46 (Winter 1980–1) pp. 43–61.

CHAMBRE, HENRI, 'Presse, radio et conduite des hommes', *La Nef*, vol. 13, no. 12 (March 1956) pp. 168–79.

——, 'L'Union soviétique, 1953–1963', *Revue de l'Action Populaire*, no. 171 (September–October 1963) pp. 964–76.

——, 'La protection des droits de l'homme en Union Soviétique', *Revue de l'Action Populaire*, no. 174 (January 1964) pp. 88–94.

——, 'Soviet ideology', *Soviet Studies*, vol. XVIII, no. 3 (January 1967) pp. 314–27.

CHARVIN, ROBERT, 'Trois points d'interrogation', *La Nouvelle Critique*, no. 108 (November 1977) pp. 49–55.

CHAULIEU, PIERRE, 'Les rapports de production en Russie', *Socialisme ou Barbarie*, 1ère Année, no. 2 (May–June 1949) pp. 1–66.

——, 'L'exploitation des paysans sous le capitalisme bureaucratique', *Socialisme ou Barbarie*, 1ère Année, no. 4 (October–November 1949) pp. 19–44.

——, 'La révolution prolétarienne contre la bureaucratie', *Socialisme ou Barbarie*, vol. IV, no. 20 (December 1956–February 1957) pp. 134–71.

——, 'La voie polonaise de la bureaucratisation', *Socialisme ou Barbarie*, vol. IV, no. 21 (March–May 1957) pp. 59–76.

CHAVANCE, BERNARD, 'Sur les rapports de production en URSS (A propos d'un article de Paul Sweezy)', *Les Temps Modernes*, vol. 33, no. 375 (October 1977) pp. 513–26.

——, 'La nature du système soviétique, questions et enjeux', *Les Temps Modernes*, vol. 37, no. 419 (June 1981) pp. 2198–213.

——, 'Trois types d'économie socialiste: Union Soviétique, Yougoslavie, Chine. Pour une approche comparative', *Critiques de l'économie politique*, Nlle série, no. 19 (April–June 1982) pp. 29–69.

——, 'Pourquoi le capitalisme étatique? Réponse à: "Marxisme en crise cherche sociétés socialistes"', *Babylone*, no. 2/3 (Winter 1983–4) pp. 126–42.

CHEVENEMENT, JEAN-PIERRE, 'Comprendre', *République Moderne*, no. 2 (Fall 1985) pp. 5–7.

COCKBURN, PATRICK, 'Moscow legalises private enterprise in service sector', *The Financial Times* (20 November 1986) p. 1.

COHEN, FRANCIS, 'La supériorité de la civilisation socialiste', *Cahiers du Communisme*, 26ème Année, no. 11 (November 1949) pp. 1355–66.

——, 'L'URSS et le monde – Réflexions', *Cahiers du Communisme*, 41ème Année, no. 12 (December 1965) pp. 51–66.

——, 'La révolution socialiste d'octobre soixante ans après', *Cahiers du Communisme*, 53ème Année, no. 10 (October 1977) pp. 86–94.

——, 'Démocratie et réalités sociales dans l'Europe socialiste', *La Pensée*, 217–18 (January–February 1981) pp. 100–21.

——, 'Structure sociale, classes et différenciations dans le socialisme existant (notes préliminaires)', *La Pensée*, 225 (January–February 1982) pp. 91–102.

——, 'Connaissance des pays socialistes', *Cahiers du Communisme*, 59ème Année, no. 7–8 (July–August 1983) pp. 90–7.

——, 'Mutations sociales et contradictions', *Recherches internationales*, no. 9 (July–August–September 1983) pp. 77–94.

——, 'Les sept semaines de Gorbatchev', *Révolution*, no. 270 (3–9 May 1985) p. 17.

COLLIGNON, JEAN-GUY, 'De l'isolationnisme au comparatisme – méthodes et approches anglo-saxonnes pour l'analyse du système politique soviétique', *Revue française de science politique*, vol. 26, no. 3 (June 1976) pp. 445–82.

COMITE DE DIRECTION, 'Le Monde communiste', *Les Cahiers de la République*, 4 (December 1956) p. 41.

CONSEIL DE DIRECTION, 'Notre programme', *Le Monde slave*, no. 1 (November 1924) pp. 1–20.

CONTE, FRANCIS and LAVROFF, DIMITRI G., 'La constitution de l'Union des républiques socialistes soviétiques du 7 Octobre 1977', *Revue du droit public et de la science politique en France et à l'étranger*, vol. 94, no. 3 (May–June 1978) pp. 679–715.

CROUZATIER, JEAN-MARIE, 'Analyses occidentales du régime soviétique', *Revue du droit public et de la science politique en France et à l'étranger*, vol. 101, no. 2 (March–April 1985) pp. 339–60.

CROZIER, MICHEL, 'The Cultural Revolution – Notes on the Changes in the Intellectual Climate of France', *Daedalus*, vol. 93, no. 1 (Winter 1964) pp. 514–42.

DAVIES, NORMAN, 'Study visit in France: a short Report', *International Newsletter* (International Committee for Soviet and East European Studies), no. 15 (July 1982) pp. 42–7.

DE FOUQUET, PIERRE, 'Marxisme et socialisme étatique', *Revue d'études comparatives Est-Ouest*, vol. 12, no. 1 (March 1981) pp. 83–119.

DE GAUDEMAR, JEAN-PAUL, 'U.R.S.S.: le travail fait système', *Les Temps Modernes*, vol. 36, no. 417 (April 1981) pp. 1792–815.

DELAHAYE, YVES, review of H. Chambre, *Le Marxisme en Union soviétique Idéologie et institutions Leur évolution de 1917 à nos jours* (Paris: Seuil, 1955) in *Revue française de science politique*, vol. VI, no. 1 (January–March 1956) pp. 201–5.

DELANNOI, GIL, '*Arguments*, 1956–1962 ou la parenthèse de l'ouverture', *Revue française de science politique*, vol. 34, no. 1 (February 1984) pp. 127–45.

DELIMARS, E., 'Mentalité des cadres en U.R.S.S.', *Le Contrat Social*, vol. V, no. 3 (May–June 1961) pp. 159–64.

——, 'Le Kremlin et le peuple russe', *Le Contrat Social*, vol. VII, no. 3 (May–June 1963) pp. 153–60.

DE ROCHEGONDE, G., 'La lutte pour le pouvoir en Union Soviétique (1)', *Revue de défense nationale*, vol. 21 (June 1965) pp. 995–1007.

——, 'La lutte pour le pouvoir en Union Soviétique (fin)', *Revue de défense nationale*, vol. 21 (July 1965) pp. 1212–22.

DESCAMPS, CHRISTIAN, 'Claude Lefort le peuple et le pouvoir', *Le Monde Dimanche* (7 November 1982) pp. ix–x.

DE SEDE, GERARD, 'Une pseudo-sociologie du communisme', *La Revue internationale*, 6ème Année, no. 22 (April–June 1950) pp. 143–5.

DESERT, MYRIAM, 'Quels cadres pour les contremaîtres soviétiques?', *Cahiers du monde russe et soviétique*, vol. xxv, nos. 2–3 (January–March 1984) pp. 149–60.

DHOMBRES, DOMINIQUE, 'M. Gorbatchev engage une profonde réforme du mode de sélection des responsables', *Le Monde* (29 January 1987) pp. 1 and 4.

DOMENACH, JEAN-MARIE, 'L'intelligentsia française et la perception de l'Est communiste', *Cadmos*, 4ème Année, no. 13 (Spring 1981) pp. 18–27.

DROUARD, ALAIN, 'Réflexions sur une chronologie: Le développement des sciences sociales en France de 1945 à la fin des années soixante', *Revue française de sociologie*, vol. xxiii, 1 (January–March 1982) pp. 55–85.

DUCHENE, GERARD, 'Le poids du militaire', *Le Débat*, no. 24 (March 1983) pp. 178–90.

——, 'Technologie militaire et besoins civils en URSS', *Babylone*, no. 2/3 (Winter 1983–4) pp. 36–47.

DUHAMEL, OLIVIER and PARODI, JEAN-LUC, 'Images du communisme: 1 La dégradation de l'image de l'Union soviétique', *Pouvoirs*, 21 (1982) pp. 169–80.

DUVERGER, MAURICE, 'Les régimes de type russe', *La Vie intellectuelle*, 16e Année (February 1948) pp. 46–62.

——, 'Démocratie libérale et démocratie totalitaire', *La Vie intellectuelle*, 16e Année (July 1948) pp. 56–70.

——, 'La seconde étape', *Le Monde* (28 June 1956) pp. 1 and 6.

——, 'La démocratie en U.R.S.S.', *L'Express*, no. 698 (2 November 1964) p. 16.

EISENMANN, LOUIS, 'Slavonic Studies in France', *The Slavonic Review*, I, 2 (December 1922) pp. 295–305.

FAVRE, PIERRE, *'Regards sur la science politique française – La science politique française et ses problématiques'*, Paper delivered to the Association Française de Science Politique, Paris, 19 June 1980, 47 pages.

——, 'La science politique en France depuis 1945', *International Political Science Review*, vol. 2, no. 1 (1981) pp. 95–120.

FEJTO, FRANÇOIS, 'Le Parti et l'Etat', *La Nef*, vol. 13, no. 12 (1956) pp. 34–53.

——, 'The Motives and Prospects of Khrushchev's Policy', *The Review*, vol. iv, no. 1 (1962) pp. 31–45.

——, 'L'Union soviétique après le XXIVe Congrès', *Contrepoint*, no. 5 (Winter 1971) pp. 73–92.

FERRO, MARC, 'Y a-t-il "trop de démocratie" en URSS?', *Annales*, 40ème Année, no. 4 (July–August 1985) pp. 811–27.

——, 'URSS D'une société sous contrôle à une société en auto-surveillance', *République Moderne*, no. 2 (Fall 1985) pp. 11–14.

FICHELLE, ALFRED, 'Origines et développement de l'Institut d'études slaves (1919–1949)', *Revue des études slaves*, vol. 27 (1951) pp. 91–103.

FRAGER, DOMINIQUE, 'I. URSS: quelle stratégie? – Interview de Cornelius Castoriadis', *Critique socialiste*, no. 43 (April 1982) pp. 11–17.

FRAPPAT, BRUNO and WOLTON, DOMINIQUE, 'L'optimisme glacé

de Raymond Aron', *Le Monde Dimanche* (21 September 1980) pp. I and xvii–xviii.

FRIEND, JULIUS W., 'Soviet Behavior and National Responses: The Puzzling Case of the French Communist Party', *Studies in Comparative Communism*, vol. xv, no. 3 (Autumn 1982) pp. 212–35.

FRITSCH-BOURNAZEL, RENATA, 'Les Forces armées et la "société socialiste avancée"', *Pouvoirs*, 6 (1978) pp. 55–64.

FURET, FRANÇOIS, 'Quand Aron raconte notre histoire . . .', *Le Nouvel Observateur*, no. 982 (2 September 1983) pp. 46–8.

GARDER, MICHEL, 'Où va l'Union soviétique?', *Revue politique et parlementaire*, no. 757 (June 1965) pp. 42–50.

——, 'Un régime condamné', *Contrepoint*, no. 2 (October 1970) pp. 121–33.

——, 'De l'armée impériale russe aux forces armées soviétiques (1917–1977)', *Esope*, no. 387 (16 October 1977) pp. 1–17.

GAUCHET, MARCEL, 'La logique du politique', *Critique*, vol. 30, no. 329 (October 1974) pp. 907–26.

GELARD, PATRICE, 'Des enjeux nouveaux', *La Nouvelle Critique*, no. 108 (November 1977) pp. 56–60.

——, 'La Constitution d'octobre 1977', *Problèmes politiques et sociaux*, no. 326 (23 December 1977) pp. 27–38.

——, 'Le consensus en Union soviétique', *Pouvoirs*, 5 (1978) pp. 133–40.

——, 'De Brejnev à Tchernenko et les dix-huit mois de Iouri Andropov', *Pouvoirs*, 33 (1985) pp. 141–52.

GEORGE, PIERRE, 'L'U.R.S.S. au seuil du VIe Plan quinquennal', *Cahiers internationaux*, 8ème Année, no. 73 (February 1956) pp. 61–8.

GERBOD, PAUL, 'L'image de la Russie en France de 1890 à 1917', *L'Information historique*, 41ème Année, no. 3 (May–June 1979) pp. 115–22.

——, 'D'une révolution, l'autre: les Français en Russie de 1789 à 1917', *Revue des études slaves*, vol. LVII, no. 4 (1985) pp. 605–20.

GOGUEL, FRANÇOIS, 'La science politique en France', *Revue de l'enseignement supérieur*, no. 4 (October–November–December 1965) pp. 91–8.

GRAPIN, JACQUELINE, 'La perception de l'Union soviétique par les Américains et les Européens', *Défense nationale*, 39e Année (October 1983) pp. 93–104.

GREMION, PIERRE, 'Le rouge et le gris – Les intellectuels français et le monde soviétique', *Commentaire*, vol. 6, no. 24 (Winter 1983–4) pp. 767–80.

GROSSER, ALFRED, 'I. Recherche et enseignement', *Tendances* (December 1960) pp. 471–6.

HARDY, YVES and GABAI, PASCAL, 'La gauche française et les contestataires soviétiques', *Le Monde diplomatique* (December 1977) pp. 12–14.

HASSNER, PIERRE, 'Western European Perceptions of the Soviet Union', *Daedalus*, vol. 108, no. 1 (Winter 1979) pp. 113–50.

——, 'Le pacifisme est-il l'aveu d'un pessimisme total?', *Le Nouvel Observateur*, no. 920 (26 June 1982) pp. 37–8.

——, 'American Foxes and French Hedgehogs? A French Perspective on East European Studies', *Studies in Comparative Communism*, vol. xv, no. 4 (Winter 1982) pp. 365–72.

——, Le miroir totalitaire – Le totalitarisme soviétique vu de l'ouest', *Commentaire*, vol. 7, no. 26 (Summer 1984) pp. 195–204.

HELLER, MICHEL, 'Boris Souvarine 1895–1984', *Survey*, vol. 28, no. 4 (Winter 1984) pp. 198–204.

——, 'Teeth 'n' Smiles – Gorbachov for Beginners', *Survey*, vol. 29, no. 1 (Spring 1985) pp. 12–18.

——, 'Union soviétique: Les illusions du changement', *Géopolitique*, 10 (Summer 1985) pp. 50–61.

HILTON, RONALD, 'Russian and Soviet Studies in France: Teaching, Research, Libraries, Archives, and Publications', *The Russian Review*, vol. 38, no. 1 (January 1979) pp. 52–79.

HOWARD, DICK, 'Introduction to Castoriadis', *Telos*, no. 23 (Spring 1975) pp. 117–31.

——, 'An interview with C. Castoriadis', *Telos*, no. 23 (Spring 1975) pp. 131–55.

——, 'Introduction to Lefort', *Telos*, no. 22 (Winter 1974–5) pp. 2–30.

HUBERT, PIERRE and LABBE, DOMINIQUE, '50 ans de timbres soviétiques (1918–1969)', *Revue française de science politique*, vol. xxiii, no. 6 (December 1973) pp. 1157–70.

IMSECO, *Rapport scientifique* (May 1986) 65 pages.

'INTELLECTUELS (LES) COMMUNISTES ET LE CULTE DE STALINE', *Est-Ouest* (Supplément), 273 (16–28 February 1962) 57 pages.

JELEN, CHRISTIAN and UNGER, LEOPOLD, 'L'Etat kleptocratique ou comment gagner de l'argent à l'Est', *L'Express*, no. 1465 (11 August 1979) pp. 58–64.

—— and LANNES, SOPHIE, 'U.R.S.S. Les hommes-fourmis. L'Express va plus loin avec Michel Heller', *L'Express*, no. 1757 (15 March 1985) pp. 42–9.

JENSON, JANE and ROSS, GEORGE, 'The Uncharted Waters of De-Stalinization: The Uneven Evolution of the Parti Communiste Français', *Politics and Society*, vol. 9, no. 3 (1980) pp. 263–98.

K., M., 'L'Afrique, enfin', *Le Monde* (1 March 1983) pp. 1 and 17.

KAHN, MICHELE and MINK, GEORGES, 'Les ouvriers en URSS; statut économique et social', *Le Courrier des Pays de l'Est*, no. 234 (November 1979) pp. 3–38.

KANET, ROGER, Review of H. Carrère d'Encausse, *Le pouvoir confisqué – gouvernants et gouvernés en U.R.S.S.* (Paris: Flammarion, 1980) in *Slavic Review*, vol. 40, no. 2 (Summer 1981) pp. 294–5.

KENDE, PIERRE, 'L'intérêt personnel dans le système d'économie socialiste', *Revue économique*, no. 3 (1959) pp. 340–64.

——, 'Culture politique et société civile', *Communisme*, no. 8 (1985) pp. 90–104.

KERBLAY, BASILE, 'Le régime juridique des brevets d'invention en U.R.S.S.', *Cahiers de l'Economie Soviétique*, no. 8 (April–June 1947) pp. 3–10.

——, 'Soviet studies in Western Europe: France', *Survey*, no. 50 (January 1964) pp. 97–106.

——, 'Le pouvoir soviétique et la paysannerie', *Sociologia Ruralis (Assen)*, vol. xii, no. 2 (1972) pp. 167–80.

—— *et al.*, 'Où va le régime soviétique?', *Esprit* (November 1973) pp. 655–9.

——, 'Les enseignements de l'expérience soviétique d'agriculture collectiviste (Résultats, problèmes et perspectives)', *Revue d'études comparatives Est-Ouest*, vol. x, no. 3 (September 1979) pp. 7–30.

——, 'Les problèmes de la socialisation dans le milieu rural soviétique', *Cahiers du Monde Russe et Soviétique*, vol. xxi, no. 3–4 (July–December 1980) pp. 249–77.

KRIEGEL, ANNIE, 'Débat – L'avenir de l'Union soviétique', *Pouvoirs*, 6 (1978) pp. 121–30.

——, 'Qui détient le pouvoir en U.R.S.S.?', *Le Figaro* (13 November 1980) p. 2.

——, 'Le système communiste mondial: mythe ou réalité?', *Pouvoirs*, 21 (1982) pp. 5–24.

KUPFERMAN, FRED, 'L'oeil sur Moscou', *L'Express*, no. 1766 (17 May 1985) pp. 40–1.

LANGROD, GEORGES, 'Le rôle du parti unique dans l'Etat soviétique', *Revue politique et parlementaire*, vol. cciv (April–June 1951) pp. 47–52.

——, 'Le régime de la grande méfiance', *Politique – Revue internationale des doctrines et des institutions*, vol. 1, no. 1 (January–March 1958) pp. 82–9.

——, 'Les formes de la participation des masses dans le gouvernement et l'administration de l'U.R.S.S.', *Annuaire de l'U.R.S.S. Droit–Economie–Sociologie–Politique–Culture*, vol. i (1962) pp. 101–39.

——, 'Le rôle administratif des Soviets et son évolution', *L'URSS, Droit–Economie–Sociologie–Politique–Culture*, vol. ii (1964) pp. 53–76.

LAPALOMBARA, JOSEPH, 'Monoliths or Plural Systems: Through Conceptual Lenses Darkly', *Studies in Comparative Communism*, vol. viii, no. 3 (Autumn 1975) pp. 305–32.

LARUCHETTE, JEAN, 'L'U.R.S.S. et les libertés individuelles – Point de vue juridique', *Etudes*, vol. 346 (June 1977) pp. 725–39.

——, 'Les Soviétiques et leur emploi', *Etudes*, vol. 350, no. 4 (April 1979) pp. 469–86.

LAURAT, LUCIEN, 'Convergences Est-Ouest?', *Est et Ouest*, vol. 15, no. 309 (16–30 November 1963) pp. 16–18.

——, 'Libéralisme et "libéralisation"', *Le Contrat Social*, vol. xi, no. 1 (1967) pp. 18–22.

LAURENT, JACQUES, 'Connaissons-nous l'armée soviétique?', *L'autre Europe*, no. 3 (1984) pp. 9–17.

LAUTMAN, JACQUES, 'Les sciences sociales et le C.N.R.S., entre la culture et la demande bureaucratique', *Commentaire*, vol. 6, no. 21 (Spring 1983) pp. 186–97.

LAUTREDOU, FLORENCE, 'Le discours pédagogique soviétique ou l'Affect fait Idéologie', *Essais sur le discours soviétique*, 5 (1985) pp. 85–100.

LAVABRE, MARIE-CLAIRE and PESCHANSKI, DENIS, 'L'image de l'U.R.S.S. diffusée par le parti communiste français: soixante ans d'almanachs', *Revue des études slaves*, vol. LVII, no. 4 (1985) pp. 637–47.

LAVAU, GEORGES, 'Le rapport entre l'idéologie et la politique extérieure', *Pouvoirs*, 21 (1982) pp. 125–38.

LAVIGNE, MARIE, 'Une symmétrie beaucoup plus formelle que réelle', *Le Monde diplomatique* (August 1975) pp. 11–12.

——, 'Quelques changements dans les magasins . . . et dans le zèle', *L'Expansion*, no. 233 (17 February 1984) pp. 18–22.

——, 'L'économie politique du socialisme en U.R.S.S. 1953–1983', *Revue des études slaves*, vol. LVII, no. 2 (1985) pp. 225–38.

LAZITCH, BRANKO, 'Souvarine: souvenirs sur Lénine Trotski et Staline', *L'Express*, no. 1484 (22 December 1979) pp. 76–85.

—— and LANNES, SOPHIE, 'La technique du pouvoir en U.R.S.S.', *L'Express*, no. 1430 (2 December 1978) pp. 194–225.

LEBORGNE, DANIELLE, '1930–1980: 50 ans de croissance extensive en U.R.S.S.', *Critiques de l'économie politique*, Nlle série, no. 19 (April–June 1982) pp. 71–98.

—— and LIPIETZ, ALAIN, 'Est, Ouest: deux modes de régulation du capitalisme', *Reflets et Perspectives de la vie économique*, tome XXII, no. 4/5 (1983) pp. 369–76.

LECA, JEAN, 'La science politique dans le champ intellectuel français', *Revue française de science politique*, vol. 32, no. 4–5 (August–October 1982) pp. 653–78.

LEFORT, CLAUDE, 'Le totalitarisme sans Staline', *Socialisme ou Barbarie*, vol. IV, no. 19 (July–September 1956) pp. 1–72.

——, 'What is Bureaucracy?', *Telos*, no. 22 (Winter 1974–5) pp. 31–65.

——, 'La première révolution anti-totalitaire', *Esprit*, no. 1 (January 1977) pp. 13–19.

——, 'Reculer les frontières du possible', *Esprit*, no. 1 (January 1981) pp. 96–106.

LEGRAS, JULES, 'La politique de nationalités du gouvernement soviétique en Ukraine', *Le Monde slave*, 3ème Année, no. 11 (November 1926) pp. 317–19.

LEMERCIER-QUELQUEJAY, CHANTAL, 'L'Islam en Union soviétique: survivances et renaissance', *L'Alternative*, no. 9 (March–April 1981) pp. 12–16.

LEMERT, CHARLES C., 'Literary politics and the *champ* of French sociology', *Theory and Society*, vol. 10, no. 5 (September 1981) pp. 645–69.

LEROY LADURIE, EMMANUEL, 'L'Union soviétique analysée par Alain Besançon', *Le Monde* (11 April 1980) p. 18.

LESAGE, MICHEL, 'Note sur l'évolution de la structure du secrétariat du Comité central du parti communiste de l'Union Soviétique', *Annuaire de l'U.R.S.S. Droit–Economie–Sociologie–Politique–Culture* (1966) pp. 39–46.

——, 'Les études soviétiques et est-européennes en France', *Canadian Slavonic Papers*, vol. XI, no. 3 (Fall 1969) pp. 295–303.

LOURAU, RENE, 'La bureaucratie comme classe dominante', *L'Homme et la Société*, no. 21 (July–August–September 1971) pp. 259–78.

LOWIT, THOMAS, 'Y-a-t-il des Etats en Europe de l'Est?', *Revue française de sociologie*, vol. xx, no. 2 (April–June 1979) pp. 431–66.

——, 'Le parti polymorphe en Europe de l'Est', *Revue française de science politique*, vol. 29, no. 4–5 (August–October 1979) pp. 812–46.

——, 'Classe ouvrière et structures syndicales en Europe de l'Est', *Les Temps Modernes*, vol. 37, no. 419 (June 1981) pp. 2214–32.

MAKINSKY, MICHEL, 'La relation armée-pouvoir en U.R.S.S.', *Défense nationale*, 40ème Année (July 1984) pp. 105–18.

——, 'La fonction propagande et la stratégie globale de l'U.R.S.S.', *Défense nationale*, 41ème Année (July 1985) pp. 75–91.

MALLET, SERGE, 'Bureaucratie et technocratie dans les pays socialistes', *L'Homme et la Société*, no. 10 (October–November–December 1968) pp. 147–71.

MARCOU, LILLY, 'Réflexions', *Révolution*, no. 203 (20–6 January 1984) p. 12.

MARIE, JEAN-JACQUES, 'La bureaucratie et l'opposition face à la convergence', *Le Monde diplomatique* (August 1975) pp. 10–11.

MARKIEWICZ-LAGNEAU, JANINA, 'La fin de l'intelligentsia? Formation et transformation de l'intelligentsia soviétique', *Revue d'études comparatives Est-Ouest*, vol. vii, no. 4 (December 1976) pp. 7–71.

MARTINEZ, LOUIS, 'La "langue de bois" soviétique', *Commentaire*, vol. 4, no. 16 (Winter 1981–2) pp. 506–15.

MAULNIER, THIERRY, 'Le bien-être et la puissance', *Preuves*, no. 74 (April 1957) pp. 61–7.

MAUSS, MARCEL, 'Socialisme et bolchévisme', *Le Monde slave*, 2ème Année, no. 2 (February 1925) pp. 201–22.

MAZON, ANDRE, 'Slavonic studies in France', *The Slavonic and East European Review*, vol. xxv, no. 64 (November 1946) pp. 206–13.

'Memento de la "guerre froide"', *Bulletin d'études et d'informations politiques internationales* (16–30 November 1951) pp. 13–15.

MENDRAS, MARIE, 'La France dans la politique occidentale de l'U.R.S.S.', *Politique étrangère*, no. 3 (Fall 1985) pp. 653–68.

MEQUET, G. and PIERRE, ANDRE, 'La femme en Russie soviétique', *Le Monde slave*, 4ème Année, nos. 11–12 (November–December 1927) pp. 419–41.

MOND, GEORGES H., 'Le contrôle politique de l'administration en U.R.S.S.', *Annuaire de l'U.R.S.S. Droit–Economie–Sociologie–Politique–Culture* (1966) pp. 107–30.

——, review of M. Lesage, *Les régimes politiques de l'U.R.S.S. et de l'Europe de l'Est* (Paris: Presses Universitaires de France, 1971) in *Revue de l'Est*, vol. 2, no. 3 (July 1971) pp. 183–8.

MONGIN, OLIVIER, THIBAUD, PAUL and ROSANVALLON, PIERRE, 'L'exigence révolutionnaire – Entretien avec Cornelius Castoriadis', *Esprit*, no. 2 (February 1977) pp. 201–30.

——, 'Hannah Arendt – Penser ce que nous faisons', *Esprit*, no. 42 (June 1980) pp. 3–6.

MONNEROT, JULES, 'Le totalitarisme: la droite et la gauche', *La Nef*, vol. 5, no. 41 (April 1948) pp. 21–37.

MORIN, EDGAR, 'From the Stalinist era to the Stalinistic era (Fragments)', *The Review*, vol. 5, no. 3 (1963) pp. 1–12.

MORRISSON, CHRISTIAN, 'Les moyens des sciences sociales en France', *Revue Economique*, vol. xxvi, no. 6 (1975) pp. 1004–20.

MOUSKHELY, MICHEL, 'La révolution communiste en marche – A propos du nouveau programme', *Res Publica*, vol. iv, no. 4 (1962) pp. 328–44.

NAVILLE, PIERRE, 'Les sociétés soviétiques', *La Nef*, vol. 13, no. 12 (March 1956) pp. 15–24.

——, 'Modèles historiques et modification de la structure de la classe ouvrière', *L'Homme et la Société*, no. 21 (July–August–September 1971) pp. 133–40.

——, 'Le parti nécessaire', *Critique socialiste*, no. 38–9 (1980) pp. 21–9.

——, 'Grèves et revendications ouvrières en U.R.S.S.', *Critique socialiste*, no. 40 (1980) pp. 95–103.

NIVAT, GEORGES, '"Langue de bois" et "Langue de vie" dans la Russie d'aujourd'hui', *Cadmos*, 7ème Année, no. 26–7 (Summer–Fall 1984) pp. 109–19.

NOVE, ALEC, 'The Class Nature of the Soviet Union Revisited', *Soviet Studies*, vol. xxxv, no. 3 (July 1983) pp. 298–312.

OLBERG, PAUL, 'Le Komsomol', *Le Monde slave*, 8ème Année (tome ii), no. 2 (May 1931) pp. 280–8.

——, 'La seconde révolution agraire russe', *Le Monde slave*, 8ème Année (tome iii), no. 2 (August 1931) pp. 304–16.

OST, CAROLINE and LOURMEL, GILLES, 'La stratocratie: une interprétation hâtive', *Critique*, vol. 37, no. 411–12 (August–September 1981) pp. 744–61.

PANKOW, WLODZIMIERZ, 'L'été polonais – un système de pouvoir en crise', *Revue française de sociologie*, vol. xxiv, no. 2 (April–June 1983) pp. 271–83.

PAPAIOANNOU, KOSTAS, 'La fondation du totalitarisme – Note sur la conception léniniste du parti', *Res Publica*, vol. iv, no. 4 (1962) pp. 345–62.

——, 'Classe et Parti II', *Le Contrat Social*, vol. vii, no. 5 (September–October 1963) pp. 274–84.

——, 'La conception léniniste du Parti', *Est et Ouest*, no. 587 (1–15 February 1977) pp. 1–6.

PAQUOT, THIERRY, 'Charles Bettelheim et la "révolution capitaliste" d'Octobre', *Le Monde Dimanche* (3 October 1982) pp. ix–x.

PELTIER, CONTRE-AMIRAL, 'L'homme nouveau du monde soviétique', *Revue de défense nationale*, vol. 18 (July 1962) pp. 1127–44.

PERGENT, J., 'La D.O.S.A.A.F., formation territoriale soviétique', *Est et Ouest*, vol. 15, no. 305 (16–30 September 1963) pp. 14–18.

PIERRE, ANDRE, 'Le XIVe Congrès du parti communiste russe', *Le Monde slave*, 3ème Année, no. 2 (February 1926) pp. 274–93.

——, 'En U.R.S.S. – La vie politique, économique et intellectuelle (janvier–

février 1929)', *Le Monde slave*, 6ème Année (tome I), no. 3 (March 1929) pp. 457–80.

——, 'La vie politique, économique et intellectuelle en U.R.S.S. (février–mars 1929)', *Le Monde slave*, 6ème Année (tome II), no. 4 (April 1929) pp. 145–60.

——, 'La vie politique, économique et intellectuelle en U.R.S.S. (mars–avril 1929)', *Le Monde slave*, 6ème Année (tome II), no. 5 (May 1929) pp. 302–20.

——, 'La vie politique, économique et intellectuelle en U.R.S.S. (avril–juin 1929)', *Le Monde slave*, 6ème Année (tome III), no. 7 (July 1929) pp. 135–60.

——, 'La vie politique, économique et intellectuelle en U.R.S.S. (juillet 1929)', *Le Monde slave*, 6ème Année (tome III), no. 8 (August 1929) pp. 303–20.

——, 'La vie politique, économique et intellectuelle en U.R.S.S. (aout 1929)', *Le Monde slave*, 6ème Année (tome III), no. 9 (September 1929) pp. 441–53.

——, 'La vie politique, économique et intellectuelle en U.R.S.S. (septembre 1929)', *Le Monde slave*, 6ème Année (tome IV), no. 10 (October 1929) pp. 103–21.

——, 'La vie politique, économique et intellectuelle en U.R.S.S. (octobre 1929)', *Le Monde slave*, 6ème Année (tome IV), no. 11 (November 1929) pp. 271–84.

——, 'La vie politique, économique et intellectuelle en U.R.S.S. (novembre 1929)', *Le Monde slave*, 6ème Année (tome IV), no. 12 (December 1929) pp. 450–66.

——, 'La presse de l'U.R.S.S. en 1932', *Le Monde slave*, 9ème Année (tome III), no. 7 (July 1932) pp. 115–29.

——, 'L'Académie des Sciences de l'U.R.S.S.', *Le Monde slave*, 10ème Année (tome III), no. 7 (July 1933) pp. 90–104.

'POLITIQUE (LA) DE STALIN', *Le Monde slave*, 7ème Année (tome I), no. 1 (January 1930) pp. 1–15.

'POLITIQUE (POUR UNE) A L'EGARD DE L'UNION SOVIETIQUE', *Commentaire*, vol. 5, no. 19 (Fall 1982) pp. 381–5.

POMIAN, KRZYSZTOF, 'Le Parti: vérités et mensonges', *Les Temps Modernes*, vol. 33, nos. 376–7 (November–December 1977) pp. 588–607.

RABAUT, JEAN, 'Le goulag et la France', *Le Monde Dimanche* (17 October 1982) pp. x–xi.

RITTERSPORN, GABOR, 'Facing the war psychosis', *Telos*, no. 51 (Spring 1982) pp. 22–31.

——, 'Rethinking Stalinism', *Russian history*, vol. 11, no. 4 (Winter 1984) pp. 343–61.

ROBITAILLE, LOUIS-BERNARD, 'Le pouvoir au bout du char', *Le Nouvel Observateur*, no. 895 (2 January 1982) pp. 14–19.

ROMER, JEAN-CHRISTOPHE, 'Le facteur militaire dans la politique soviétique', *Projet*, no. 167 (July–August 1982) pp. 844–51.

ROY, CLAUDE, 'Le premier homme', *Le Nouvel Observateur*, no. 994 (25 November 1983) pp. 54–5.

RUPNIK, JACQUES, 'L'union soviétique dans l'opinion française (1944–1984)', *L'autre Europe*, no. 6 (1985) pp. 87–91.

SAPIR, JACQUES, 'L'armée dans la société soviétique', *République Moderne*, no. 2 (Fall 1985) pp. 24–35.

SICARD, EMILE, 'I. Réflexions sur les études françaises de Sociologie des peuples slaves', *Sociologie et Droit Slaves*, no. 1 (December 1945) pp. 14–36.

——, 'I. Réflexions sur l'Information scientifique, juridique et sociologique, concernant les pays et les peuples slaves', *Sociologie et Droit Slaves*, no. 2 (March–April–May 1946) pp. 99–116.

——, 'I. Sociologie et Histoire des peuples et des Etats slaves', *Sociologie et Droit Slaves*, no. 1 (1947) pp. 4–14.

SINGER, BRIAN, 'The early Castoriadis: Socialism, Barbarism and the bureaucratic thread', *Canadian Journal of Political and Social Theory*, vol. 3, no. 3 (Fall 1979) pp. 35–56.

——, 'The later Castoriadis: Institution under interrogation', *Canadian Journal of Political and Social Theory*, vol. 4, no. 1 (Winter 1980) pp. 75–101.

SMOLAR, ALEKSANDER, 'La planification comme processus d'apprentissage. Le cas soviétique', *Revue d'études comparatives Est-Ouest*, vol. ix, no. 3 (September 1978) pp. 63–111.

SOCHOR, LUBOMIR, 'La succession au trône et la kremlinologie', *L'Alternative*, no. 20 (January–February 1983) pp. 3–9.

——, 'Peut-on parler de la "société civile" dans les pays du bloc soviétique?', *Communisme*, no. 8 (1985) pp. 79–89.

——, 'Le "socialisme réel", une idéologie tournée vers le passé', *Les Temps Modernes*, 41ème Année, no. 468/9 (July–August 1985) pp. 158–238.

SOCIALISME OU BARBARIE, 'La vie de notre Groupe', *Socialisme ou Barbarie*, 1ère Année, no. 4 (October–November 1949) pp. 59–69.

SODARO, MICHAEL J., 'Moscow and Mitterrand', *Problems of Communism*, vol. xxxi, no. 4 (July–August 1982) pp. 20–36.

SOKOLOFF, GEORGES, 'La dynamique Gorbatchev', *Politique étrangère*, no. 3 (Fall 1985) pp. 611–24.

SOUVARINE, BORIS, 'Aveux à Moscou', *La Vie Intellectuelle* (10 April 1938) pp. 55–67.

——, 'Le stalinisme', *Le Contrat Social*, vol. ix, no. 3 (May–June 1965) pp. 149–59.

——, 'Après le jubilé', *Le Contrat Social*, vol. xi, no. 6 (November–December 1967) pp. 331–5.

——, 'Un demi-siècle d'amitié', *Est et Ouest*, vol. 25, no. 515 (16–30 September 1973) pp. 1–4.

STRMISKA, ZDENEK, 'Programme socialiste et rapports sociaux en U.R.S.S. et dans les pays socialistes', *Revue d'études comparatives Est-Ouest*, vol. vii, no. 3 (September 1976) pp. 107–233.

SZAWLOSKI, RICHARD and TERLECKA, HANNA, 'Western Research on Russia until 1939: I. Developments up to 1914', *Canadian Slavonic Papers*, vol. ix, no. 2 (1967) pp. 145–69.

——, Review of *Annuaire de l'URSS. Droit–Economie–Sociologie–Politique–Culture*. Volumes for 1965, 1966 and 1967 (Paris: Editions du Centre

National de la Recherche Scientifique. 1966–1967–1968) in *Soviet Studies*, vol. xxi, no. 2 (October 1969) pp. 259–62.

TARSCHYS, DANIEL, 'The Soviet political system: Three models', *European Journal of Political Research*, vol. 5, no. 3 (September 1977) pp. 287–320.

TATU, MICHEL, 'Réflexions sur la structure du pouvoir en Union Soviétique', *Politique étrangère*, vol. 32, no. 2 (1967) pp. 196–208.

——, 'Political prospects in Soviet Russia', *Pacific Community*, vol. 2, no. 1 (October 1970) pp. 212–23.

——, 'Les institutions communistes face aux crises: les militaires seront-ils le recours?', *Défense Nationale*, 37ᵉ Année (November 1981) pp. 45–55.

THIBAUD, PAUL, 'Le plus dur et le plus fragile des régimes – Entretien avec Cornelius Castoriadis', *Esprit*, no. 63 (March 1982) pp. 140–6.

——, 'Le socialisme mûr – Entretien avec Michel Heller', *Esprit*, no. 74 (February 1983) pp. 41–5.

THIVENT, AGNES, 'L'ignorance française', *Le Monde Dimanche* (31 November 1982) pp. i and xi.

TIRASPOLSKY, ANITA, 'Les responsables du pouvoir en Union soviétique', *Projet*, no. 147 (July–August 1980) pp. 801–16.

TOKES, RUDOLF L., 'Comparative Communism: The Elusive Target', *Studies in Comparative Communism*, vol. viii, no. 3 (Autumn 1975) pp. 211–29.

TRAIN, JEAN, 'L'étude du Russe en France', *Cahiers du Monde Russe et Soviétique*, vol. 1, no. 1 (May 1959) pp. 180–3.

URGENSE, 'Un taylorisme arythmique dans les économies planifiées du centre', *Critiques de l'économie politique*, Nlle série, no. 19 (April–June 1982) pp. 99–146.

VERDES-LEROUX, JEANNINE, 'Souvarine le premier', *Esprit*, no. 89 (May 1984) pp. 21–37.

VIDAL, DOMINIQUE, 'L'U.R.S.S. vue par les Français', *Révolution*, no. 247 (23–28 November 1984) p. 12.

——, 'Les pays socialistes et nous – 1976/1984 – Entretien avec Francis Cohen', *Révolution*, no. 246 (16–22 November 1984) pp. 56–9.

VIGNE, ERIC, 'Lectures du stalinisme', *Communisme*, 3 (1983) pp. 129–34.

VINCENT, MICHEL, 'L'armée dans la société soviétique', *Faire*, 45/6 (1979) pp. 46–50.

VINEUIL, JEAN, 'U.R.S.S.: expansion ou stabilisation?', *Preuves*, no. 147 (May 1963) pp. 60–5.

——, 'Les hommes de Moscou', *Preuves*, no. 167 (January 1965) pp. 64–9.

WILCZKOWSKI, C., 'L'aspect czariste du régime stalinien', *Travaux de l'Action populaire*, Nlle série, no. 16 (January 1948) pp. 54–8.

——, 'Structure sociale soviétique', *Revue de l'Action Populaire*, no. 60 (June–July 1952) pp. 466–75.

WILD, GERARD, review of H. Carrère d'Encausse, *L'Empire éclaté – la révolte des nations en U.R.S.S.* (Paris: Flammarion, 1978) in *Le Courrier des Pays de l'Est*, no. 225 (January 1979) pp. 46–7.

X., B., 'La récolte en U.R.S.S. en 1933', *Le Monde slave*, 10ᵉᵐᵉ Année (tome iii), no. 7 (July 1933) pp. 104–14.

XXX, 'Des musulmans tranquilles – L'Islam en Chine et en URSS', *Etudes*, vol. 363, no. 5 (November 1985) pp. 437–50.

ZALESKI, EUGENE, 'Le pouvoir économique en U.R.S.S.', *Pouvoirs*, 6 (1978) pp. 73–8.

Index

185